16LIVES
ÉAMONN CEANNT

The 16LIVES Series

MARY GALLAGHER – AUTHOR OF 16LIVES: ÉAMONN CEANNT

Mary Gallagher was born in Dublin and studied in UCD where she graduated with a BA in Economics and History, then a Master's in Public Administration. She also has a National Diploma in Business Studies (Business Strategy) from the Irish Management Institute. From 1995 to 2005, she was a member of the Governing Body of the Institute of Technology Carlow. Following a public-service career in the IDA, Enterprise Ireland and the National Sports Campus Development Authority, she completed a National Certificate in Genealogy and Family History, and a Master's in Modern Irish History. She is a grand-niece of Éamonn Ceannt.

LORCAN COLLINS – SERIES EDITOR

Lorcan Collins was born and raised in Dublin. A lifelong interest in Irish history led to the foundation of his hugely popular 1916 Rebellion Walking Tour in 1996. He co-authored *The Easter Rising: A Guide to Dublin in 1916* (O'Brien Press, 2000) with Conor Kostick. His biography of James Connolly was published in the *16 Lives* series in 2012. He is also a regular contributor to radio, television and historical journals. *16 Lives* is Lorcan's concept and he is co-editor of the series.

DR RUÁN O'DONNELL – SERIES EDITOR

Dr Ruán O'Donnell is a senior lecturer at the University of Limerick. A graduate of UCD and the Australian National University, O'Donnell has published extensively on Irish Republicanism. His titles include *Robert Emmet and the Rising of 1803*; *The Impact of the 1916 Rising* (editor); *Special Category, The IRA in English Prisons 1968–1978*; and *The O'Brien Pocket History of the Irish Famine*. He is a director of the Irish Manuscripts Commission and a frequent contributor to the national and international media on the subject of Irish revolutionary history.

● ● ● ● ● ● ● ● ● ● ● ● ● ● ● ● ● ● ●

16LIVES
ÉAMONN CEANNT

Mary Gallagher

Waterford City and County
Libraries

THE O'BRIEN PRESS
DUBLIN

First published 2014 by
The O'Brien Press Ltd,
12 Terenure Road East, Rathgar,
Dublin 6, Ireland.
Tel: +353 1 4923333; Fax: +353 1 4922777
E-mail: books@obrien.ie.
Website: www.obrien.ie
ISBN: 978-1-84717-271-6
Text © copyright Mary Gallagher 2014
Copyright for typesetting, layout, editing, design
© The O'Brien Press Ltd
Series concept: Lorcan Collins

8 7 6 5 4 3 2 1
18 17 16 15 14
All quotations, in English and Irish, have been reproduced with original spelling and punctuation.

Printed and bound by CPI Group (UK) Ltd, Croydon, CR0 4YY
The paper used in this book is produced using pulp from managed forests.

PICTURE CREDITS

The author and publisher thank the following for permission to use photographs and illustrative material:

Front cover image: Kilmainham Gaol Collection. **Back cover:** courtesy of Mary Gallagher. **Inside-front cover:** courtesy of Prof Davis Coakley. **Picture section 1:** p1 (both), p4, p5 (top), pp6–7, courtesy of Mary Gallagher; p2 (both), courtesy of Nora Sleator; p3 (both), p5 (bottom), p8, courtesy of the National Library of Ireland. **Picture section 2:** p1 (both), courtesy of the National Library of Ireland; p2, p3 (top), p6 (both), p7, courtesy of Mary Gallagher; p3 (bottom), courtesy of Lorcan Collins; p4 (both), p5 (both), courtesy of Prof Davis Coakley; p8, courtesy of Michael Sheehy.

If any involuntary infringement of copyright has occurred, sincere apologies are offered and the owners of such copyright are requested to contact the publisher.

DEDICATION

For my family and friends

ACKNOWLEDGEMENTS

I am very grateful to Honor O Brolchain for introducing me to Michael O'Brien, who trusted me to write this biography of my grand-uncle, Éamonn Ceannt. I am equally grateful to my editor, Ide Ní Laoghaire, who rescued my initial draft from the byways of historical context and family anecdotes. Lorcan Collins and Ruán O'Donnell, the series editors, together with Emma Byrne, Nicola Reddy and the team at O'Brien Press, were always helpful and supportive.

My thanks are also due to the archivists and staff at the National Library of Ireland, National Archives of Ireland, the Bureau of Military History, the Archives Department of University College, Dublin, the Allen Library, the Royal Dublin Society, Dublin City Library and Archive, and South Dublin County Libraries. They were unfailingly helpful and courteous. I am particularly grateful to the librarians in my local library, Ballyroan Library, who acquired many of the books and references I needed. On-line access to original sources made my life immeasurably easier. The ability to search for the unusual name of Ceannt gave me access to a wide range of sources I might otherwise have missed. They include the Census of Ireland 1901 and 1911, the witness statements from the Bureau of Military History, the Irish Court of Petty Sessions Court Registers at findmypast.ie and a wide range of national and local newspapers at Irish Newspaper Archives Online.

When William Henry wrote the first biography of Éamonn, *Supreme Sacrifice: The Story of Éamonn Ceannt: 1881–1916*, (2005), he approached my late sister, Joan, and myself for assistance. We were delighted to help but came to recognise the limitations of our knowledge. In the past few years I have had the opportunity to rectify that and I hope William will forgive any shortcomings in the information with which we then provided him.

Before attempting to write Éamonn's life story, I had the great pleasure of returning to my alma mater, University College Dublin. My thanks are due to the School of History and Archives, in particular Professor Michael Laffan, Dr Lindsey Earner-Byrne, Professor Diarmaid Ferriter and their colleagues. I am also grateful to my fellow students, particularly Margaret Ayres, Tom Burke, Declan O'Keefe and Conor Mulvagh. My thanks are similarly due to Sean Murphy and my fellow students in the certificate course in Genealogy and Family History for a thorough grounding in genealogical research methods.

Éamonn naturally wrote many of his letters, diaries and articles in his beloved Irish, and I am particularly grateful to Siobhán Ní Mhathúna and my cousin, Tuhye Gillan, for their help in translating them.

My thanks are also due to Dr Joe McPartlin, Trinity Centre, St James's Hospital, who organised a seminar, 'Easter 1916 at the South Dublin Union', in April 2014. Dr Patrick Geoghegan, Trinity College, chaired and the speakers were myself, Prof Davis Coakley and Paul O'Brien. Prof Coakley very kindly showed me around the site of the SDU at St James's Hospital.

Finally, I want to place on record my deep gratitude to my family – living and departed. My late grandfather, Michael Kent, wrote our family story in his diaries from 1911–1920. His daughter, Joan Kent, preserved them, tenderly wrapped in brown paper and hidden away on top of a wardrobe. She also kept Bill Kent's letters to Michael, from the Boer War to Flanders, and many other family photographs and memorabilia. My sister, Nora Sleator, her husband Louis, and my nieces Niamh and Clodagh have supported me patiently throughout the long months of research and writing, as have the extended Ceannt, Gillan and Sheehy families. My equally patient and supportive friends regularly ask, 'how's Éamonn getting on?' I hope this book will answer their question!

16LIVES Timeline

1845–51. The Great Hunger in Ireland. One million people die and over the next decades millions more emigrate.

1858, March 17. The Irish Republican Brotherhood, or Fenians, are formed with the express intention of overthrowing British rule in Ireland by whatever means necessary.

1867, February and March. Fenian Uprising.

1870, May. Home Rule movement founded by Isaac Butt, who had previously campaigned for amnesty for Fenian prisoners.

1879–81. The Land War. Violent agrarian agitation against English landlords.

1884, November 1. The Gaelic Athletic Association founded – immediately infiltrated by the Irish Republican Brotherhood (IRB).

1893, July 31. Gaelic League founded by Douglas Hyde and Eoin MacNeill. The *Gaelic Revival*, a period of Irish Nationalism, pride in the language, history, culture and sport.

1900, September. *Cumann na nGaedheal* (Irish Council) founded by Arthur Griffith.

1905–07. *Cumann na nGaedheal*, the Dungannon Clubs and the National Council are amalgamated to form *Sinn Féin* (We Ourselves).

1909, August. Countess Markievicz and Bulmer Hobson organise nationalist youths into *Na Fianna Éireann* (Warriors of Ireland) a kind of boy scout brigade.

1912, April. Asquith introduces the Third Home Rule Bill to the British Parliament. Passed by the Commons and rejected by the Lords, the Bill would have to become law due to the Parliament Act. Home Rule expected to be introduced for Ireland by autumn 1914.

1913, January. Sir Edward Carson and James Craig set up Ulster Volunteer Force (UVF) with the intention of defending Ulster against Home Rule.

1913. Jim Larkin, founder of the Irish Transport and General Workers' Union (ITGWU) calls for a workers' strike for better pay and conditions.

1913, August 31. Jim Larkin speaks at a banned rally on Sackville (O'Connell) Street; Bloody Sunday.

1913, November 23. James Connolly, Jack White and Jim Larkin establish the Irish Citizen Army (ICA) in order to protect strikers.

1913, November 25. The Irish Volunteers are founded in Dublin to 'secure the rights and liberties common to all the people of Ireland'.

1914, March 20. Resignations of British officers force British government not to use British army to enforce Home Rule, an event known as the 'Curragh Mutiny'.

1914, April 2. In Dublin, Agnes O'Farrelly, Mary MacSwiney, Countess Constance Markievicz and others establish Cumann na mBan as a women's volunteer force dedicated to establishing Irish freedom and assisting the Irish Volunteers.

1914, April 24. A shipment of 35,000 rifles and five million rounds of ammunition is landed at Larne for the UVF.

1914, July 26. Irish Volunteers unload a shipment of 900 rifles and 45,000 rounds of ammunition shipped from Germany aboard Erskine Childers' yacht, the *Asgard*. British troops fire on crowd on Bachelor's Walk, Dublin. Three citizens are killed.

1914, August 4. Britain declares war on Germany. Home Rule for Ireland shelved for the duration of the First World War.

1914, September 9. Meeting held at Gaelic League headquarters between IRB and other extreme republicans. Initial decision made to stage an uprising while Britain is at war.

1914, September. 170,000 leave the Volunteers and form the National Volunteers or Redmondites. Only 11,000 remain as the Irish Volunteers under Eoin MacNeill.

1915, May–September. Military Council of the IRB is formed.

1915, August 1. Pearse gives fiery oration at the funeral of Jeremiah O'Donovan Rossa.

1916, January 19–22. James Connolly joins the IRB Military Council, thus ensuring that the ICA shall be involved in the Rising. Rising date confirmed for Easter.

1916, April 20, 4.15pm. *The Aud* arrives at Tralee Bay, laden with 20,000 German rifles for the Rising. Captain Karl Spindler waits in vain for a signal from shore.

1916, April 21, 2.15am. Roger Casement and his two companions go ashore from U-19 and land on Banna Strand in Kerry. Casement is arrested at McKenna's Fort.

6.30pm. *The Aud* is captured by the British navy and forced to sail towards Cork harbour.

1916, 22 April, 9.30am. *The Aud* is scuttled by her captain off Daunt Rock.

10pm. Eoin MacNeill as chief-of-staff of the Irish Volunteers issues the countermanding order in Dublin to try to stop the Rising.

1916, April 23, 9am, Easter Sunday. The Military Council of the Irish Republican Brotherhood (IRB) meets to discuss the situation, since MacNeill has placed an advertisement in a Sunday newspaper halting all Volunteer operations. The Rising is put on hold for twenty-four hours. Hundreds of copies of *The Proclamation of the Irish Republic* are printed in Liberty Hall.

1916, April 24, 12 noon, Easter Monday. The Rising begins in Dublin.

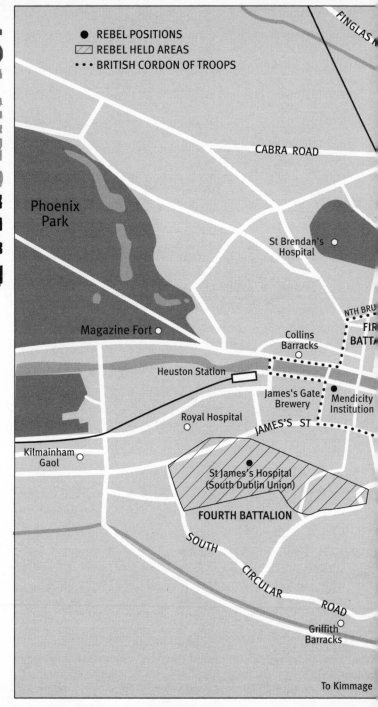

● REBEL POSITIONS
▨ REBEL HELD AREAS
••• BRITISH CORDON OF TROOPS

FINGLAS N

CABRA ROAD

Phoenix
Park

St Brendan's ○
Hospital

NTH BRU

FIR
BATT

Magazine Fort ○

Collins
Barracks
○

Heuston Station

James's Gate
Brewery

Mendicity
● Institution

Royal Hospital
○

JAMES'S ST

Kilmainham ○
Gaol

St James's Hospital
(South Dublin Union)
●

FOURTH BATTALION

SOUTH

CIRCULAR

ROAD

Griffith
Barracks ○

To Kimmage

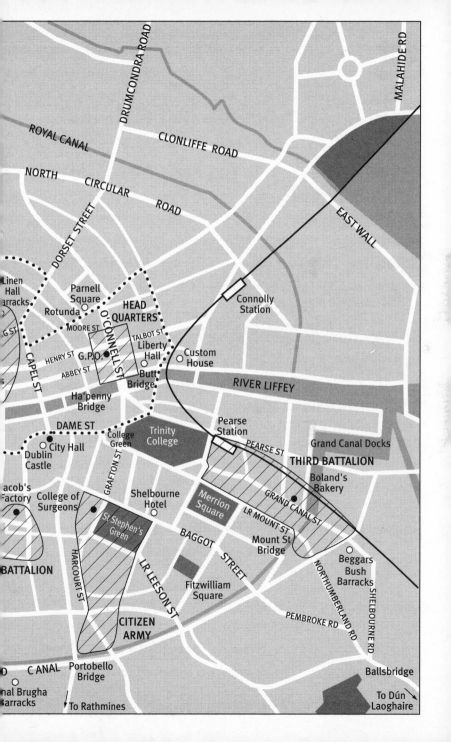

16LIVES – Series Introduction

This book is part of a series called *16 LIVES*, conceived with the objective of recording for posterity the lives of the sixteen men who were executed after the 1916 Easter Rising. Who were these people and what drove them to commit themselves to violent revolution?

The rank and file as well as the leadership were all from diverse backgrounds. Some were privileged and some had no material wealth. Some were highly educated writers, poets or teachers and others had little formal schooling. Their common desire, to set Ireland on the road to national freedom, united them under the one banner of the army of the Irish Republic. They occupied key buildings in Dublin and around Ireland for one week before they were forced to surrender. The leaders were singled out for harsh treatment and all sixteen men were executed for their role in the Rising.

Meticulously researched yet written in an accessible fashion, the *16 LIVES* biographies can be read as individual volumes but together they make a highly collectible series.

Lorcan Collins & Dr Ruán O'Donnell,
16 Lives *Series Editors*

CONTENTS

Chapter One

• • • • • •

1881–1899

A Constabulary Childhood

When Éamonn Ceannt (Edward Thomas Kent) was born in Ballymoe, County Galway, on 21 September 1881 to Royal Irish Constabulary (RIC) Constable James Kent and his wife, Johanna, few could have imagined that he would live to become Commandant of the 4th Battalion of the Irish Volunteers, that he would sign the Proclamation of the Irish Republic and that he would be executed by firing squad following a hastily convened field court martial on 8 May 1916.

The year 1881 started badly in the west of Ireland with an exceptionally hard winter. Although the deprivation was not comparable with the period of the Great Famine, well within living memory, hunger was widespread and starvation was an ever-present threat. But for James and Johanna Kent the situation was less bleak than for many of their neighbours. James had a good pensionable job with regular pay and subsidised accommodation.[1]

James Kent had been born on 14 July 1839 in Rehill, near Mitchelstown, County Cork.[2] He joined the RIC on 15 January 1862.[3] His family farmed in Lyrefune, a townland of Ballyporeen, County Tipperary.[4] When he joined the RIC he gave his occupation as 'labourer' and was recommended as a young man of good character and a suitable member of the RIC by his parish priest. Like most of his contemporaries, he had received an elementary education in reading, writing and arithmetic.[5] A tall, well-built man, he was in excellent health and easily met the physically demanding conditions for the force. For a landless younger son like James, the RIC presented a welcome opportunity for improvement.[6]

His wife, Johanna, was from Buttevant, County Cork, and they met when he was posted in nearby Kanturk. By the time Éamonn was born in 1881, they had been married for nearly eleven years.[7] Although money would have been tight in the early years of their marriage, James was now approaching the maximum salary of £70 per annum for a constable with nearly twenty years' service.[8]

Like many of her contemporaries, Johanna spent the early years of her married life caring for their young children. At the start of 1881 they had five children under the age of eleven: William Leeman (Bill), John Patrick (JP), Ellen (Nell), James Charles (Jem) and Michael (Mick). Their fifth son, Edward Thomas (Ned) – who was subsequently to adopt the Gaelic translation of his name, Éamonn Ceannt – was born in September that year and their youngest son, Richard (Dick), two years later. Even if she had the time or inclination, the regulations of the force prevented Johanna from taking up any occupation for profit outside the home, such as dressmaking, nor could she take in lodgers.[9]

As for James, he was part of a quasi-military force of men whose daily lives were highly regulated. They were always 'on duty' and were expected to be available at all hours. They could not serve in their own home localities or those of their spouses. When they were assigned to a new location, their priority was to get to know their new community. As a young recruit, James would have received training in the elements of police duties, including proficiency in 'the use of arms and military movements', and would have operated under a Code of Regulations that required him to know his neighbours, including their political views.[10] Like most of his contemporaries, James's duties entailed collecting information, patrolling the countryside, and acting as an officer of the courts, reporting such things as prosecutions for allowing two donkeys to wander on the public highway,[11] or for having a dog without a licence,[12] or for being drunk on the public street.[13] Until the late 1870s the Irish countryside had been quiet, from a policing point of view, and the life of a policeman a 'rather mundane and tedious occupation'.[14] Such evictions as took place were the responsibility of the sheriff and his bailiffs, with little police involvement.[15] In the early 1880s the environment within which James Kent and his RIC colleagues worked changed irrevocably. The Land League, set up by Michael Davitt in Mayo in 1879, was soon established as a national movement under Charles Stewart Parnell and, although the League was committed to peaceful means, agrarian strife was on the increase, putting considerable strain on the RIC.[16] The effectiveness of the new tactics of the 'boycott', in which landlords or their agents were shunned by whole communities, did not stop some of the extreme agitators from resorting to the old agrarian tactics: haystacks were burned and the lives of landlords and their agents were sometimes at risk. In 1880, at the height of the land war, over two thousand families were driven from their homes and 'outrages' totalled 2,590. [17]

In this tense climate, the role of the RIC became increasingly politicised and their duties multiplied to include keeping evicted farms under observation to prevent trespass, attending and recording public meetings, protecting individuals thought to be at risk and arresting and escorting prisoners. All of these extra duties, while making the members of the force unpopular with their neighbours, also led to significant extra work, 'without the least compensation or consideration'.[18]

During these difficult times in the west of Ireland, the mighty British Empire was at the height of its power. The evolving technologies of steam and telegraph made it possible to control an ever greater proportion of the global land mass and to dominate world trade. Yet in one small corner of the Empire the seeds of its future decline were being sown. The ultimate success of the Irish National Land League would lay the foundations for a movement that, with Éamonn as one of its leading members, would shake the Empire to the core.

A month after Éamonn's second birthday, his father was promoted to Head Constable and, in December 1883, was transferred from Ballymoe to County Louth, where the family was initially based in Drogheda. Just 56km from Dublin and 120km from Belfast, Drogheda was a thriving port with a strong industrial base. This move, from the heart of impoverished rural Galway to the relatively prosperous east coast, must have been both exciting and stressful for them, and indeed, Éamonn's brother Michael remembered that shortly after they arrived in Drogheda, the toddler, Éamonn, 'wandered and was lost for part of a day and night!' Éamonn started in the Christian Brothers' School at Sunday's Gate, Drogheda, around the age of five. He got homesick the first day and was sent home with Michael. Their mother was astonished when she saw them playing happily in the garden.[19] Éamonn was a sensitive child – 'a little oddity', according to Michael – and he had quite a temper. His mother was known to call him a 'little weasel' when he was in bad form. The family later moved out to the country district of Ardee[20] and Éamonn attended the De La Salle Brothers' School there.

Éamonn loved the countryside and, with his brothers, enjoyed 'rolling hoops, fishing, rambling over the bog, and hailing with joy the occasional circus and the crowds that came to the Mullacurry Races'.[21] Still, life for Éamonn and his family would have been quite regulated as Constabulary wives and children were expected to behave in accordance with Constabulary regulations.[22]

After three decades in the RIC, James Kent retired from the force in 1892, aged fifty-three.[23] He was entitled to take voluntary retirement after his thirty years' service, with a pension based on his full salary. Like many of his contemporaries, however, this was not the end of his working life. Also, the influence of the RIC on its retired members did not conclude upon their departure from the force. With no absolute 'right' to a pension, they could find their income cancelled for improper behaviour over the remaining years of their lives: 'in the case of retirees, it was a matter of – once a policeman, always a policeman'.[24]

James was ambitious to see his children educated and able to better themselves in life, and in 1892 the family moved to Dublin. The eldest, Bill, stayed in Drogheda with the Christian Brothers[25] and JP had already followed in his father's footsteps and joined the RIC at the age of eighteen.[26] James still had a young family, however. Richard, the youngest, was only nine years of age, and Éamonn was just about to start secondary (Intermediate) school.

The years during which the Kent family had lived in County Louth coincided with the strengthening of the Home Rule movement as Charles Stewart Parnell turned his attentions from land reform, where the battle was almost won, to building a disciplined party structure for the Irish Parliamentary Party (IPP) in Westminster in pursuit of Home Rule.

The move to Dublin brought the Kent family to the most wealthy and influential part of Ireland. Dublin was the capital city and Dublin Castle represented British rule in Ireland. The city was an important administrative and commercial centre with a population of about 350,000. Politically, however, it was a 'Deposed capital, a city bereft of its parliament, a backwater in Irish politics'.[27] Nonetheless, the city was changing. While the wealthy areas of Rathmines and Pembroke on the south side still housed the Protestant ascendancy and the wealthy professional classes, and the city's teeming tenements had the dubious distinction of being among the worst in Europe, Dublin also had a growing Catholic middle class that was beginning to make its mark on the city's commercial and cultural life.

During the second half of the nineteenth century, the number of people who moved to Dublin from rural Ireland was insignificant compared to the numbers who left Ireland

altogether, and most long-term migrants to Dublin, like the
Kent family, had a reasonable degree of financial security.[28]
The move to Dublin presented James Kent with the opportunity to supplement his pension within a more prosperous environment while, at the same time, giving his growing
family access to improved educational and career prospects.
Living in an imperial port city also enabled the young Kents
to glimpse the wider world outside Ireland. In an echo of
the day on which James Joyce's young Dubliner and his pal
Mahony skipped school to watch graceful three-masted
schooners on the Liffey discharge their cargo and to examine 'the foreign sailors to see had any of them green eyes',[29]
Éamonn and his friend Jack O'Reilly 'used to go down to
the quays when a foreign boat came in, to converse with the
sailors'.[30]

The family's first home was 26 Bayview Avenue, Fairview, a brick-fronted one-storey-over-basement house
between Ballybough Road and North Strand Road. It was
just twenty minutes' walk from the centre of Sackville Street
(now O'Connell Street).[31] Also a short walk away from the
family's new home was the Christian Brothers' O'Connell
School, North Richmond Street, where Éamonn and the
younger brothers of the family resumed their education. The
school had been established in 1829 by Edmund Rice, the
founder of the Christian Brothers, and named after Daniel
O'Connell, who laid the foundation stone.

'North Richmond Street, being blind, was a quiet street except at the hour when the Christian Brothers' School set the boys free',[32] so wrote one of Éamonn's contemporaries in the school, the young James Joyce, who attended O'Connell's School for a few months in 1893 before moving on to the Jesuit Belvedere College. Another contemporary in the school was Sean T O'Kelly (Ó Ceallaigh), later President of Ireland.[33] Éamonn and Sean's paths would cross many times in later years. Other near contemporaries, whose fates would closely echo that of Éamonn, were Sean Heuston and Con Colbert. Colbert would fight in Éamonn's 4th Battalion Irish Volunteers during Easter Week 1916 and the two men, together with Sean Heuston, would all die by firing squad on the same day, 8 May 1916.

Theirs was the first generation of poorer Catholic boys to have the opportunity to receive a secondary, or, as it was called at the time, Intermediate, education. Throughout the last two decades of the nineteenth century, there had been growing pressure to provide a competitive examinations system in Ireland that would open up access, for Catholics in particular, to jobs in the civil service and to professional careers. The Intermediate Education (Ireland) Act had been passed by Parliament in 1878. The Act established an examining board with an annual sum of £32,500, which was distributed by way of money prizes for pupils and results fees for schools.[34]

Valuable 'Exhibitions', worth up to £50, were awarded to students with the highest marks. From the start, Éamonn's school results were excellent. In the Preparatory Grade Examinations of 1894, 'Edward T Kent' was awarded an Exhibition of £20, tenable for one year – one of fourteen such awards to the O'Connell School that year. Since they were paid directly to the family, the Exhibitions made a significant contribution to the family finances. He also received a Composition Prize of £2 in French.[35] Although the curriculum included the Celtic language, Éamonn didn't study the subject – there may have been a pragmatic reason for his decision, as the weighting for marks allocated to subjects varied, with the classics (Latin and Greek), together with English and mathematics, each being worth 1,200 marks; German and French, 700; while Celtic (i.e. Irish) was worth only 600.[36] The following year he was less successful, being awarded a Third Class Book Prize (£1).[37] During that year, however, tragedy had struck the Kent family when Johanna, Éamonn's mother, died on 6 February from acute phlebitis (blood clots in the leg) at the age of fifty-four.[38] Éamonn was only thirteen at the time, while Dick, the youngest in the family, was eleven and was just joining Éamonn at the O'Connell School. Éamonn, always a shy, reserved boy, received the news of his mother's death with 'silence and immobility'.[39]

In spite of his loss, Éamonn kept his attention on his studies in the year ahead, and in 1896 he was again awarded an

Exhibition – Junior Grade – of £20, tenable for three years. Getting a good education remained a priority for the Kent family. In his notebook for that year, Éamonn wrote that:

> a good school education is the all important thing for a young person about to embark on his fortunes in the world and is absolutely essential to succeed. Fathers who are careful for the interests of their children are often sorely perplexed in looking about for their future state in life. Even when no state has been definitely decided upon they take as their motto – education first – employment after … We must read if we wish to acquaint ourselves with the doings of the world – we must write if we wish to express our opinions or communicate with friends … The more we know, the more we wish to know: we are never tired getting additional knowledge – after our school days are over. [40]

These were far-sighted words from a young boy who, in later life, was renowned for never going anywhere without a book in his pocket and for haunting the National Library of Ireland for material on his researches into Irish music, language and culture.

At the age of fifteen, Éamonn was already thinking about his future career. His friend Peter Murray was advising him on the 'true road to civil service success',[41] while his own notebook records his thoughts on 'Why I should not like to be a soldier'. It's likely that the idea of a career in the army was a topic of conversation for the Kent family as Éamonn's eldest brother, Bill, joined the Royal Dublin Fusiliers shortly afterwards. Éamonn, on the other hand, was already clear that taking the queen's shilling would not figure in his plans. With no Irish army in prospect in 1896, he wrote, with some maturity, if not foresight, that he did not want to be a soldier:

because the paths to glory lead but to the grave;

because I consider the pen is far mightier than the sword;

because I am Irish and no Irishman should serve in a foreign army;

because as much honour and eminence may be gained in a civil profession;

because I have no desire to be a target for foreign adversaries;

especially because I am Irish and no Irishman can serve his country while in a foreign service.[42]

In spite of his academic achievements, Éamonn was a normal teenager. In his school diary he recorded the events of his sixteenth year. Éamonn started the school year that September by getting up every morning at 6.15am to get organised for the day though moaning about having to go to school on a 'regular wintry morning, dark, gloomy and cold'.[43]

With a bright future ahead of him, it was only occasionally that he gave a thought to Irish history. The Christian Brothers were exceptional during the nineteenth century for teaching Irish history as a subject in its own right. They did so from their own textbooks, which highlighted the themes of 'Irish resistance to English invasion; of Irish suffering resulting from English persecution; of Irish struggle against English oppression'. Moreover, they stressed the splendour of the old Gaelic civilisation which the arrival of the English had gradually suppressed and displaced.[44] Éamonn's teacher, Mr Maunsell, tended to 'wax enthusiastically about love of country', but it was not sufficient to generate much enthusiasm from the young Éamonn. On 6 October 1896, he mentioned in his notebook only that it was the 'anniversary of a man named Parnell's demise'. Éamonn was far more interested in the fact that he 'made [his] first debut as an orator today before an audience of two in the drawing school'. He was practising for a speech that his teacher Mr Duggan had asked him to deliver at the school prize-giving banquet the following day. To his own surprise, not to mention that of his family, he made an excellent speech. He called it 'a very pleasant evening. I perpetrated a – a speech …'

In the new year, 1897, Éamonn was back into the school

routine – though, as for many adolescents, early rising had become more of a problem. In January, he admitted that 'I have got into the fashion of late rising and nothing can induce me to rise before it is absolutely necessary.' All in all, life in January that year was a bit bleak. The school was gloomy, with snow lying on the roof and thick on the ground. The journey home was beset with snowball fights and, while he 'eluded the gang in Richmond Cottages', he was obliged to 'run the gauntlet for the Sackville Avenue crowd' – and run he did. He remarked in his diary that 'he that fights and runs away, will live to fight another day!'

Things only got worse in February. '*Me miserum*! Alas and alak! Misfortune never came singly,' he moaned as the boys were prohibited from playing football, causing Éamonn to wish, 'may it always thunder, rain, hail or snow when the originator of this barbarous scheme walks out!' On top of that, he was finding lessons 'simply dreadful' and 'the leather [for corporal punishment] on the point of being used', which would have been unusual in his case.[45]

There were some bright spots that term, however. In March the comic *Chums* notified Éamonn that he had been awarded a prize of an illustrated volume in their pocket-money competition.[46] His brother Michael also won a prize. The prizes were a copy of *Fame and Glory in the Soudan War* and a 'chivalrous narrative entitled *Under Bayard's Banner*'. Both arrived in the post on St Patrick's Day, and both would influence Éamonn in later life, although not in the way their authors had intended.

The following month, April, Éamonn tried out his name in Irish in his school diary – 'Eamun Tomas Ceannt'. By this stage in the school year, exams were looming. The summer term meant cramming for the exams and Éamonn hoped that 'eleven hours a day, three days a week, and nine and a half hours the other three' should leave him in 'a pretty fair condition to spout our knowledge in seven weeks' time'.

In spite of his fears before the exams, Éamonn's academic success continued and he was again awarded a Middle Grade Exhibition of £30 for two years. The school year came to an end and the summer holidays began. The following day the Kent family left Bayview Avenue and moved to their new home at 27 Fairview Avenue, Clontarf.

In 1898 Éamonn was awarded a Retained Senior Grade Exhibition of £30, allowing him to progress through to final exams.[47] Not many of his contemporaries were as fortunate. Most boys in the Intermediate education system benefited only from its early stages, and just 4.4% of the total number of students examined in Éamonn's final year progressed to senior level.

Like many of his later associates in the Irish–Ireland movement and in the republican movement, Éamonn left school and set out on life as a typical example of a Christian Brothers' boy. He was well tutored, academically bright and ambitious. The question was, how would he put this to use?

Ireland was no meritocracy at the start of the twentieth century, and in spite of their education and the opening of access to jobs in the public sector and local government, many young Catholic men from poorer and lower middle-class backgrounds found their expectations frustrated.

Chapter Two

• • • • • •

1900–1905

A Busy and Enquiring Mind

As the new century opened, the prospect of Home Rule for Ireland seemed far away. The British Empire was fighting the Boer War in South Africa, and Eamonn's brother Bill was out there, fighting on the British side. Young Éamonn, however, showed his emerging independence of spirit when he persuaded their sister, Nell, to make a Boer flag for him, which he hoisted on a tree at the end of the garden. It remained there until his father saw it and ordered it to be removed.[1] Showing his true colours already, Éamonn would, as an adult, oppose recruitment into the British Army with every fibre of his being.

The young Kents were setting out on their various career paths. JP was serving with the RIC in Wicklow; Nell, who had trained as a dressmaker,[2] was keeping house for her father and younger brothers in Fairview Avenue; Jem was working with his father as an assistant house agent; while

Michael and Éamonn were considering their career options and Richard was still at school. Their father was supplementing his RIC pension by working as a house agent with an address at 138 Dorset Street. All members of the family living in Dublin were recorded in the 1901 census as speaking both Irish and English.[3] His father's knowledge of the Irish language had come as a surprise to Éamonn when he himself started to learn it.[4]

After leaving school, Éamonn considered a number of careers including that of newspaper reporter. He went so far as to do an interview with the editor of the *Independent* but 'upon learning that he would be on duty by day and by night with little freedom, he changed his mind'.[5] He refused to join the civil service 'on the plea that it was British', but later 'consented to enter for the Corporation, remarking that the funds for the Corporation came from the Citizens of Dublin'. In the meantime, Éamonn tutored boys at Skerry's Academy, which prepared students for civil service and university exams. [6]

The enactment of legislation for the reform of local government in 1898 had transformed Dublin Corporation.[7] The electorate was increased from around 8,000 to almost 38,000 and the Act removed the requirement for councillors to be property owners.[8] Although the administration of local government was taken out of the control of large property owners and the local gentry, the franchise still excluded the majority of Dublin citizens who were lodgers paying less than four shillings a week in rent, and the many thousands who eked out an existence in the crowded tenements. Nevertheless, the change had an impact and, by 1900, the Corporation was dominated by the nationalist politicians of the United Irish League.[9]

During 1900, Dublin Corporation had decided that 'all appointments to clerkships and kindred offices under this Corporation shall be made by competitive examination'.[10] Éamonn started work in Dublin Corporation that same year and his was one of the earliest appointments under the new system. He became a clerk in the City Treasurer and Estates and Finance Office. His salary was £70 per year with an annual increment of £5, which he received regularly.[11] His brother Michael followed him into the Corporation in February 1901. Both brothers soon signed up as members of the Dublin Municipal Officers' Association (DMOA), which was set up in June 1901 for 'the purpose of recreation and mutual advancement' of Corporation employees.[12] Éamonn was later elected Chairman of the Association and remained an active member throughout his career in the Corporation.

For Éamonn, his work in Dublin Corporation would be a means to an end. He did his work efficiently and effectively; his

Constabulary upbringing and Christian Brothers education, together with his diligent personality, saw to that. Indeed, his wife Áine later recalled that 'in the seventeen years that he worked in the Corporation, only once was he late, and that was a day on which he started from home on a bicycle and the storm blew him off it'.[13]

But the career opportunities available to an educated, lower middle-class Catholic in 1900 were never likely to provide enough challenge or reward for someone like Éamonn. A colleague recalled that 'a brain such as his, always crowded with ideas, novel and interesting, seemed to chafe at the humdrum of routine and sameness'.[14] He had to find his challenges elsewhere. For him, as for many of his contemporaries, that meant the nascent Irish–Ireland movement and, in particular, the Gaelic League. Before long Éamonn had developed an abiding passion for Irish language and music.

His interest was sparked by a chance visit, on St Patrick's Day, to Gill's booksellers in Sackville Street where he came across a book called *Simple Lessons in Irish* by Fr Eugene O'Growney of St Patrick's College, Maynooth.[15] This led to his joining the Gaelic League (Conradh na Gaeilge). The League had been established in 1893 by a small group of language enthusiasts that included O'Growney, Douglas Hyde, the son of a Roscommon clergyman, and Eoin MacNeill from County Antrim, then a young civil servant. The objective of the League was to revive the Irish language, which had been in decline throughout the previous century. It also aimed to foster an interest in Irish music and dance. From the beginning the League was both non-sectarian and non-political. After a slow start the influence of the League accelerated until, by 1904, there were nearly six hundred branches. Its most remarkable achievement at that time has been described as establishing 'in the imaginations of some of the most ardent spirits of the new century, a sense of shared endeavour in the restoration of life to something precious that had come close to extinction'.[16]

This was certainly true as far as Éamonn was concerned. It also introduced the young man to a new circle of friends and acquaintances who would fundamentally shape his future direction in life. Among them was Frances (Áine) O'Brennan, the woman who, initially his student in the Gaelic League, was to become his wife and soulmate.

Éamonn attended his first meeting of the Central Dublin Branch of the Gaelic League on 18 September 1899 in the Rotunda. This was one of the most active branches in the League. Among the existing members were Eoin MacNeill and a young Patrick Pearse – two years Éamonn's senior, Pearse was already a member of the Central Branch and had been co-opted onto the Coiste Gnótha (Executive Council) in 1898.[17] This was heady company for Éamonn, a 'tall, pale, serious-looking youth' who was described by a contemporary Gaelic Leaguer as quiet, reticent and anxious to avoid the limelight.[18]

But from the start he was determined to master the Irish language. He initially inclined towards the Munster pronunciation but, as a contemporary recalled, 'having paid a visit to Connaught, he adopted the standard of that province for his pronunciation and ever afterwards, Connaught had for him a strange fascination'.[19] At the Feis Laighean agus Midhe for 1901, 'There were three entries of Irish essays on "The National Festival" confined to students of not more than three years' standing. Mr Edward T Kent carried off the First Prize.'[20]

He was also becoming known for his organisational skills and willingness to take responsibility for the routine work of the League. Within a year, Éamonn had been elected a member of a small sub-committee of the Central Dublin Branch, which was responsible for arranging monthly *scoraíochtaí* (music and dramatic events). These events had been started the previous January and 'brought music and life from the libraries and theorists and placed it before the public … They have fought the music halls by showing that relaxation and sociability and enjoyment are possible in Dublin in a healthy natural atmosphere.'[21]

A contemporary on the sub-committee, Máire, recalled later that 'when the question of programmes, posters etc. arose, the quiet voice said, "I'll attend to that, Máire" and that work was well done. I need have no anxiety whatever about it … [Éamonn] made everything run smoothly, but never got, nor expected, the slightest thanks from anyone.'[22]

Throughout this time many of those who attended the branch meetings saw only the reserved side of Éamonn's personality, a side of which he was well aware. But those who worked closely with him also saw his innate sense of fun. A contemporary later remembered two young men – Éamonn and Patrick Pearse – rushing to tell her an anecdote about the naming of Sackville Street (now O'Connell Street). Shy Éamonn was 'stepping long legged over the forms towards me, and Pearse hurrying around the table'. Both young men were 'choking with laughter'.[23]

On 18 November 1900, the Fairview/Clontarf Branch of the Gaelic League was established, with Éamonn as its first Secretary.[24] When classes started, over '100 pupils attended and received tuition from Mr T O Russell, Mr E T Kent and Miss M Kennedy, B.A. … The subscription [was] one shilling per person, no charge being made for the children.'[25] He was later, in 1903, elected President of the branch.[26]

In January 1902, Éamonn was co-opted onto the Leinster Feis Committee and was appointed, as its Secretary, to the Sub-Committee for Music and Dancing.[27] In the years between 1903 and 1905 he was a regular representative of the Central Dublin Branch at the League's annual Árd Fheiseanna. The Árd Fheis was the event at which delegates debated and decided the policy of the League and at which the Coiste Gnótha was elected. During these years Éamonn was one of the branch's nominees for election to the Coiste Gnótha but was never elected.[28]

This was a very busy time for Éamonn. Not alone was he working all day in the Corporation but in the evenings he was keeping all the records of the Clontarf Branch, attending meetings of the Central Dublin Branch, writing reports for the press, teaching students and publicising the events organised by both branches. He also found time for 'his share of hurling practice in the Phoenix Park and enjoyed many a swim at The Bull, Dollymount'.[29]

He had a particular talent for arranging concerts and entertainments to attract new members to the League. He designed and distributed posters to promote the entertainments. His brother Michael remembered in particular that 'when we used to go along at night posting up the concert posters in Clontarf, Éamonn led the way with the war pipes, keeping us going with grand old Irish airs'.[30]

All the members of the Kent family were musical and none more so than Éamonn. Michael later remembered buying 'a cheap fiddle (7s. 6d.) to practise on at home ... Éamonn took it up and could play "St Patrick's Day" on it before I could at all.'[31] Before long, Éamonn was proficient in both the fiddle and the whistle.[32]

Patrick Nally, a colleague in Dublin Corporation, sparked

Éamonn's interest in the union or *uilleann* pipes. Éamonn described the *uilleann* pipes as consisting 'of bag, chanter, drones and regulator, the wind being supplied by a bellows placed under the right arm. It is an exceedingly sweet and very perfect instrument.'[33] Nally arranged for Éamonn to purchase a set of pipes, and he immediately started to study them.[34]

He became a member of the Dublin Pipers' Club (Cumann na bPíobairí), established on 17 February 1900. The objectives of the club were:

1. The cultivation and preservation of Irish Pipe Music;
2. The popularisation of the various forms of Irish Pipes; and
3. The cultivation of Irish dancing in connection with Irish pipe music.

One of the important patrons and, later, President of the club, was Edward Martyn; Martyn, together with William Butler Yeats and Lady Gregory, had previously established the Irish Literary Theatre. The club held public musical evenings each Friday night, promising aspiring members that:

Irish Dancing, Fiddle, Flute and Pipe-playing are practised. Pipers and other musicians visiting Dublin also attend and enliven the proceedings. Irish, the official language of the Cumann, is spoken as much as possible on these occasions and is also used largely in correspondence. Pipers, both amateur and professional, are supplied to concerts in any part

of the country if reasonable notice be given to the Hon.
Secretary. An index of pipers is kept, containing a record
of all known pipers, at home and abroad, living and dead.[35]

Characteristically, Éamonn set about researching the history of the pipes and promoting them publicly by every
means possible. He also gave talks, illuminated with magic
lantern slides,[36] and wrote a set of articles on the history
of the pipes from their origins in 'the simple reed such as
children construct for themselves from the rushes that grew
by the river banks', through their development in the four-
teenth, fifteenth and sixteenth centuries.[37] Éamonn did not
confine his enthusiasm for the pipes to the island of Ireland.
Correspondence with *The Sphere* newspaper in London,
in December 1903, confirmed the paper's intention to use
Éamonn's article on the Irish bagpipes and 'to pay for it and
for the photographs at the ordinary rates'.[38]

In the text of a pamphlet written by Éamonn, the club
promised that 'any person with good lungs and fair musical capacity can become fairly proficient in six months'.[39]
For those lacking Éamonn's musicality and enthusiasm, this
seems optimistic, but in his notebook, Éamonn identified the
problem and set about finding a solution.

Gentlemen often expressing a desire to learn the Pipes
have been prevented by not meeting with a proper Book
of Instructions, which has induced the author to write the

following Treatise, which, it is presumed, with the favourite Collections of Tunes added thereto, will be acceptable to the Lovers of ancient and Pastoral Music.

The unpublished text provided pages of detailed instructions on everything the aspiring piper needed to know. The Pipers' Club itself provided tuition for student pipers and, in his address as Secretary to the AGM on 27 February 1903, Éamonn remarked that the class 'left no excuse to those who were eternally complaining that they could not get tuition on the instrument'.[40]

Éamonn also put his considerable organisational skills at the disposal of the new club. As its Honorary Secretary, he organised the meetings of the club and took the minutes in Irish. 'He was in constant demand as an adjudicator at both pipe and fiddle competitions,' recalled his wife, Áine.

Éamonn and Áine's growing relationship and their joint interest in the pipes was typical of the cross-fertilisation of interests between members of the Gaelic League and the other organisations committed to the preservation of all things Gaelic. In many cases interests merged as they did when, on 21 October 1901, Éamonn appeared on stage as the blind piper in Douglas Hyde's play, *Casadh an tSúgáin*, in the Gaiety Theatre. The play, which was the first in Irish to be presented in a Dublin theatre, was produced by the Irish Literary Theatre.[41] The tune Éamonn played during the play was 'The Lasses of Limerick'.

The Pipers' Club was also closely associated with the Oireachtas of the Gaelic League,[42] which comprised musical and Irish-language competitions, and, on 28 May 1903, the club's members were praised in the League's newspaper, *An Claidheamh Soluis,* for 'showing us unmistakably that the instrument and the musicians to whom Irish–Ireland owes the preservation of its best airs are not yet dead'.[43]

Éamonn used every opportunity to promote his interest in the pipes and his commitment to the Irish language. A colleague in the Gaelic League remembered a time, in 1902 or 1903, when 'there were droves of young enthusiastic Gaels going off to Aran and elsewhere to "perfect themselves" in Irish'. A group of these men set off, 'to become native speakers in a fortnight'. Sadly disillusioned with their progress, they were returning to Dublin through Galway. Hearing of their arrival in Galway, Éamonn joined them. 'With the skirl of the pipes', Éamonn solemnly preceded them through Eyre Square and all the way to the station. Heads were popping, children running alongside and everyone gasping at the sight. The young Irish students 'would have been glad if the ground opened up to swallow [them], or if they could have wrung Éamonn's neck'. At the station, Éamonn marched up and down until a cheer was raised as the train moved off.[44]

Although he had left County Galway while just a small child, Éamonn came to love the county as an adult. He spent many holidays in Connemara, adopted the Connaught dialect, and always thought of himself as a Galway man. In a speech he gave to the Clontarf Branch of the Gaelic League, he described his first visit to Galway as a Gaelic Leaguer. He recounted how:

> Whenever a Gaelic Leaguer enters [the village of] Menlo, he finds himself surrounded by a chattering crowd of children – chiefly boys. Give one a penny and he'll tell a story or recite a poem with an accent and pronunciation that will fill you with delight as well as envy. Someone once remarked in surprise that in France even the little children speak French fluently. Wonderful. In Menlo the little children know more Irish than all the members of the Craobh Chluaintairbh put together.

With a naïve delight, common among his fellow Gaelic Leaguers, he described how he would cycle out along the coast, calling out in Irish to all those he met. He often took the opportunity to talk to little groups of youngsters galloping up *bóiríní* (little roads) from the sea with loads of seaweed – 'curious unsophisticated youngsters they are, ragged and rough and all browned by the sea and wind. Wind from the Atlantic.'

The women he met were 'fine, stout, rosy cheeked, weather beaten dames'. He described one young woman

> … as she crossed a rock bearing in her hand a pail of water from the well. Her hair and eyes were black; a small dark

shawl was thrown over her blue bodice. And a pair of bare feet projected from beneath the usual red petticoat, the contrast being highlighted still more by a white apron partly tucked up round the waist. There was something gypsy-like in her love of bright colours and her taste in selecting them. It struck me at the time that many of our fine ladies could have learned a lesson in dress from that poor hard working, supple, active, graceful country woman.[45]

One wonders whether the gently reared and well-shod ladies in his Dublin audience would have shared his enthusiasm!

In the early years of the century, the Gaelic League and the Pipers' Club provided their members with a very active social life filled with music, song and dance. These were ideal opportunities for young men and women to meet and develop relationships based on deep mutual interests. The League was particularly attractive to women because it accepted members irrespective of gender.

Frances O'Brennan (who adopted the name Áine) was the youngest of the four daughters of Frank O'Brennan and his wife Elizabeth (née Butler). Áine's family had nationalist tendencies on both her mother's and her father's side: her father, who died before she was born, was a Fenian, and her mother's father was believed to have been a member of the United Irishmen.[46]

Áine, like her future husband, was one of the new generation who benefited from the Intermediate Education Act of 1878. Although initially confined to boys, the provisions of the Act were extended to girls in the face of opposition from the IPP and the Roman Catholic bishops – this followed the intervention by a deputation led by women's rights campaigner Isabella Tod. Among the schools to benefit from the new legislative environment was the Dominican College in Eccles Street which Áine, together with her sisters Mary, Kathleen and Elizabeth (Lily), attended. Shortly after leaving school, Áine joined the Gaelic League and it was on a League outing to Galway, when Éamonn was nineteen and Áine twenty, that they met for the first time. They journeyed back from Galway together and, not long afterwards, Áine also joined the Pipers' Club where she became Treasurer.[47]

Their relationship blossomed slowly at meetings of the League and the Pipers' Club, on walks in the country and by the seaside. In August 1903, Éamonn and Áine kissed for the first time on the strand at Shankill, County Dublin. 'Kisses never were sweeter,' Éamonn later remembered, as he lay on the grass with Áine looking down into his face on 'a magnificent, warm, sunshiny August day'.[48]

In the manner of the time, they corresponded very regularly – and Áine kept Éamonn's letters, although he does not appear to have kept hers! Éamonn's letters were bilingual – frequently starting in Irish and progressing in English. That same August,

1903, Éamonn was holidaying as usual in Connaught and wrote regularly from O'Sullivan's Hotel in Spiddal and from the Hotel of the Isles in Gorumna. Missing her, he sent her railway vouchers to join him at the Connacht Feis.

At the time Éamonn was still living in the family home in Clontarf. Áine was living with her mother and sisters off the South Circular Road, at Dolphin's Barn, and working at Messrs Cooper and Kenny, Auditors and Accountants, in 12 College Green, just up the road from Éamonn in Dublin Corporation's municipal buildings.[49]

Early December 1903 saw the young couple comparing notes on their respective head colds while Éamonn reported on his sister Nell's illness in hospital and his brother Michael's progress with a slight attack of blood poisoning after cutting his arm with a knife. They wondered whether their absence from the club would occasion comment. If it had, it would have been warranted, as, by this time, Éamonn and Áine were passionately in love and Éamonn was looking forward to 'turning over the pages of the book of our lives together'.[50] He compared Áine's love for him to that of the impudent, coquettish little Grace for the big, slow-moving, grave Hugh in the popular Charles Kickham novel *Knocknagow* – 'the way a little girl can make her way into a big man's heart. "That's you and I."'[51]

On Sunday, 20 December 1903, Éamonn asked Áine to marry him, in Irish, as he recorded: '*An bpósfaigh tú mé?*'

and his sweetheart 'whispered her consent to be my little wife'. Although Éamonn felt unworthy of Áine's great love, he longed to become her acknowledged protector and husband.[51] Éamonn and Áine didn't immediately share their good news with others but agreed to defer its announcement until the following July.

One of Éamonn's preoccupations as the New Year (1904) started was how he was going to be able to afford to rent a house and to support a wife. While his salary in the Corporation was adequate, he didn't feel it would be enough, particularly since the convention of the day would require Áine to give up her own job. By Easter 1904 he was wishing that 'some good fairy would indicate a hidden – but accessible – "crock of gold" whereby we might brave the dangers of housekeeping and enter on a new life, the married state'.[53] Then with his usual determination, Éamonn turned his busy brain to money-making schemes. Having acquired a typewriter, which he called an 'infernal machine', in April 1904, he began writing advertisements to order. Another scheme entailed manufacturing and selling a kind of Reckitt's Blue, used for whitening clothes in the laundry, to be called Kent's Irish Blue.[54]

In May 1904, Éamonn took measurements for the engagement ring. By now they were longing to make their love for each other public – not least because 'when we're engaged we needn't be so dependent on the weather and chance meetings' and Áine's sisters had begun to suspect their engagement. They formally announced it on 12 July 1904.

With their marriage imminent, Éamonn was determined that, before the year was out, Kent's Irish Blue would make an appearance on the market. His diary for the year, written in Irish, recounts his detailed product research. He wrote to companies throughout Britain and Ireland seeking quotes for boxes and labels, moulds and dyes, mills and gas engines. Áine did the 'market research', providing Éamonn with 'a list of people who would buy the Blue. People from all over Ireland.' [55]

The early months of 1905 were exceptionally busy with Éamonn's Blue experiments, the Pipers' Club, the Gaelic League and his meetings with Áine. On 18 January, Éamonn read a paper to the Árd Craobh of the Gaelic League entitled 'Ceol Éireannach' (Irish Music).[56] Still, they both found time for reading. Éamonn was reading a book by the American author F. Marion Crawford entitled *Cecilia: A Story of Modern Rome*. Áine was reading a book that Éamonn had recommended to her, *The Days of Auld Lang Syne*, written by Ian Maclaren, a Scottish theologian. Evenings and weekends were spent together – house hunting, walking, or at Áine's family home. Both Áine and Éamonn, devout Catholics, attended weekly Mass and Confession, though sometimes Áine had to remind Éamonn to attend the latter.

By the end of March, the strain of keeping too many balls

in the air was beginning to tell on Éamonn and he decided to submit his resignation as Secretary to the committee of the Pipers' Club. His diary recorded that he 'wrote the minutes and left the book in room seven. I'm sorry to be leaving the Club but I won't be gone altogether.'[57] The committee, at its meeting on 8 April 1905, unanimously agreed that 'such a thing couldn't be thought of and that [he] should be asked to reconsider [his] decision'. They could not see how the Cumann would get on without him and asked him to come along to the next meeting on the following Monday to argue the point.[58] What the committee didn't know was that during these days the Kent siblings were keeping vigil by the bedside of their brother Jem, who had been admitted to Our Lady's Hospice at Harold's Cross with tuberculosis. He was twenty-nine years of age and he died on 13 April, at 11.30pm. Although tuberculosis was rampant among young adults in Dublin at the time, his death came as a terrible blow to his family. Éamonn's diary for the previous few days was empty – without words. Then on Thursday, 13 April, he wrote: 'Séamus [Jem] died in the hospital out in Harold's Cross at 11.30pm. God rest him.'[59]

Éamonn's friends in the Pipers' Club expressed their deepest sympathy for the sad loss of his brother, but remained dismayed by his decision which, in the absence of anyone else willing to take on the role of Hon. Secretary, seemed to be leaving them 'completely stranded. It looks as if there were nothing for it but for the club to break up.'[60] Éamonn stayed firm on his decision but agreed to remain on the committee. In the Annual Report for 1905–1906 of Cumann na bPíobairí, the committee noted that:

> The most important happening from a Club point of view during the year was the resignation of Mr E.T. Kent from the Secretaryship. Mr Kent had been one of the founders of the Club, he had been Secretary for many years and whatever the Club has done for Irish music and Irish ideals during those years has been largely the result of his endeavours. However, though unable to retain the Secretaryship, the Club has had the advantage of his advice and experience on the Committee and he is at the present moment engaged in the preparation of a Tutor for the Pipes.[61]

Better days were ahead for Éamonn and Áine, who had set a date for their wedding – 7 June 1905. On 1 May, Éamonn signed a tenancy agreement with Messrs Darby and Baily for 44 Reuben Avenue, Dolphin's Barn, which was close to Áine's family home. Éamonn noted in his diary that they really liked the house: that 'the kitchen is fantastic, and the garage isn't bad.'[62] Their rent was two pounds sterling a month.[63] At £24 per annum, this was a significant enough expense out of Éamonn's salary, which by now had increased to £90 per annum.[64]

But at last they had a home of their own and, with great

excitement, they set about furnishing it. Áine kept receipts for chairs, a wardrobe and a set of fire irons from P A Walsh, Auctioneers; a hair mattress, bolsters, pillows, carpet and oil-cloth from James H Webb and Co., Cornmarket (paid for by her mother, Mrs O'Brennan); picture cord, picture hooks, bamboo pole, curtain hooks and pins, a watering can, hatchet, trowel and stair rods (again thanks to Mrs O'Brennan); and a drawing room suite and table from PA Wren, Auctioneers and Valuers, Bachelor's Walk, in the amount of £3 12s.10d., paid for by Éamonn.[65]

Plans for the wedding itself were also progressing. Wedding carriages, rosettes and ribbons were ordered by Miss O'Brennan from the James's Street branch of A O'Neill and Son, Carriage and Funeral Establishment, 171 North Strand. Éamonn bought a gold Albert (pocket) watch from Hopkins and Hopkins for £2 10s., and, from J McDowell, Practical Watchmaker and Jeweller, 3 Upper Sackville Street, a wedding ring and keeper ring for £1 15s. and pearls for £4. Although he was known in his family to have little interest in clothes, he was determined to be a credit to Áine on their wedding day and recorded in his diary that he also bought green material for a suit, together with six shirts, three evening shirts, two fashionable shirts, six pairs of shirt studs, six collars, six kerchiefs and twelve shirt fronts.

The long-anticipated wedding took place in St James's Church, James's Street. The Rev. Francis MacEarney of

Westland Row conducted the ceremony in Irish and the witnesses were Mairtín MacMurchadha (a friend of Éamonn's from the Pipers' Club) and Eilís ní Bhraonáin (Áine's sister, Lily). Éamonn refused to use English money to represent 'all his wealth' in the ceremony, and instead procured some French francs for the occasion.[66]

The only shadow on this happy time emerged a month later, when there was a testy exchange of correspondence between Éamonn and Dr George Stritch, the Registrar for Dublin South City, about the language to be used on the wedding certificate. When the meticulous Éamonn pointed out that he might be fined £10 if the certificate was not correctly registered, the Registrar finally clarified that adding the English versions of the particulars given by Éamonn in Irish

> was made in your own interest for purposes of identification thereafter and in order that the English forms of the names might be inserted in the Marriage Indexes of this Department as well as the Irish forms.

He then stated that if Éamonn objected to this, he would leave it as it stood. Not surprisingly, Éamonn wanted it left as it was in Irish. [67]

It was not only the Dublin bureaucrats who had problems with Gaelic names – or indeed, with the very idea of Éamonn's being married! Éamonn's friend from his schooldays, Peter Murray, himself married and living in London, was astonished when he received notification of the marriage:

> ... Ned Kent married, married – Ned Kent. Well to be Yankee – it licks creation. Shy – bashful, retiring Ned, who used to blush when asked the boundaries of Europe – not merely engaged, mind you – but – married! Well, I'm blowed. I really am.
>
> I am ashamed to confess that your wedding-card was, in part, unintelligible to me, and I am still doubtful if the fortunate lady's name was Annie Brennan or not (excuse me for anglicising it) ...[68]

At the start of the new century, Éamonn was an average young Dubliner with much the same dreams as the hundreds of other clerks who bicycled daily into work from Dublin's new suburbs to its city offices. By the summer of 1905, his twenty-fourth year, the shy and retiring young man had a secure job, a loving wife and a home of his own. He had a wide circle of acquaintances and a growing reputation among the minority Irish–Ireland movement as an organiser, activist, teacher and musician.

A committed Gaelic Leaguer, he had adopted the principles of the League regarding the preservation and use of the language, music and dance of Gaelic Ireland and put these principles into effect with enthusiasm through his teaching and his pipe playing. He had begun to emerge from his youthful shell and make his voice heard in League circles. In November 1905 when the League's newspaper, *An Claidheamh Soluis*, wondered how successful the organisation was in achieving one of its primary aims – making good speakers of Irish – Éamonn pointed out that the League had not provided any forum at which the adult student could showcase his or her oral proficiency and he suggested the 'establishment of a competition ... in which a gold medal would be awarded to the best adult non-native speaker of Irish'.[69] The committee took up his suggestion and decided to include a competition for 'Dialogue – for non-native speakers over 18 years of age, Prize £2'.[70]

However, he remained independent of spirit and was willing to take a stand against the more dogmatic disciples of the League when they came in conflict with his innate kindness and practical Christianity. At a time when artists who appeared at any functions organised by, or under the auspices of, Dublin Castle, were ostracised by the Leaguers, a Gaelic League contemporary of Éamonn's recalled his standing up bravely for a young singer who was booed from the stage of the Rotunda Hall with the accusation of having appeared at a Castle function:

> It was a brave, a very brave thing to face that hostility, and to risk his own reputation. He was as likely as not to be called 'Castle hack' for his action. There came a great quietness, as the audience listened to him. He did not stand but

spoke with his arms folded. His voice sounded aggressive and harsh, because he was trying to overcome his natural shyness, and it shook with intensity, as he told of the struggle of women like her, with a great gift cramped by poverty, to earn any kind of a living. And then, with a fine scorn, he pointed out that we all went to hear great artists of Irish blood and applauded them, without regard to their principles. Why not apply the same rule to all? Why indeed? The truth and the logic hit guilty consciences, and the audience went to the other extreme of applause, when the music was done. The artist took it all calmly.[71]

By 1905, however, his diaries and correspondence still provide little to suggest that his interest in all things Gaelic would necessarily translate to any radical form of political activity. As Áine would later recall: 'After the Parnell split there was no interest in politics by the young folk. There were too many divisions. The Gaelic League, where there were no politics spoken, was a mecca for everybody.'[72] It was the intensity of Éamonn's commitment, however, that gave the clue to his future direction. The League may have been determinedly apolitical, but many of its leading members were not. The shy young man had made his name in the League on the back of his enthusiasm, combined with his work ethic and ability to get things done. By the age of twenty-four he had spent nearly five years in the company of many advocates of an Irish-Ireland. He was reading Griffith's *United Irishman* and Moran's *Leader* newspapers, both of which called for the revival of native Irish industry. He was, through his Kent's Irish Blue, experimenting actively with self-sufficiency and economic nationalism. Once the young couple had set up home and settled into married life, the establishment of Sinn Féin would provide him with a new and political outlet for his energies.

Chapter Three

• • • • • • •

1906–1908

Finding His Public Voice

For Éamonn and Áine, the year 1906 brought great joy with the birth of their son, Rónán, in June. Following his birth, however, Áine contracted septic poisoning (septicemia) which, in that pre-antibiotic era, nearly cost her life. Death in childbirth was all too common in the early twentieth century and Éamonn's friend Peter Murray, writing his congratulations from London, remarked on the coincidence of 'both our wives nearly losing their lives as a consequence [of childbirth] and, from the same terrible cause, septic poisoning'. He added that he expected Rónán would speak Gaelic, while his own little daughter, Betty, would speak only 'Anglo Saxon'.[1] His expectation proved true and Éamonn spoke to Rónán almost exclusively in Irish.

With his home and family life settled, the Gaelic League and the Pipers' Club continued to occupy Éamonn's free time. The Gaelic League was concerned about whether it was achieving its main objective of making Irish a spoken language among a significant proportion of the population. Patrick Pearse, as editor of *An Claidheamh Soluis*, reflected the League's concern that 'the vast majority of those who undertake the study of Irish, whether in League classes or in the schools, do not become Irish speakers'. Pearse blamed imperfect teaching and hoped that a way would soon be found to support the training of teachers in Dublin and other League centres.[2] Training colleges for teachers of Irish already existed in Munster, Connaught and Ulster and the need for a similar resource in Leinster became a matter of public debate early in 1906. With influential support coming from Eoin MacNeill on behalf of the League, and from the Roman Catholic Archbishop of Dublin, Rev. William Walsh, a committee consisting of Agnes O'Farrelly, Eoin MacNeill, Patrick Pearse and E Moonan was established to prepare plans for a Leinster College of Irish (Coláiste Laighean).

By September 1906 the project had become a reality. A location had been chosen, 52 Upper Sackville Street, and advertisements were placed in the national media for the appointment of the chief professors and a registrar. The part-time post of Registrar, carrying a stipend of £30, was responsible for the clerical administration of the college during the annual sessions, the first of which ran from 1 October 1906 to 31 March 1907.[3]

The opportunity to apply for the post could not have

come at a better time for Éamonn. Rónán's arrival had strained the family budget and, although Éamonn's salary had continued to increase, his experiments with Kent's Irish Blue were probably a drain on, rather than an addition to, the household finances. Also, Éamonn's administrative and Irish-language skills were ideally suited to the post. On 19 September, he was informed that the committee had unanimously selected him for the position.[4] However, a problem arose regarding the opening of the college as planned and a notice in *An Claidheamh Soluis* alerted students that 'it has been found necessary to postpone the opening of the classes.'[5] The *Freeman's Journal* explained:

The reason the College is in darkness is because when the Registrar, Éamonn Ceannt, called to the offices of the Gas Company to arrange the installation of gas he provided all the necessary details and signed with his name, Éamonn Ceannt, the name under which he was appointed to the college, does all his private business and is known to his friends. The officials of the company however asked if it were not an Irish name and if it were that he must 'translate' it. Apparently an unfamiliar name of any other 'nationality' would have been accepted. Mr Ceannt could not solve the problem by 'translating' his proper name, and the officials of the company informed him that the requisition would not be accepted nor the gas supplied. Hence the present obscurity.[6]

Ultimately Éamonn was successful in getting the lights turned back on. Archbishop William Walsh and Dr Douglas Hyde, the President of the Gaelic League, presided over the opening of the college on 15 October.[7]

In their letter of appointment the committee had informed Éamonn that he would also be eligible for 'any other appointments that it may become necessary for them to make', once all concerned had a clearer idea of the workload of the Registrar. Never work-shy, by November Éamonn, who had won Third Prize for Teaching Method at the Oireachtas the previous August,[8] was teaching an intermediate class in the college on Mondays and Thursdays from 9pm–10pm. His hours as Registrar were from 7pm–9pm every weekday evening.[9]

Éamonn took his responsibilities seriously. In his teaching notebook he listed his thoughts on the teaching of Irish. He stressed the advisability of introducing a large number of simple phrases, the benefits of repetition and of giving answers under the breath – he called this a kind of ventriloquism. He was conscious of the sensitivities of his pupils and stressed the importance of laughing *with* them, never *at* them, and of 'keeping the business lively'. To this end, he reminded himself that 'sitting down won't do. Stand, walk, *act* the part. Use gestures freely.' For a man who was naturally shy and introverted, he recognised the need for personal magnetism in a teacher. Apparently it worked, because his pupils remembered his classes with great fondness.[10]

In spite of the punishing evening workload on top of his day job in the Corporation, and with the financial cushion of his college stipend, Éamonn, Áine and Rónán found time that same month to move from 44 Reuben Avenue to a nearby house at 47 Reuben Avenue.[11]

In January 1907, while Éamonn attended the annual dinner of the Dublin Municipal Officers' Association (DMOA) in the Dolphin Hotel on Essex Street (now part of Temple Bar), a riot was taking place across the river in the Abbey Theatre, where JM Synge's new play, *The Playboy of the Western World*, had just premiered. The riot brought into stark relief the widening gulf between the Anglo-Irish Ireland of William Butler Yeats, Lady Gregory and their supporters, and the Irish-Ireland of Douglas Hyde, Arthur Griffith and their followers. The play outraged Irish nationalists. Already concerned that the Abbey – the national theatre – was failing to subordinate its aesthetic and artistic objectives to the nationalist cause, they saw the play as a slur on the purity of Irish womanhood and the Irish peasant, both of which they were accustomed to idealising. The riots also raised the issue of whether there could, or should, be an Irish literature in English, as opposed to in Irish alone.[12] Some Irish–Ireland critics acknowledged that the dispute might be temporary; if, and when, Ireland was free and independent, things might be different, but until then, they insisted that it was up to the national theatre to do its duty for the national cause.[13]

Writing to Patrick Pearse as editor of *An Claidheamh Soluis* in April, Éamonn left his readers in no doubt about where he stood on the matter. He explained that for a long time he had believed that 'a straight line divided Gaelic literature, past, present and future from all literary productions by Irishmen in English'. He criticised Pearse for two recent articles in *An Claidheamh Soluis* praising a writer of fine English (Yeats) as 'the most powerful mind in the "present literary movement"'. Éamonn's point was that the newspaper of the Gaelic League was

> no place for the booming literary efforts of English-writing people born in Ireland, however 'beautiful' their English or national their personal aspirations and acts. There is a place for everything. The English-writing Irishman has a huge field open to him. The English-writing dramatist will, unfortunately, have little difficulty finding an audience anywhere in Ireland … His Gaelic brother is not so fortunate. His audience is necessarily more restricted. He needs encouragement and deserves it.

He also criticised *An Claidheamh Soluis,* and implicitly Pearse, for demeaning the acting skills of amateur Irish actors. According to Éamonn, Pearse had taken as his standard 'the professional players employed at the notorious "Abbey" and was recommending that the Gaelic actor should go to the "Abbey" or elsewhere to acquire the technique of acting'. He concluded:

> The League at present is in a certain danger of losing its
> force by trying to cover too much ground. I protest that it
> has not time to waste on Anglo Irish poets, dramatists, or
> literature. Their time has gone. Let the Gael have the field
> henceforth.

In a typically robust response, Pearse, referring to Éamonn's
letter, stated that a 'bombshell burst at our feet on Monday
last', and that he saw nothing heretical in a Gaelic Leaguer
holding the opinions set out in his own articles, although he
acknowledged magnanimously that another Gaelic Leaguer
might legitimately disagree.[14] He maintained, however, 'in
all seriousness that the Gaelic Leaguer who confines himself to Irish – if there be any such – *does not* appreciate the
full extent of the present day literary movement'. He also
hoped that Éamonn's 'mental obfuscation', which prevented
him from appreciating 'the very clear and indeed almost self
evident argument with regard to [acting] art and technique',
would prove temporary.[15]

The mildly jocular tone of Éamonn's letter and Pearse's
somewhat patronising response suggest that the two young
men were able to disagree in principle without resorting to
personal animosity. Both continued to be closely associated
with the Leinster College of Irish, Pearse on the committee
and Éamonn in his dual role of Registrar and teacher.

Éamonn and Áine spent the summer holidays in the west of Ireland. With the family's overstretched budget in mind, he had turned down a gold medal for his recent Oireachtas prize for Teaching Method in favour of an award of £1 plus railway and carfare to south Connemara.[16] They left little Rónán with Áine's sister Lily, and went to stay in the Seaview Hotel, Spiddal.

He wrote to Lily from the hotel: 'To dearest Lily, of the long locks, defender of the orphan [Rónán], waterer of the flowers, sender of *Póga* [kisses], seeker of a man, greetings!' In ungrateful brotherly fashion, he hoped Rónán was waking her up early and told her that the '*fear an tighe* [man of the house]' was on the look-out for a girl with £200 a year – just in case she was interested![17]

The following September, possibly finding the hours too demanding or the work not sufficiently interesting, Éamonn stepped down from the post of Registrar of the Leinster College and returned as a staff professor.

During 1907 the apolitical Gaelic League was beginning to worry that the public was confusing it with an emerging political movement called the Sinn Féin League. The Gaelic language term *sinn féin* (we ourselves/ourselves alone) referred to the principle that Irish men and women should achieve political and economic independence through self-reliance. As far as the Gaelic League was concerned, this concept represented the essence of its own broad platform and, in an editorial in *An Claidheamh Soluis*, Pearse pointed out that it could fairly be claimed that 'all Gaelic Leaguers are Sinn Féiners'. He accepted however that, while individual Gaelic Leaguers were at liberty to become political Sinn Féiners, they should not use League platforms to promulgate any political programme.[18]

The debate over the 'ownership' of the term *sinn féin* was due to the establishment of a new political movement, formed from the amalgamation of Cumann na nGaedheal and the Dungannon Clubs. It adopted the name The Sinn Féin League. Cumann na nGaedheal had been formed in 1900 as a loose grouping of bodies that shared the objective of Irish independence; and Bulmer Hobson, Denis McCullough and a group of Ulster nationalists with strong connections to the secretive Irish Republican Brotherhood (IRB), who were committed to armed rebellion, had formed the Dungannon Clubs in 1905. The President of the Sinn Féin League was PT Daly, also a member of the IRB.[19] The party was committed to the restoration of Irish independence.

Another group to claim the name 'Sinn Féin' was the National Council. Arthur Griffith, a Dublin journalist, together with Maude Gonne and others, had established the National Council in protest against King Edward VII's visit to Dublin. By 1905 it had been restructured as a political party and was fielding candidates in local elections with some success. In 1906 Griffith changed the name of his newspaper, *The United Irishman*, to *Sinn Féin*. Then, in September 1907, following the North Leitrim by-election of June 1907, the Sinn Féin League merged with the National Council, 'united under the title of the National Council for the common purpose of achieving by Sinn Féin methods the establishment of the independence of Ireland'. The amalgamated party soon began to describe itself as the 'Sinn Féin Organisation', later referred to as the Sinn Féin Party.[20] The organisation was an uneasy alliance between two very different groups who were, in fact, united primarily in their opposition to the IPP and its pursuit of Home Rule by constitutional means.

On the one side were the supporters of advanced republican separatism, and IRB activists, such as Bulmer Hobson, Denis McCullough and, latterly, Seán MacDiarmada. With the addition of Tom Clarke, a veteran Fenian, who returned from America in November 1907, these men would form the nucleus of a revived IRB. On the other side were the supporters of the politically more conservative Arthur Griffith. In his book *The Resurrection of Hungary*, Griffith had proposed a dual mandate of political and economic nationalism. Politically, it suggested a system by which Ireland and Britain would remain under a single monarch but would have separate and independent parliaments. To achieve this, he proposed that Irish Members of Parliament would abstain from attendance at Westminster and that an Irish parliament would be set up in Dublin. Economically, Griffith supported the development of indigenous Irish manufacturing industries under the protection of a high-tariff barrier against imports.

Éamonn was attracted to the new Sinn Féin Organisation – he had already joined it when it was the Sinn Féin League. His sister-in-law recalled later that he was never a Home Ruler,[21] and Sinn Féin's political commitment to Irish independence and to the development of Irish industry meshed closely with his own principles. Éamonn's pursuit of these principles was also evident in his attempts to radicalise the DMOA, his professional representative body. At the start of 1908, Éamonn was elected to the position of Vice Chairman of the Association.[22]

During 1908, the uneasy alliance between the Sinn Féin Organisation and the Gaelic League led to public friction when articles in Griffith's newspaper, *Sinn Féin*, appeared to suggest that the political party supported one side of an internal wrangle within the Gaelic League. The wrangle led to Éamonn publicly announcing his support for the political objectives of the Sinn Féin Party.

In June 1908, Éamonn presided over a meeting of the Sinn Féin Central Branch (Árd Craobh) during which, as Pearse later reported in *An Claidheamh Soluis*:

> [he] … avowed himself as a Sinn Féiner, both in the broad
> sense in which the word was used by Gaelic Leaguers long

before the motto Sinn Féin was adopted by a political party,
and also as an official Sinn Féiner in the narrower [sense as]
… a follower of the political programme of the [Sinn Féin]
National Council … [23]

By 1908 the Gaelic League had reached its peak in
terms of the number of branches in Ireland, with a single-
year highest membership estimated to have been between
33,550 and 47,000 people.[24] On the surface this was a great
success but the League was concerned that there were still
many Irish men and women for whom the idea of Irish as
a national language was an irrelevance or, at best, a cause
worth throwing a half a crown at every so often – if only
to get rid of importunate collectors. It was for this reason
that Éamonn had, the previous November, made himself
available to the Propagandist Committee to help promote
the cause.

In August 1908, he took matters a step further. In an article in *An Claidheamh Soluis*, which Pearse commended to his
readers as deserving of careful consideration, Éamonn suggested the League had forgotten its 'propagandist' methods.
He argued that the rousing processions – marching to the
sound of pipes and the beat of the drum – were no longer
enough. The League had become too inwardly focused and,
he said, the 'outside public have grown cold. No one will
deny they have. They need constant rousing, constant appeals
from press and platform.' He was particularly concerned

at the inability of the League to convert the 'professional and monied' class to the cause. Practical as always, he was not suggesting that the busy doctor should go back to his schooldays but that he would be persuaded to divert to the League a small part of the patronage and money he ordinarily devoted to the 'local bazaar, the annual ball, the agricultural show, the boat club, the races'. Éamonn argued that the League should study the psychology or art of obtaining money and he pointed out that 'a man will give less to a collector at his own door on a dark March evening than he would dare to offer in the light of day and in the presence of a large and enthusiastic meeting. Method means money and money is of vital importance to the League.' He proposed that the League should adopt a publicity programme across all branches, great and small, and thus show 'a little more "go", a little less timidity and diplomacy and a great deal more faith in our strength'.[25]

Éamonn had already accused the Coiste Gnótha itself of failing to communicate effectively with its own members about important topics of the day. He was particularly concerned by the fact that reports of the Coiste 'are of the most meagre description', and that 'from whispers which occasionally reach even as far as my ears I know that a great deal of information is withheld from Leaguers which Leaguers are entitled to have'.[26]

The appearance of his letters in *An Claidheamh Soluis*,

his talks on League publicity platforms, and the time he spent presiding over meetings of the largest Central Dublin Branch, were giving Éamonn a higher public profile in the League. In August, at its Árd Fheis, this led to his election to the Coiste Gnótha of the League. Now he was at the centre of the League and would no longer have to rely on whispers for his information.

For Éamonn, the high point of the year 1908 came in September when he accompanied the Catholic Young Men's Society's (CYMS) pilgrimage to Rome as its official piper. St Kevin's parish, near where Éamonn lived, organised the pilgrimage and the chief organiser was PJ Daniels, a colleague in Dublin Corporation.

The International Federation of the CYMS had arranged for athletics tests to be held in the Vatican gardens. All the nations of Europe were represented, with the exception of England and Russia. In the absence of an English contingent, the Irish were anxious that their participation would 'mark as strongly as possible the separate individuality of Ireland as a Nation'.[27] To that end, throughout the visit Éamonn wore an Irish piper's costume believed to be an eleventh-century design, which his sister, Nell, had made for him.[28]

The pilgrims and athletes were accompanied by a delegation of members from Dublin Corporation, which had decided to make an address in Irish to Pope Pius X on the occasion of the fifth anniversary of his coronation.[29] Among

the representatives was Sean T O'Kelly, a Sinn Féin member
of Dublin Corporation, who had been a contemporary of
Éamonn's at school. A fellow Gaelic Leaguer, O'Kelly was
chosen to give the address to the Pope because he was the
only Irish speaker among the members of the Corporation.[30]
O'Kelly's day job was as the business manager of *An Claidheamh Soluis*.

Éamonn himself had decided not to speak a word of
English on the trip, so he spoke Irish or French, with a
smattering of Italian.[31] His private diary, written in Irish,
describes his travels and reveals something of the evolution of his political thinking at the time. The group left
the North Wall to strains of 'God Save the Pope', played by
Éamonn on the pipes. After a rough passage they arrived
in Liverpool, took the train to London, and the steamer
to Dieppe. The first thing Éamonn saw on his arrival in
Dieppe was a large cross on the quay. He believed this was a
sign, 'showing to all and sundry that the country of France
wasn't without religion'. This apparently provided some
reassurance to Éamonn that republicanism could co-exist
with Roman Catholicism.

He was shocked by the fleshpots of Paris, but, as the travellers made their way by train through the French towns and
countryside, he concluded that there was a lot to be seen,
heard and learned by travelling abroad. He recommended
fellow Irish speakers to leave their 'English' spectacles at

home when travelling. He advised them to travel, to expand their horizons and to let the world know that Ireland had its own language, music and culture. In particular he reminded them to emphasise to all they met that 'this country is not a part of England but a country in its own right'.[32]

The travellers received 'a great welcome in Rome'.[33] They arrived in the rain early on the morning of Tuesday, 22 September, and marched behind Éamonn, playing the pipes, to their hotel. Éamonn was happy to discover that, unlike at home when he wore his Irish piper's costume, 'the dogs were not barking at me and the boys in the street were not calling out any bad names at me.'[34]

On Thursday, 24 September, the pilgrims marched to the Vatican for their audience with the Pope, with Éamonn and his pipes again leading the way. At the Vatican, the Pope first received the members of the official Corporation delegation for a private audience in his study. Sean T O'Kelly read out his official address in Irish – a Latin translation having been provided for the Pope, with illumination copied from the Book of Kells.[35] About 250 people lined up on three sides of the Grand Hall around the papal throne. The Pope greeted the visitors and allowed them to kiss his hand before ascending to his throne and reading out an address to the Irish people. After the Pope's address, the assembled pilgrims sang a 'Song for the Pope' and, as the last chorus of the song echoed in the hall, the skirl of 'O'Donnell Abú' on the pipes could be heard. Éamonn marched into the 300-foot-long hall, walking its full length up to the steps of the throne and back down again. He did this three times until he came to a stop within a few paces of the throne. The Pope called him forward to examine the pipes and was startled when 'a most unearthly sound was emitted' by the bag and chanter. Having regained his composure, he asked Éamonn to play again, and Éamonn obliged with 'The Wearing of the Green'. The Pope then came down and patted him on the back before walking informally among the rest of the pilgrims.[36] The pilgrimage received widespread coverage in the newspapers back in Dublin, as well as in the provincial media. Éamonn's picturesque costume and his pipes were frequently highlighted.

Éamonn's political views were also beginning to bring him some notoriety. His old school friend Peter Murray wrote from London to say that he 'just about knows what a Sinn Féiner is [he has read *The Resurrection of Hungary*],' and expressed the 'hope that the shy bashful super-quiet Ned Kent of my schoolboy days … will never be called upon to wield a pike for what used to be called "The Ould Country"; and that he will wield any other more peaceful weapon for his native land gallantly and well.'[37]

In December 1908, the first Christmas Aonach (Fair) was organised by Seán MacDiarmada on behalf of Sinn Féin. The idea behind the Aonach, dear to Éamonn's heart, was to encourage Irish consumers to buy Irish for Christmas.

The organisers hoped to create jobs in Ireland by turning people from foreign manufacturers, and to provide 'for the permanent support in decency and comfort of 50,000 of our people'.[38]

Chapter Four

• • • • • • •

1909–1911

An Active Activist

During the following year, 1909, Éamonn remained active within both the Gaelic League and Sinn Féin. The topic that dominated the affairs of the Gaelic League during 1909 was their demand that Irish be a compulsory subject for entry to the new university colleges. The Roman Catholic bishops opposed the League's stance, fearing that middle-class Catholics who did not speak Irish would be discouraged by the language requirement and would continue to send their sons to Trinity College. The fact that the League itself realised that it had had little success in creating Irish speakers from among the professional and monied classes suggests that the bishops' fear was justified.

As a member of the Coiste Gnótha, Éamonn was at the centre of this debate. He attended a special meeting of the Coiste Gnótha on 27 January at which Douglas Hyde insisted that Irish must be recognised as an essential element in a free national university and criticised those in the media who painted 'a distressing picture of crowds of students driven away from the National University through a fear or hatred of having to learn the national language'. Hyde reminded the members of the non-sectarian League that the Catholic bishops' statement 'should be treated with respect but should not be regarded as being authoritative'.[1]

The position of the Catholic bishops did not reflect the views of the clergy as a whole, many of whom were very active in the League. The following month, March 1909, Éamonn represented the League at a language demonstration on St Patrick's Day in Galway during which:

> The Rev. Fr. Considine (presiding) dealt with the contention that coercion was implied in the demand for compulsory Irish in the University, and said that the Ten Commandments might also be condemned on the same principle (laughter and cheers).[2]

The bishops ultimately put pressure on priests who had spoken out in favour of the League's demand for compulsory Irish. The debate raged through the summer months and a number of priests resigned from the League.[3]

The position of the hierarchy remained unyielding and, at the end of July, Fr O'Herlihy of Maynooth, who had published a pamphlet supporting 'An Irish University, Or Else', was dismissed from his Chair of Irish at Maynooth.[4]

In the autumn, both Patrick Pearse and Éamonn began to distance themselves from the internal politics of the Gaelic League. In September, Pearse announced his resignation as editor of *An Claidheamh Soluis* but agreed to remain on until a replacement was appointed.[5] By then he was heavily committed to his school, St Enda's, which had opened in Cullenswood House. However he didn't sever his ties completely, and was again co-opted onto the Coiste Gnótha.[6] Éamonn didn't attend the meetings of the Coiste Gnótha in June or July and, although his name appears as a representative of the Árd Craobh to attend the Árd Fheis, he was not nominated for re-election to the Coiste Gnótha. When Coláiste Laighean reopened the following October, he was no longer listed as one of the teachers.[7]

In Éamonn's case this may have reflected his increasing interest in the Sinn Féin political party, although the level of his political activism at this time is unclear. Áine Ceannt later recalled that Éamonn resigned from his position in Coláiste Laighean 'to devote more time to Sinn Féin'.[8] In June 1908 he was certainly presiding over meetings of the Central Branch. However, Sean T O'Kelly, himself a founder member of Sinn Féin, wrote that although Éamonn was well known 'personally to be strongly in favour of complete separation from England', he did not recall his taking part actively in Sinn Féin activities.[9]

The Sinn Féin Party itself had experienced mixed fortunes

following the 1907 by-election and, although the number of branches had increased from 21 in 1906 to 128 in 1908, the party had reached its peak and was beginning a slow decline. This decline was evident even in Dublin Corporation, where the party had achieved some success since the local government elections of 1906. After 1910, the party saw its numbers fall from 12 to 4 seats on the Council of Dublin Corporation.[10]

On 23 December 1909 Éamonn attended the Dublin Municipal Officers' Association dinner. The menu card for the event, which Éamonn kept, bore a cartoon that shows that the members of the DMOA were very unhappy with their employers – the Lord Mayor and Council Members of the Corporation. Titled 'Christmas Dreams', it depicts Corporation officials grovelling for increased pay and scrambling up a precarious 'Ladder of Promotion' to a heavenly cloud where, in extreme old age, the committees (made up of Council members) and pensioned officials 'cease from troubling and are at rest'. [11]

Dissatisfaction among the officials had been simmering for some time. The members of the Council, dependent on votes from the ratepayers, were anxious to reduce the cost of running the Corporation and keep rates at a minimum. Alderman Dr J C McWalter regularly proposed postponing the annual salary increments and promotions (classifications) of clerks. In February 1908, the Council, by a large majority, decided to postpone a series of such increments and promotions. Although the decision was never implemented, many officials suffered hardship during the long-drawn-out process of resolutions and counter-resolutions. Éamonn's brother Michael was one of those whose promotion was continually postponed.

The DMOA was particularly concerned with the actions of the Sinn Féin members on the Council who had not alone voted with these proposals to defer increments, but who were also proposing changes to the basis for promotion, in the interests of improving the calibre of officer at senior level. The DMOA accused the Sinn Féin members, in election and other pronouncements, of treating the rank and file of the Corporation officials like a body of social parasites.[12] They accused them of 'endeavouring to keep men who have entered by competitive examinations for an indefinite period at a max salary of £100 per annum so that … no recognition of increased duties and responsibilities can be given until the possibly remote period … when the rates are reduced'.[13] In March 1909, the Council decided to appoint a committee to consider the appropriate terms and conditions of new and existing officers.[14]

During this time, Éamonn, with his colleague Henry Mangan, was actively trying to instil a spirit of militancy into the executive committee of the Association by encouraging it to strengthen its position in negotiations with the Council.

One of his initiatives was a proposal to merge the DMOA with, initially, the County Council Officers' Association and, later, with the Civil Service Guild. This proved a step too far for the executive but, during 1909, Éamonn's other proposal to adopt a more aggressive approach towards the negotiations on salaries with the Council was approved.[15]

By this time Éamonn himself, in the City Treasurer's office, was earning £110 per annum. Although more than adequate in comparison with the many unemployed and unskilled workers in the city, this compared with Edmund W Eyre's salary, as City Treasurer, of £1,250 per annum.[16] Eyre was Éamonn's boss and, in November, Éamonn, seeking promotion, had asked him for a testimonial. Eyre wrote that Éamonn had discharged his very varied duties to perfect satisfaction. He mentioned, in particular, that he had been able, 'with perfect confidence to call on you to take up work which involved the receipt and payment of considerable sums of money and to find that my reliance on your capacity was always justified'. Personally, he said, he would be sorry 'to lose such an able and reliable assistant but was unable to retard Éamonn's progress to positions of higher trust and better remuneration'.[17]

At the start of 1910, Éamonn, although still relatively junior in rank, was unanimously elected Chairman of the DMOA. Before long he was embroiled in long and difficult negotiations on behalf of his fellow clerks.

In March, the Finance Committee of the Corporation presented to the Council their proposals for changes to the conditions of employment of clerks who, like Éamonn, had entered the Corporation by competitive examination. The committee essentially agreed with the DMOA that the system of increments should not be changed.[18] They recommended an increased scale rising to a maximum of £250 per annum, which would only ratify the existing conditions of service and bring the scale back into parity with the maximum pay scale for civil servants of the same rank. In spite of their limited nature, the committee's recommendations led to a flurry of choleric letters to the newspapers. At one extreme, there was the ubiquitous Alderman JC McWalter, who called it 'one of the most amazingly impudent documents ever issued to any Corporation'; and at the other, an anonymous civil servant who cast aspersions on the quality of work done by Corporation clerks and their educational qualifications.[19] The DMOA took public umbrage at this slight on 'a deserving and hard worked body of officials'.[20] At the end of this public debate the need to appease the ratepayers won out. The Council rejected its Finance Committee's recommendations 'in view of the present high rates in the city, and the general want of employment'.[21]

Éamonn, as Chairman of the DMOA, was centrally embroiled in the dispute. John Monks, a colleague of Éamonn's in the City Treasurer's office and an activist in the DMOA, recalled in later years that, as Chairman, Éamonn 'gave evidence of his genius for organisation and his year of office was characterised by a number of schemes that were initiated and brought to a successful issue for the betterment of the officials'. He credited Éamonn, 'a staunch believer in the need for organisation in defence of one's rights', with initiating what would ultimately be a successful campaign for increasing the maximum salary payable to First Class clerks. He said this successful outcome was 'in no small degree attributable to the help he rendered, to the advice he gave, and to the plans he laid down for bringing about the reform'.[22] The DMOA's battle for comparability with the civil service continued for many years and ultimately became the principal aim of local government trade unionism.[23]

Even though the DMOA campaign took up most of his time during 1910, leaving him little to spare for the Gaelic League and Sinn Féin, Éamonn still practised what he preached about the philosophy of self-sufficiency. The Ceannt family's household accounts for March 1910 include payment of four shillings for Buff Orpingtons and Wyandottes (types of hens) and Áine kept the script of a talk which Éamonn gave on the 'Intensive Cultivation of the Soil' and the options available to achieve higher yields.[24] Indeed, his brother Michael often referred jokingly to Éamonn's home as 'The Farm', and mentioned Éamonn's experiments with mushroom growing as another example of his varied interests.[25]

By early 1910 the prospects of Ireland achieving Home Rule by constitutional means were improving. As before, this was more to do with the arithmetic balance of power in Westminster than with any genuine commitment to Home Rule on the part of the Liberal Government. In April of 1909, the Conservatives had used their veto in the House of Lords to block the Liberal Government's 'People's Budget'. The budget proposed a series of innovative measures to reduce poverty, such as the provision of old age pensions and social insurance. The aristocratic members of the House of Lords were incensed by the increase in income tax, land taxes and death duties required to finance these reforms and vetoed the budget at the end of November 1909. Parliament was dissolved and a general election was called. Following the election, in January 1910, the IPP found itself holding the balance of power. Their freedom of action was, nevertheless, constrained. The budget had been unpopular in Ireland too, particularly among the party's powerful financial supporters, including publicans and distillers, and any further support for it would require convincing proof from the Government as to their commitment to Home Rule. This was not forthcoming and, throughout the remainder of 1910, punctuated by the death of King Edward VII in May and his succession by George V, the Liberals and Conservatives met in private session to try to resolve the crisis. When this proved impossible, a second general election was called, in December 1910. Once again, the IPP found itself holding the balance of power.

It appeared to be only a matter of time before the veto of the Lords would be broken and Irish Home Rule would at last be conceded. In reality, though, it was only the start of a long and uncertain process; the Parliament Act, which finally restricted the Lords' power, was not passed until August 1911. Even then, the House of Lords retained the right to delay certain Bills, including the Home Rule Bill, for up to a maximum of two years. Home Rule may have seemed firmly on the cards – but it was not yet. [26]

While the majority of Irish people, particularly those who were Catholic and nationalist, welcomed the prospect of a peaceful, if long-drawn-out, transition to Home Rule, there were two important groups who were very unhappy with the idea. For the southern unionists, mainly Protestants,[27] the recent papal decree of *Ne Temere*, which severely restricted the conditions under which a marriage between a Catholic and a non-Catholic could take place, was a stark warning that Home Rule could indeed mean 'Rome Rule'. This religious concern was compounded by the potential loss of economic links and social status.

For Ulster unionists,[28] the concern ran much deeper. The Ulster Unionist Council had, during 1910, established a secret committee to investigate the possibility of obtaining arms to take the fight against Home Rule to a new level of physical force. At the end of November 1910 they secretly contacted munitions works in England, Austria and Germany. On 23 September 1911, at a monster meeting in the Craigavon home of Capt. James Craig, MP for County Down, Sir Edward Carson, MP, the leader of the Irish Unionist Party, warned the crowd of 50,000 that 'we must be prepared – and time is precious in these things – the morning Home Rule passes, ourselves to become responsible for the government of the Protestant Province of Ulster'.[29]

As far as Arthur Griffith and the Sinn Féin Party were concerned, the country's renewed confidence in the constitutional politics of the IPP meant that the Sinn Féin support base was continuing to dwindle. Griffith, politically naïve but recognising reality, imposed a 'self denying ordinance' on himself and his party to give John Redmond, leader of the IPP, a fair chance to achieve Home Rule. Áine Ceannt recalled that 'the Sinn Féin National Council decided not to say one word either way as they did not want to be responsible when it would be rejected, and they felt that it would never come into being.'[30] The party had not contested either of the general elections in 1910 and, although it gained seats on a number of local authorities, it lost seats in its main stronghold of Dublin Corporation.[31] In addition to the loss of its mainstream supporters, some of its advanced nationalist supporters, such as Bulmer Hobson and his colleagues from the Dungannon Clubs, were transferring their energies to the more radical IRB. Although they were insignificant in numbers, and intentionally secretive, their influence was rising and they soon infiltrated a range of nationalist movements, with results that few of those complacently awaiting Home Rule in 1911 could ever have anticipated.

The IRB was a secret, oath-bound brotherhood, dating back to the mid-nineteenth century. They aimed to establish an independent, democratic Irish republic and were often referred to, collectively with their counterparts in the United States, as The Fenians. Following the end of the American Civil War in 1865, a small group of Irish American veterans supported the leaders of the IRB in Ireland in staging what would prove an abortive rebellion. In the appalling weather of 5–6 March 1867, 'groups of brave, unorganised, miserably armed men turned out in Dublin, Cork, Tipperary and Limerick, and to a lesser extent in Clare, Waterford and Louth'.[32] Betrayed by informants, they were quickly rounded up. By the early twentieth century, the IRB had 'become old and flabby while they awaited the decision of the Irish people to again wage war against England'.[33]

By early 1911, however, the IRB was being transformed by a younger generation of advanced nationalists. In addition to Bulmer Hobson, who had been a member since 1904,[34] these included Denis McCullough, Seán MacDiarmada and Tom Clarke. Clarke was a Fenian of long standing who, inspired by the 1867 Rising, had taken part in a dynamiting campaign in

London, for which he served fifteen years in English prisons on explosives charges. He was eventually released following a public campaign led by, among others, the IPP leader John Redmond. He travelled to the United States where he worked for Clan na Gael (the successor to the US Fenian movement) under John Devoy. He returned to Ireland with his wife, Kathleen, in 1907, and was immediately co-opted onto the Supreme Council of the IRB. Kathleen's father was the veteran Fenian John Daly of Limerick, and, with financial support from Kathleen's family, Clarke set himself up in tobacconist/newspaper shops at Amiens Street and Parnell Street. The shops soon provided a meeting place for IRB members from around the country.[35]

In November 1910, as the second British general election was getting underway, the IRB launched a new monthly paper, *Irish Freedom*, with Clarke as Chairman of the editorial committee, which also included Hobson and Pat McCartan; the Hon. Secretary and Treasurer was Seán MacDiarmada.[36] The editorial in the first edition clearly stated the paper's separatist and republican credentials. The organisation may have been tiny, and certainly invisible to the national consciousness, but it was these credentials that over the next few years would prove the final spur for Éamonn Ceannt's politicisation.

One event in particular brought attitudes into the open and sharpened differences between various political groupings. This was the coronation of the new king and the prospect of a royal visit to Ireland. On Thursday, 22 June 1911, the coronation of King George V and his consort, Queen Mary, took place in Westminster Abbey. The *Irish Times* reported that the day 'was celebrated in practically every European capital and in every town of note which possesses a British Colony'. Even tiny villages shared in the celebrations – for example, in Robertstown, County Kildare, where Éamonn's brother JP was stationed at the RIC barracks, 'the people of the Robertstown district erected an immense bonfire and had a display of fireworks … Almost everyone sent in a load of turf, and those who had not turf contributed otherwise … The fireworks consisted of the usual selection – 50 rockets, red, white and blue lights, Roman candles, maroons, shells, wheels and Chinese fliers etc.'[37] Such was the excitement and frenzy of celebration. The royal couple planned a six-day visit to Ireland a short time afterwards.

Although the royal visit had enthusiastic popular support, many advanced nationalists opposed it. Éamonn was a member of the United National Societies Committee, which was set up to 'frustrate attempts to make Dublin Corporation grant an address to the King'.[38] Áine recalled that the committee met at Sinn Féin headquarters and included Michael Joseph O'Rahilly, commonly known as The O'Rahilly, a Sinn Féiner and member of the Gaelic League, and Sean Fitzgibbon, also a Sinn Féiner and a colleague of Éamonn's in Dublin Corporation. She also mentioned Seán MacDiarmada, who, together with The Rahilly, was joint Honorary Secretary of the group.[39] She thought that they were all Sinn Féiners or members of the National Council, but it appears that the committee also included an unlikely mix of the United Irish League, Ancient Order of Hibernians, Sinn Féin and the Wolfe Tone Clubs (who were a front for the IRB).[40] Áine also recalled that 'to one meeting PH Pearse came, accompanied by Tomás MacDonagh, and that was the first time that Pearse, to my knowledge, took any interest in Irish affairs outside the Gaelic League'.[41]

At the start of an intense campaign to influence members of the Corporation, the committee decided to hold a Great National Demonstration in Beresford Place to coincide with the king's coronation on 22 June. The IRB newspaper, *Irish Freedom,* called on 'every Nationalist in Dublin, no matter to what Party he belongs, to turn out for this meeting'.[42] The committee arranged for a banner and poles advertising the meeting to be erected at the College Green end of Grafton Street. The *Sunday Independent* reported that:

> Between 12 and 1a.m. yesterday (17 June 1911) a number of young men drove up in a brake to the crossing of Grafton, Suffolk and Nassau Streets and erected two poles draped in black and white, from which were suspended streamers bearing the mottos: 'Do not miss the great Independence demonstration at Beresford Place, Thursday evening, 22 June', and 'Thou art not conquered yet dear land.'[43]

Áine Ceannt later recalled that Éamonn had been centrally involved in the escapade:

> As Éamonn Ceannt and Sean Fitzgibbon were in the Corporation they knew how to get the road opened,[44] so one morning the loyal people of Dublin were astounded to see across the road a flag announcing, 'Thou art not conquered yet dear land.' The result was, of course, that the poles were removed by the police. Seán MacDiarmada ... consulted with Éamonn Ceannt as to what they should do and Sean said that he would go into College Street police station and claim the poles as his property. The authorities offered to give him the poles if he would sign a receipt for them. Sean ... did not know what to do, so he looked at the notepaper that was presented to him, saw that it was foreign, and his reply to them was, 'I would not write on foreign notepaper.' He left as soon as he could. I do not know what happened to the poles afterwards.[45]

The ramifications of the Grafton Street poles continued to reverberate for some time afterwards.[46] Shortly after the event, a pair of humorous postcards was on sale throughout the city and from the offices of *Sinn Féin*. One of the cartoons portrayed the poles and banner, while the other depicted nine burly, mustachioed policemen engaged in removing the poles. Entitled 'Deeds that won the Empire – the capture of the poles', the text of the postcard appears to be a satirical reference to a chronicle of the Chevalier Bayard, which was largely read and circulated among young boys and which, asserted the editor of *Sinn Féin,* 'gives false views of the means by which the Empire was founded'. [47] In 1897 Éamonn and his brother Michael had won prizes from *Chums* – and the prizes included a 'chivalrous narrative entitled *Under Bayard's Banner',* by Henry Frith. Clearly, Éamonn had a long memory. The police, on the other hand, had no sense of humour and a Mr Séamus Ó Dubhtaigh was arrested for selling the postcards – 'police spite', according to the editor of *Irish Freedom.*[48]

It is not clear whether Éamonn's role was that of adviser on the Corporation procedures involved or whether he was indeed MacDiarmada's accomplice on the midnight escapade. Certainly his name does not appear in relation to the Corporation enquiry and there is no suggestion that he was in any way disciplined in relation to the matter. Just a few months later he was granted an allowance of £10 to provide holiday cover for his colleague Mr Monks, who was the pay clerk in the City Treasurer's office – to account for the significant extra responsibility in relation to very large amounts of cash.[49]

The royal couple visited Dublin the following month, arriving in Kingstown (Dún Laoghaire) on Saturday, 8 July. The town was festooned with Venetian poles and banners – this time in celebration. The newspapers recorded that the couple was welcomed by cheering crowds along the route to Dublin Castle.

Éamonn's brother Michael recorded in his diary that:

> The day had been scorching hot, the sun blazed down unceasingly … The trams were crowded with a holiday crowd; all off for the day, with little parcels and lunch baskets, and gay attire, straw hats, light dresses etc. 'Twas a public holiday, duly proclaimed all over Ireland for the King of England, George V, was about to land on our shores and pay his first visit to Erin since his coronation as King on 22 June. Mostly everybody – out of curiosity and to be with the crowd and hear the bands – went off that day along the route from Kingstown into Dublin, and the people who went far along the route had to start off early.[50]

In the face of the public celebrations the IRB leadership, together with Sinn Féin, decided to keep a low profile during the visit itself. They organised a pilgrimage to Wolfe Tone's grave in Bodenstown, County Kildare, where they were addressed by Major John MacBride of the Irish Boer Brigade and by Bulmer Hobson of the IRB.[51]

Although he was no longer a member of the Coiste Gnótha of the Gaelic League, Éamonn remained active as an ordinary member of the organisation. A few weeks after the royal visit, *An Claidheamh Soluis* published an article written by him called 'The Irish Pipes'.[52] It was the first of two articles on the subject, the other appearing in the paper on 16 September.[53] In October he wrote a memorial on the death of Pádraig Mac an Ailge, a founder member of Cumann na bPíobairí who had written the first books on the direct method of teaching Irish.[54]

Éamonn's own interest in teaching methods also continued and when the Gaelic League, having eventually won the battle for Irish as a compulsory subject for entry to the universities, decided to campaign against the attitude of the National Board of Education to the teaching of Irish in Intermediate (secondary) schools and teacher-training colleges, he was actively engaged in the debate.[55]

In September he was speaking on this subject at a meeting of the League in Dalkey. The motion, which he seconded, called for 'the immediate reconstruction of the National Board so as to bring it into line with the educational requirements of the nation, and stating that in the case of all new appointments to the Board, they considered that a knowledge of education combined with a sympathy for National feelings should be the sole qualifications'.[56] In December he was talking at the Brownstown (County Kildare) Branch of the League during which, according to a report on the event:

> He very ably dealt with the attitude of the National Board and its anglicising effects on the country. He said that it was the system that controls the educational destinies of all the children of Ireland in the primary schools. The schools were

called National because they were anti National, and they were established with the one aim and object of wiping out every vestige of nationality in Ireland and substituting 'happy English children' for happy Irish children … The National Board taught the people of Ireland to despise their country and, therefore, to despise themselves, to look upon the country as a place not worth remaining in … Mr Ceannt said that what we want is a Board responsible to the people of Ireland, a Board in sympathy with the wants of the people. It is of the utmost importance that we should have control of education in Ireland under the coming measure of Home Rule. He suggested that Dr Douglas Hyde should be appointed minister of education in Ireland and the rest left in his hands. It was the first time that the suggestion was made in public and he hoped that it would be carried out. In concluding, Mr Ceannt said – 'you cannot teach the children of Ireland unless the teachers have got Irish themselves and what we ask the National Board is that it will not put its stamp on them and turn them out as teachers unless they know Irish going into the Training Colleges … We want them to make Irish a compulsory subject for entrance to training.'[57]

In September 1911 the League held its annual language procession. The procession was an important part of the League's fund-raising effort since it included the annual Dublin collection. The procession was composed of the following sections: language, athletics, educational, national and friendly societies, temperance, industrial and representative. One of the speakers that year was James Larkin, who had founded the Irish Transport and General Workers' Union (ITGWU) in January 1909 and was becoming known as a radical labour leader. While he attended as a member of the Executive Trades Council, his presence on the platform led to outrage from some members of the League. Hyde took exception to finding he was sharing a platform with Larkin and was critical of Pearse for supporting him.[58] Éamonn, like Pearse, defended Larkin's participation. He was particularly impressed by the fact that Larkin was learning Irish, leading the *Irish Independent* to suggest that Éamonn was innocent of the danger that Larkin represented.[59] But Éamonn's defence of Larkin was no innocent plea. He had already that year made it clear that his attitude towards the growing labour movement was quite independent of the views of either the Gaelic League or Sinn Féin.

Both of those bodies saw the emerging trend towards strikes and lockouts as a threat to the development of industry in Ireland. At the end of August 1911, foundry owners in Wexford locked out their workers in a dispute over membership of the ITGWU. Writing in *Sinn Féin,* Arthur Griffith warned that native industry would close if the workers continued their dispute.[60] He predicted that

'Irish industry may be slain by strikes and lockouts. But from this day to the day of judgement no Irish industry will be created by these weapons of destruction.'[61]

In the 30 September edition of *Sinn Féin,* Éamonn wrote a blistering criticism of Griffith's argument. The child who had been born in the middle of the Land War and the man who had spent years on the DMOA fighting for the position of his fellow Corporation clerks revealed his profound belief in the entitlement of men and women to organise in defence of their rights:

Permit me as an individual Sinn Féiner to dissociate myself from the general tone of your recent pronouncements on the Wexford labour trouble …

You appear to see Larkin at the bottom of all the trouble. You do not condescend to analyse any of the principles for which Larkin professes to stand. Sufficient for you that Larkin is an agitator causing trouble between employer and employed. In a similar manner, the English Tory and his Irish allies described Irish politicians as vile Agitators, who caused trouble between the good, kind landlords and their willing slaves, the tenant farmers of Ireland. But the tenant farmers of Ireland were not deceived. True, trade was upset, industries languished and 'outrages' were reported daily in the Press. Still, notwithstanding the misrepresentation and abuse, the Agitators held on. Today the land of Ireland is to an ever-increasing extent vested in the farmers of Ireland.

Industries are beginning to flourish and the fat years bid fair to follow the lean.

None has now the hardihood to deny that the hardships and miseries of the land justification were justified. No one asserts that the tenant farmers were wrong in giving prominence to their class interests. And yet it cannot be denied that the farmers were only a class after all. It is an open secret that Parnell, who was an aristocrat, had no desire to tack on a land programme to his political programme. But [Michael] Davitt and [Laurence] Kettle induced him to do so. They saw that the interests of any large class of the community could not be overlooked. Parnell's political sagacity was acquired in the hard school of practice, not in the easy chair of theory. Would it not be wise to take a leaf out of Parnell's book, if you will not take it out of Larkin's book, as gravely suggested by Paraig MacPiarais to the Gaelic Leaguers on Language Sunday.

… No political party can now afford to ignore the claims of the so-called lowest classes in the social scale, the unskilled workers. Those claims were heretofore overlooked simply because the men were not organised. I see no reason why 'Sinn Féin' should not help to organise them rather than give them the cold shoulder.

More serious than your cold-shouldering of the Wexford men is your practical denial to them of the right to join a particular trade union. Do you seriously hold that the employers of Wexford have the right to dictate whether their men shall or shall not join a particular union? That appears to be the point at issue. Taking that to be the cause of the trouble, my sympathies go unreservedly to the men. The right of free speech, of public meeting, and of organising for a lawful purpose ought to be unquestioned and unquestionable. The particular brand of union which the men shall join, be it a Social Union, a Political Union or a Trade Union is a matter entirely for the men themselves. Neither the editor of *Sinn Féin* nor the employers have the right to dictate to them on this point.

Now to come to your objection to what you call Mr Larkin's organisation. Mr Larkin is an Irishman who has founded in Ireland an Irish union governed by Irishmen. The organisers appear to include one Englishman who went to jail recently for uncomplimentary references to King George V; Mr P.T. Daly, an ex prominent Sinn Féiner, still presumably a Nationalist; James Connolly whom you know to be a Nationalist of long standing, and who spoke at the Independence demonstration on June 22nd; Mr Larkin, a newcomer whose son learns Irish at Scoil Íte. All four appear to have been associated with labour all their lives. There is no reason to doubt their bona fides. Their methods may seem strange to those who are up in the clouds and give not half a thought to the cause of the labour volcanoes that are bursting forth all over the Continent of Europe. But practical politics cannot afford to wait while these dreamers are awakened to their new, their startlingly new, surroundings. It is the business of Sinn Féin to use the grievances of the various classes in this country as a whip with which to lash the English tyrant out of Ireland. I fail to see how this can be secured by lecturing them on their failings while they are engaged in a combat with the ring of employers who are trying to control the Wexford labour market. By the way, have you no condemnation of the Employers' Federation or is there a law for them and another for their servants?[62]

Éamonn may have dissociated himself from Griffith's attitude towards the labour movement but he remained committed to the Sinn Féin Party. At the Annual Congress of Sinn Féin on 1 October 1911, perhaps with the objective of influencing the policy of the party from within, Éamonn was elected to the party's Executive Committee for the coming year.

In an article in *Sinn Féin*, immediately following the notice of the election of the Executive Committee, an editorial noted that

the 7th Congress of Sinn Féin took place this week. Before it reassembles, the promised Home Rule Bill will have seen the light and the period of political inactivity will have ended … *Sinn Féin* doubts that a satisfactory measure of

Home Rule will be achieved and congratulates itself on the decision to 'stand down' for two years to let Parliamentarianism play its hand freely – free to intervene freely again next year – if the Bill is acceptable, Sinn Féin will not resist its enactment – but …[63]

The party left its options open in the event that the provisions of the Bill proved unacceptable.

In the same edition, Griffith took a verbal swipe at 'some of the strike orators who have tried to draw a parallel between the fight of the farmers for security of tenure and fair rents and the strike of the industrial workers for higher wages'. Presumably Éamonn was prominent among this number. Griffith warned of the danger of declaring a general war against capitalism and of the particular dangers of socialism, which 'if it ever came into being would form the strictest tyranny under which man has lived'.[64] Nothing daunted, Éamonn gave a lecture to the Central Branch of Sinn Féin on 15 November on 'The Rights of Labour'.[65]

On a lighter note, in December, Éamonn was again helping to organise the Sinn Féin Aonach in the Rotunda. Éamonn's personal papers include a list of advertisements for the Aonach that were sent to various newspapers such as the *Freeman's Journal, Evening Telegraph, Irish Times, An Claidheamh Soluis, Irish Freedom* and *Sinn Féin* – total cost £27.

Áine later recalled that, during the Aonach, The O'Rahilly invited Éamonn outside 'to meet a Russian revolutionary'.

When Éamonn came out, the person waiting to meet him was actually Seán MacDiarmada, who, having just been released from hospital, had grown a beard and was lame. It seems likely that it was during this meeting that MacDiarmada recruited Éamonn into the IRB.[66] However, we may never know the exact date on which Éamonn was sworn into the IRB for the very good reason that Éamonn did not want it known. It was one thing to be a member of the Gaelic League, an apolitical and national body of respectable language enthusiasts; or a member of Sinn Féin, an official political party whose representatives sat as members of Dublin Corporation. But as an employee of that Corporation, with a brother (Michael) employed in the same body, another (Dick) a civil servant, another (JP) a member of the RIC, and another (Bill) a soldier with the Royal Dublin Fusiliers, it was unlikely that Éamonn would have wished to broadcast his membership of an illegal, oath-bound brotherhood – especially one which had been condemned by the Catholic Church. Éamonn also had a wife and child to support and no intention of putting them, or his job, at risk – just yet.

On census night, Sunday, 1 April 1911, Éamonn (29 years) had meticulously filled out the form in Irish. He was living with Áine (30 years) and Rónán (4 years) at 4 Herberton Lane, New Kilmainham, Dublin. Áine's mother, Elizabeth O'Brennan (60 years), and her sister Lily (Eilís ní Bhraonáin, 32 years) lived with them. The house had a stable and a barn among its outbuildings. All family members, with the exception of Elizabeth O'Brennan, who was born in England, were recorded as speaking Irish and English.

On New Year's Eve 1911, the year ended for the Ceannt family with Rónán's Christmas party. While Éamonn played the part of Santa Claus, Michael Kent recorded the event in his diary:

> First [the children] had tea, then all came into the Parlour, where there was a lovely Xmas tree all lighted up with coloured candles and the branches hanging with lots of toys of all shapes and colours, stockings stuffed with sweets, glowing coloured balls and everything possible to make children glad ... Suddenly without the smallest warning a curious old familiar figure appeared, smiling down on the frightened faces of all [the children]. 'Twas Santa Claus! [who] addressed the children in a ... voice so kindly and cheerful ...

> *Dear little children, I've come straight here,*
> *To wish you all a Happy New Year*
> *Just as the Christmas Bells did chime*
> *I've counted on my fingers nine*
> *Little boys and little girls ...*
> *And Rónán Ceannt from Dublin Citie,*
> *And Nora, the best girl I know,*
> *And Kathleen, wild as mountain Roe,*

All these I said I'd come to see …
This year a Motor Car I took,
Next year an Aeroplane I'll book,
But I'd travel more than fifty miles,
To be once more 'midst Childhood's smiles,
And the Irish Welcome and Hearty Cheer
I know is waiting for me here.[67]

Chapter Five

• • • • • •

1912–1913

Never a Home Ruler

In February 1912 Winston Churchill, Home Secretary in Prime Minister Herbert Asquith's Cabinet, visited Belfast to support Home Rule. The Ulster Unionists, many of whom had been openly drilling for months, were outraged that Winston, the son of Randolph Churchill – who in 1886 had infamously declared that 'Ulster will fight and Ulster will be right' – should appear on a platform in support of Home Rule. Churchill and his wife, Clementine, were safeguarded by a heavy security presence during his visit.[1] What the unionists didn't know was that Churchill, just a few days earlier in the privacy of the Cabinet room, had backed a proposal by David Lloyd George, Chancellor of the Exchequer, that the predominantly Protestant counties in Ulster be given the choice of opting out of the Home Rule legislation.[2]

In Dublin, on 31 March, huge crowds mobbed Sackville Street and the surrounding streets at a monster Home Rule rally. The leader of the IPP, John Redmond, MP, promised that Home Rule would provide a representative national government with sufficient finances for the development of Ireland, as well as enabling Ireland to bear her fair share of imperial obligations. Other Members of Parliament, including John Dillon and Joseph Devlin, also spoke at the meeting, as did Eoin MacNeill and Patrick Pearse, on behalf of the Gaelic League. Pearse praised Redmond for his achievements and urged all interested parties to bury their differences in pursuit of a better measure of Home Rule. On the other hand, he threatened 'that if we are again betrayed there shall be red war throughout Ireland'. At the end of the meeting John Redmond told the crowd to 'Go back after this meeting to your homes with high and confident hearts.'[3]

Beneath the surface, the reality was quite different. The Parliament Act of 1911 had given the House of Lords power to delay Home Rule until at least 1914. Privately, both the Government and the Conservative opposition in Westminster were beginning to acknowledge that the exclusion of Ulster, however abhorrent to the nationalists, would have to be a precondition to any legislation.[4]

On Easter Tuesday, 9 April 1912, the Ulster Unionists responded to the Dublin rally. In Balmoral, South Belfast, a crowd of 100,000 marched in formation before a platform party led by the leader of the British Conservatives, Andrew Bonar Law, MP, and the Irish Unionist leader, Sir Edward

Carson, MP. Bonar Law told the Ulster Unionists that they 'held the pass for the Empire', as a massive Union Jack was unfurled and the meeting passed a resolution against Home Rule.

The Home Rule Bill came before the Westminster Parliament on 11 April 1912. It was very modest in its aspirations and was a disappointment to both nationalists and unionists. It failed to meet the aspirations of even constitutional nationalists by leaving external affairs – war and peace – and control of taxation revenue largely in the hands of Westminster. It also still failed to convince the Ulster Unionists that they would be able to opt out of a quasi-independent Ireland under Home Rule.

Sinn Féin had boycotted the monster meeting in Sackville Street and, on 15 April, Éamonn attended a special delegate conference at which the party accepted the principles of the Bill but refused to accept its provisions as the final settlement of Home Rule. The meeting took particular exception to the financial provisions, declaring 'that the taxes imposed by the Irish Parliament must be collected by its officers and paid into its own Exchequer'.[5]

Éamonn's own views were by now more extreme than those of the party to which he belonged. Just days before the Home Rule rally, he had drafted a speech for delivery to the Socialist Party of Ireland on 'Constitutional Agitation', in which he criticised the constitutional nationalists, including Sinn Féin, for abandoning Ireland's claim to nationhood and being willing to 'take her part in the Empire on which the sun never sets'. In an important evolution of his political thinking, he claimed that 'all laws made by such foreign powers are void and are not binding on the conscience of the people of Ireland' and that 'agitation should be confined to constitutional methods only where the laws of the country have been made and are being administered by the people of that country'. He gave a number of examples to demonstrate that Ireland was not constitutionally governed, including the fact that control of the police in Ireland resided with the Lord Lieutenant who was appointed by, and responsible to, Westminster.

He acknowledged that Home Rule would provide Ireland with a parliament around which to rally, but he highlighted the influence that the very threat of physical force by Ulster Unionists had had on the politics of England:

> Ministers of England, Ministers of the Liberal Government have exhibited unmistakable signs of alarm, either real or counterfeit, in the presence of the Ulster situation … Force is winning in Ulster, winning a political battle. It is up to the Nationalists of Ireland to adopt similar means for emphasising their views. An armed opinion will prevail when opposed only by an unarmed opinion. It is the duty of all men to be skilled in the use of arms. Preparation for war is the best guarantee of peace.

Éamonn wrote that the constitutional movement had brought the shadow of independence, Home Rule, almost within grasp, but warned that, if that measure of reform was lost, then the constitutional movement would stand condemned. He concluded that 'once the weapon of peace breaks in the hands of the Parliamentary Party leaders, there shall be no further peace but a sword. Ireland needs peace. Then let her prepare for war.'[6]

It is impossible to know whether this speech, which is the clearest articulation of the evolution of Éamonn's political views to that date, and which anticipated many of his future actions, received much, if any, publicity. He was, however, taking steps that would bring him closer to like-minded activists.

On St Patrick's Day 1912, Éamonn's father died from heart failure at the age of seventy-two.[7] Éamonn had been due to give a lecture that evening at the Gaelic League Hall but, passing a resolution of deep sympathy and condolence, the League notified its members that the lecture was postponed.[8] Meanwhile, in the family home:

> The room is shaded, a big bed stands in the centre; shrouded in white coverings, top and end; with black ribbon bows at the corner knobs of the bedstead. Five candles burn in a big candlestick on a little table beside the bed, on which also is a crucifix; a little glass slab with holy water in it – & a feather. The old gilt mirror over the fireplace is covered

with a white tablecloth. The big iron safe over in the opposite corner is similarly draped. [9]

Mourned by his family, James Kent Snr was buried the
following Tuesday from St Columba's Church, Iona Road. [10]

While it is possible that his father's death gave Éamonn
more freedom to express his increasingly extreme views publicly, it seems equally likely that the evolution of Éamonn's
thinking, and its public articulation, simply coincided with
his father's death.

Since their early days in the Gaelic League, Éamonn and
Patrick Pearse had been involved together in a wide range
of activities. In addition to their mutual commitment to the
Irish language and the Gaelic League, they shared many of
the same aspirations. It is almost certainly the case, however,
that Éamonn became politicised before Pearse, who was preoccupied with his school, St Enda's, which was frequently
in financial difficulties. By 1912, however, Pearse had also
become more preoccupied with politics. On 16 March 1912
Pearse launched a new weekly news-sheet, *An Barr Buadh*
(The Trumpet of Victory). Éamonn immediately became
one of the most regular contributors to this minority publication, which relied for its readership on the small advanced-
nationalist community. The news-sheet was chronically
underfunded and it lasted for only eleven editions. Pearse
followed the launch by establishing a new political society,

Cumann na Saoirse (The Society for Freedom). As well as
the contributors to *An Barr Buadh*, the society members
included Desmond Ryan and Con Colbert, members of Na
Fianna Éireann (Na Fianna) attached to St Enda's, and Cathal
Brugha and The O'Rahilly from the Gaelic League. At the
society's first meeting on 24 April, Pearse stated that, 'a rifle
should be made as familiar in the hands of an Irishman as a
hurley'.[11]

In Éamonn's contribution to the first edition of *An Barr
Buadh* he praised the Fenians for their courage and disputed
the received wisdom that they had been a failure. He praised
them for stirring the minds of the Irish people and raising
'the old flag of Ireland, that was at that time, hanging in the
mud ... They showed that the life essence was not gone out
of the people of this country.' He also praised James Stephens, the founder of the IRB, and those who took an oath
to the Brotherhood, many finding themselves condemned
to a term in an English prison or fleeing their native land.
He called on the youth of Ireland to stir itself: 'Is it not high
time you put your courage, spirit and fitness in the service
of Ireland?'[12]

In his second article, on 12 April, he wrote about 'The
Reason for the New Society' (Cumann na Saoirse) and
associated it with the awakening of the 'true Irish' (the Irish
speakers) from their heavy sleep, and enticing them into the
political arena to show their fellow Gaels that Ireland was

worth fighting for. He recommended that every Gael should prepare himself for the day of battle and explained that the work of the new society was to collect and disseminate the message of freedom for the Gaels, 'one way or another'.[13]

In an article published on 19 April Éamonn praised Sinn Féin for its recent opposition to the provisions of the Home Rule Bill. He welcomed, 'the old spirit of Freedom … alive and bright among those Gaels', while still bemoaning the fact that 'there weren't twenty words of Irish to be heard'.[14]

In the second-last edition of *An Barr Buadh*, Éamonn wrote about 'The Irish Priest'. He praised the priests of Ireland for their devotion and loyalty, for their willingness to suffer punishment for their faith and to fight for the rights of the Irish. He was critical, however, of the bishops for the position they had taken during the battle for compulsory Irish in the new universities when, 'the bishops and the English stood shoulder to shoulder' against the Gaelic League. Éamonn advised the bishops not to oppose the Irish when the Irish were only standing up for their rights. Finally, however, he acknowledged the bishops' primacy in matters of religion, as opposed to politics. He assured them that, when it came to matters of religion, the Irish would stay true to their teaching against irreligious groups.[15]

The perilous state of finances of both the news-sheet and of Pearse's school at St Enda's soon spelled the end of both *An Barr Buadh* and Cumann na Saoirse. It has been suggested that another reason for closing the news-sheet was because Pearse, like Éamonn, had used it to criticise the Catholic bishops but could not afford to have them against him at a time when his school was in financial difficulties.[16]

With *An Barr Buadh* no longer providing an outlet for his views, Éamonn turned to the national media. In an article in the *Irish Independent* on 11 June he wrote a stinging critique on 'The Intermediate – System's Worst Attributes'.[17] Obviously with clear memories of his own schooldays, Éamonn sympathised with the new generation who were forced to get up early and work late to cram for their Intermediate exam, before their youthful hearts 'if not utterly chilled as often they are, will again glow and expand under the cheerful rays of six weeks' summer sun'. He criticised the system of rote learning and of teaching languages 'on the grammar and irregular verbs system' with the result that 'we did not speak a word of the language we professed to learn with such toilsome expenditure of energy, nor did we acquire [the] facility in reading literary masterpieces without painfully turning their every word and sentence back into the vernacular'.

Echoing the speech he had made the previous December in Brownstown, Éamonn reserved his greatest criticism for the fact that the whole system at National (primary) and Intermediate level was designed to

> ... make officials of the flower of Ireland's intellect ... Its purpose is to provide our brainy young men with more or

less well-paid soft jobs under the Government where their security of tenure enables them to shirk their responsibilities as citizens and renders them oblivious to the problems of the day.

Éamonn suggested that the system be reformed to echo the principles under which Pearse had established St Enda's, a school which Éamonn's son, Rónán, attended. They included, 'several hours exercise in the open air at least twice a day. Home lessons should be reduced to a minimum. Languages should be taught on the direct method introduced by the Gaelic League.' Although Éamonn had clearly been one of the brilliant pupils who was 'crammed and petted' in the interests of exam results, he made a plea on behalf of the less quick-witted schoolchildren who were neglected under the prevailing system.[18]

Throughout the summer of 1912, the Ulster Unionists continued to demonstrate their opposition to Home Rule in no uncertain terms. They had influential support in Westminster. Bonar Law, the leader of the British Conservative Party, went so far as to assure the Ulster Unionists that he would go to any length of resistance to support them.

A semi-religious Solemn League and Covenant was drawn up under the auspices of James Craig, the Irish Unionist MP. On 28 September 1912, a day designated as Ulster Day, nearly a quarter of a million Ulster Unionist men signed a pledge to 'use all means which may be found necessary to defeat the present conspiracy to set up a Home Rule Parliament in Ireland'. Nearly a quarter of a million women Unionists also signed a parallel declaration. Those who signed the Covenant pledged to refuse to recognise the authority of any Home Rule parliament.

The Prime Minister failed to force the Home Rule Bill through the House of Commons in November in the face of a Cabinet that was in disarray on the issue of Ulster. By Christmas, the Unionist MPs had put down an amendment to exclude from Home Rule all nine Ulster counties. In the face of Westminster's apparent willingness to capitulate to the Ulster Unionists, there was good reason to believe that they were dangerously indifferent to the increasing embitterment of Irish nationalists.[19]

It was within this context of political stalemate that Éamonn was elected to the National Council of the Sinn Féin Party as Joint Honorary Secretary during the December 1912 Árd Fheis.[20] He also contributed an article, 'Eolas agus Misneach' (Knowledge and Courage), to the Central Branch's first Christmas annual. Grace Gifford, who married Joseph Plunkett in Kilmainham Jail shortly before his execution, illustrated the cover. It 'symbolises the militant spirit of the Dublin Central Branch'.[21]

Throughout all of this activity, Éamonn remained deeply committed to his beloved pipes. He gave a lecture at the National Museum of Ireland, Kildare Street, on 'The Bagpipes'. It was a closely researched study of the history of the instrument, illustrated by lantern slides and with a musical accompaniment using some of the sets of pipes in the National Museum's collection of musical instruments, as well as gramophone recordings of some beautiful old airs.[22] He also lectured about the pipes in the Gaelic League Hall in December.[23]

The House of Commons eventually passed the Home Rule Bill at the end of January 1913. As expected, the House of Lords immediately rejected it. Later that year, in July, the House of Commons again passed the Bill. Again the Lords rejected it. As the prospect approached of the Bill actually becoming law, the threat of the Ulster Unionists taking arms against his Government prompted King George V to consult with his Prime Minister Herbert Asquith, Irish Chief Secretary Augustine Birrell, the leaders of the Irish Unionists, and the leader of the Opposition, Andrew Bonar Law. Discussions continued throughout the king's August holiday in Balmoral. Asquith himself was by now becoming convinced that if Home Rule became law there would be bloodshed in Ulster. The equally unacceptable alternative, though, given the strength of expectation among the rest of Ireland, was that Ireland would become ungovernable 'unless by the application of forces and methods which would offend the conscience of Great Britain, and arouse the deepest resentment in all the self-governing Dominions of the Crown'.[24]

The majority of ordinary people in Ireland continued to assume that a peaceful transition to Home Rule was just a matter of time. They had no idea that soon even John Redmond might acquiesce in allowing some Ulster counties to opt out of Home Rule. For a small minority of politically aware activists, including Éamonn, however, such faith as they ever had in Home Rule had expired and, to quote Yeats, the next few years would see things changed, changed utterly.

In the midst of the political stalemate at the start of 1913, the Ulster Unionist Council followed up the Solemn League and Covenant by establishing the Ulster Volunteer Force (UVF). The UVF was open to men who had signed the Covenant and was limited to 100,000 members. Although doubt has been cast over its effectiveness,[25] many recent commentators support the historian Charles Townshend's conclusion that: 'The UVF was the decisive spur to the militarisation of nationalist politics. Whatever its limitations and internal tensions, and however short of arms it might have been, it impressed nationalists, maybe even more than it did the government.'[26] Drilling took place openly, significant amounts of money were collected, and plans were put in place to purchase arms and ammunition. By September 1913, the unionists had formed the outline of a provisional government.

On the advanced nationalist side, the IRB was continuing to recruit members from among those men, such as Éamonn, known to have separatist sympathies. This was not always easy. Diarmuid Lynch, a Gaelic Leaguer who had returned to Ireland from the US in 1908, had been approached by Sean T O'Kelly and recruited into the IRB. Lynch subsequently became Munster representative on the Supreme Council. He later recalled that looking for recruits, particularly in some rural areas, was 'like looking for a needle in a haystack. The needle was in the haystack but, in those days of dena-tionalisation, there may not have been in a whole district a single man imbued with republican ideals.'[27] The difficulties in recruitment were exacerbated by the Catholic hierarchy's condemnation of oath-bound societies.

Among even moderate nationalists, however, the propo-sition that it was necessary to take up arms was becoming widely accepted. Patrick Pearse, like Éamonn, had declared his support for this idea at the establishment of Cumann na Saoirse. Like Éamonn, his talents had been spotted by Séan MacDiarmada and, by the end of 1913, Bulmer Hobson had recruited Pearse into the IRB. The O'Rahilly, though not a member of the IRB for religious reasons, wrote in the IRB newspaper, *Irish Freedom*, in early 1912 that 'the foundation on which all government rests is the possession of arms and the ability to use them'.[28]

At a meeting of the National Council of Sinn Féin on 20 January 1913, Éamonn proposed, and The O'Rahilly seconded, the resolution 'That the Council of Sinn Féin is of the opinion that it is the duty of all Irishmen to possess a knowledge of arms.' The British Government had, some years earlier, withdrawn the law 'depriving Irishmen of the elementary right of citizens of all nations to possess weapons of offence and defence'. The Council agreed that it should educate public opinion on the matter so that 'all Irishmen would regard the possession and practice of arms as a duty'.[29] Áine Ceannt later recalled that Arthur Griffith, who had missed the meeting, was very indignant over the resolution. When speaking to The O'Rahilly, he said that he 'wanted no tinpike soldiers'. O'Rahilly replied that evidently he did not know Ceannt well because anything he undertook he meant to do, and that he was already learning to shoot.[30] Three days later Éamonn volunteered to find a suitable rifle range for practice purposes.[31]

On 24 June 1913, Éamonn bought a gun from J Lawlor and Son. It costs him £1 7s.6d. A few months later he bought five guns and two belts (of ammunition) from Dobbyns, on behalf of the Banba Rifle Club.[32] They cost £9 2s. 9d.[33] Éamonn was the Secretary of the Banba Rifle Club at Larkfield and shortly after it was formed, the club decided to write to the Miniature Rifle Association of Great Britain to be enrolled and to ask for some kind of shield for competition. This was duly received. After the Great War broke out, the Rifle Association wrote to Éamonn asking how the club was getting on and hoping that its members would volunteer to 'fight for the cause of small nations'. Irish Volunteer Thomas Slater recorded later that when Éamonn, the Secretary, replied, he suggested that 'all its members were willing to fight for the rights of small nations'.[34] Presumably Ireland was among the small nations to which Éamonn referred.

As a member of the Sinn Féin National Council, Éamonn pursued the agendas that were important to him. One of these was the campaign to limit enlistment by the British Army in Ireland. Traditionally the British Army provided an outlet for large numbers of Irishmen who otherwise had little hope of employment, or of excitement and foreign travel – like Éamonn's brother Bill. In 1913, in the face of widespread fear of an imperial German invasion of Britain, an active enlistment campaign was underway in Ireland.

In February 1913, the National Council of Sinn Féin held a Special Congress to consider the political situation in the country. On a proposal by Éamonn, the Congress resolved that 'the policy of Sinn Féin for the coming year be one of active hostility to the English Government in Ireland and that the attention of the Executive be directed especially to the fresh attempt at recruiting for the English army and navy now proceeding'.[35] Éamonn suggested that a 'car' (an ass and cart) be procured that would parade through the streets of Dublin carrying anti-enlistment slogans, particularly in the vicinity of the military and navy recruiting stations at Great Brunswick Street (Pearse Street) and Amiens Street. In April the National Council agreed the wording of the slogans: 'Before joining the British Army enquire – why so many deserters? Why do so many ex soldiers die in the work-house? The British soldier's life is the life of a slave. His end's a pauper's grave.'[36]

Shortly after Éamonn had procured the ass and cart, for two shillings a day, together with a boy to lead them, the police seized the cart, brought the driver to Store Street police station, and defaced the slogans on the cart. Nothing daunted, the National Council secured the release of the hired cart; agreed to purchase its own ass and cart for £2; and sent them out to appear again on the street.[37]

Éamonn's other agenda on the Sinn Féin National Council for 1913 was his deep and abiding passion for the Irish language. Always disappointed with Sinn Féin's lack of commitment on this front, he proposed that the Constitution of the party be amended to advance the cause of the Irish language.[38] His suggestion fell on fertile ground and, shortly afterwards, the National Council agreed that Sinn Féin should support the Gaelic League's Language Demonstration and subscribe to its collection.[39]

By 1913 the Gaelic League had been in operation for twenty years. It was still a minority interest among the population as a whole and the census returns for Irish speakers were not encouraging. The number of members and of branches had been declining, and the finances of the League remained under pressure. It had, however, had a significant impact on educational policy, and had revived interest in Irish language and culture across a broad range of social classes and religious backgrounds. The League had never been homogeneous but had persisted with its aim of acting apolitically and inclusively. The year 1913 was a critical one for the League. The Keating Branch in particular, devotees of Munster Irish, disparaged the speakers of other dialects, especially those of Connacht Irish.[40] The branch also had among its members many advanced nationalists and IRB members, including Cathal Brugha, Piaras Béaslaí and Thomas Ashe. These men saw the language as a weapon in the arsenal of the fight for political independence and were putting pressure on the apolitical stance of the League.

Éamonn, himself a member of the Central Branch and, like Douglas Hyde and Patrick Pearse, a devotee of Connacht Irish, was equally frustrated by the failure of the League to use all possible tools in its arsenal to promote the language. In February 1913, he wrote an article, 'The Political Value of the Irish Language', that was published in the *Sinn Féin* newspaper. It set out, in blunt and unequivocal terms, his view that the revival of the Irish language was paramount and that 'Ireland *without* its language cannot lay claim to nationhood though it might obtain political independence'. He claimed that this view was 'commonly accepted'.

Up to this point Éamonn was arguing within the boundaries of traditional Gaelic League ideology – that revival of the language came before politics and made politics subsidiary to the language revival. From there on, however, his views began to diverge. He asserted that:

Ninety percent of those who have actively assisted in the Gaelic League work, and all those outside the League who have given their assent to the movement, have done so from motives of nationality and from motives of nationality alone.

He said that 'the fact that the movement has not been hitherto frankly recognised as political is due to the simple device of writing over its doors – "This is a non-political movement".' Éamonn acknowledged that this slogan may have been good policy in the past but questioned whether it should remain so in the future. His answer to the question of how the language could be linked with political activity was that, instead of just paying lip service to the principle, the language should be introduced prominently and obtrusively into every department of Irish life.

Éamonn blamed the League's 'supineness, this want of self confidence', on:

… the timidity inherent in a movement led by civil servants, teachers and priests. The numerical superiority of these classes – all of whom in Ireland are subject to a strict discipline – has at times confined the League's methods within a very narrow compass.

By confining itself to acceptable methods such as persuasion, education etc., the League had, he felt, a 'dread of anything approaching, even in remote degree, the region of physical force'.

He recommended that the Gaelic League should 'go at once into the arena of national politics. Draw up your demands and force them on every candidate for Parliamentary honours. Make the language a reality in public life ... If the Home Rule mirage [should] fail to materialise, it is even more necessary than before to choose our weapons, decide our policies and re-organise our forces.' [41]

As the date for the Árd Fheis of the Gaelic League approached, dissent among members became public in the pages of *Sinn Féin*. Hyde called a special general meeting of members on 3 July. He asked the branches 'either to relieve him of the responsibility [of leading the League] or to give him a good Coiste Gnótha on whose loyalty and good sense he could rely'. [42]

The Dublin Central Branch, of which Éamonn was a prominent member, unanimously passed a resolution in support of Dr Hyde and criticised those who anonymously defamed him. Later, Éamonn informed the meeting, in his capacity as Secretary of the National Council of Sinn Féin, that certain attacks on Dr Hyde, which had been made in

Sinn Féin, 'had not been approved of in any way by the Executive of the Sinn Féin organisation'.[43]

Éamonn himself returned to the theme of 'Politics and the League' in another article in *Sinn Féin* on 12 July. He suggested that the League had three policies to choose from: 'the Parliamentarian or deputation-cum-negotiation method; the Sinn Féin or self-reliance method; and the physical force method'. He suggested that some people, and here he was referring to Hyde and his supporters, wanted to restrict the League to the first of these, the policy of 'sanity and commonsense'. Éamonn agreed that this method was effective, but only when dealing with 'our own people'. When dealing with bodies such as the national university, established by the British but not under British control, he suggested that the Sinn Féin approach of 'helping the lazy ones on with a stick has proved entirely effective'. But when it came to influencing a body such as the National Board for Education, 'the educational citadel fortified by the British Government', he insisted that it was not enough. In dealing with such a body, he asserted that physical agitation would be required.

> One National School boycotted or leveled to the ground, one inspector ejected, one Leaguer imprisoned for ignoring the English-run Insurance Act, would effect more in a month than a cairn of resolutions.

We cannot afford to throw away a single weapon, whether it be branded Sinn Féin, Physical Force or Parliamentarianism. It is open to the League to use all three, or any one of them, how and when it pleases without reference to anybody but the members who compose and control the organisation.[44]

Éamonn now found himself uncomfortably positioned between Douglas Hyde – for whom he had the utmost respect but with whose policies he was often at odds – and his increasingly politicised position on the National Council of Sinn Féin.

As the controversy within the Gaelic League raged on, the Árd Fheis and the Oireachtas competitions were held, for the first time, in Galway. The two events ran from 29 July to 1 August 1913. Initially, Hyde stayed away. Following a delegation to request his presence, however, he arrived at the meeting and was greeted with enthusiasm by the delegates. The O'Rahilly proposed Dr Hyde for re-election as President of the Gaelic League for the next year and Éamonn seconded the motion. Dr Hyde was elected to loud and prolonged applause and committed himself to doing his best for the League. He said that he hoped there would be an end to the dissention that had occurred between two parties of different political views.[45] When the election took place for the new Coiste Gnótha, Éamonn was elected with 110 votes. Other members elected from Dublin included Sean T O'Kelly (150), The O'Rahilly (141), Thomas Ashe (103) and Edward Martyn (94).[46]

Not long after, Éamonn wrote an open letter, in Irish, to An Craoibhín Aoibhinn (pen-name for Douglas Hyde). The letter appeared in *Sinn Féin* on 19 July. In the letter Éamonn greatly praised Hyde for his loyalty to the Irish cause, his work for it, his generosity, devotion and charity, and he condemned those who 'throw a stone at you from behind the hedge'. However, while criticising the approach Hyde's critics had taken, he asked that recognition be given to the fact that they were also working for the good of the Irish language and the love of Ireland. He sympathised with them for losing patience with the slow pace of progress. He deplored the way in which the crisis had caused them to attack each other. He acknowledged that he himself had lost patience and no longer shared Hyde's faith in the apolitical, consensus-building approach but asked, plaintively – what harm was there in that? He wondered if they could not find a way to work together in the future, particularly in the light of the storm clouds he saw appearing across the Irish sea and of the concern in the ranks of the League about its future direction. He wondered whether he had made Hyde angry but he didn't retract his opinions. 'Of those at the fight,' he asked prophetically, 'who knows who will come out alive?'[47]

Patrick Pearse also wrote in praise of Hyde in the IRB

newspaper, *Irish Freedom*. Unlike Éamonn, however, Pearse still had some faith in the League's consensus-building approach. Where Éamonn openly demanded a more pro-active approach, Pearse remained politically uncommit-ted. He denounced Griffith, who had never worked under Hyde nor been an active member of the League; who had never been a member of the Coiste Gnótha and did not even speak the language.[48] By the end of 1913, however, Pearse had come to the conclusion that 'the Gaelic League, as the Gaelic League, is a spent force; and I am glad of it'. He predicted that the vital work to be done in the new Ireland would be done not by the League, but by men and movements that sprang from it.[49] Following the Árd Fheis, the League returned to an uneasy peace. The new Coiste Gnótha included advanced nationalists and IRB members like Éamonn, Sean T O'Kelly and Thomas Ashe. They were now determined to force a change to the League's apoliti-cal, consensus-building stance.

Not long after Éamonn and his Gaelic League colleagues had returned from debating the future direction of League policy and procedures in Galway, the capital city was descend-ing into crisis. Within the context of rising waves of indus-trial action by workers across Europe in the years before the outbreak of the Great War, industrial unrest had spread to the island of Ireland. In 1911, James Connolly and Jim Larkin's ITGWU had organised a successful dockers' strike and had also won better conditions for the women workers in the linen mills. Further south, the Wexford Lockout of September 1911, during which Éamonn had supported the right of workers to combine and organise, had provided a foretaste of the unrest that was about to take place on the streets of Dublin.

Since its establishment, the ITGWU had proved contentious in a number of ways. Its attraction for general workers, as opposed to skilled workers who were able to join their craft union, was that it aimed to organise both general and craft workers in the interests of their mutual protection. From the start its existence pitched employers against the union, and the union against the Catholic Church and much of the political establishment – and, ultimately, against the police. Both Sinn Féin and the Gaelic League were divided as to whether Larkinism was a benevolent or malign force.

On 15 August 1913, workers employed in the *Irish Independent* were warned that they would lose their jobs if they joined the ITGWU. Some forty refused to comply and were laid off. Their employer was William Martin Murphy, one of Dublin's most successful businessmen. He had founded the Dublin Employers' Federation and was, in 1913, President of the Dublin Chamber of Commerce. Soon after the dispute in the *Irish Independent*, Murphy's employees in the United Tramway Company received the same ultimatum. On 26 August, as Dublin was *en fête* for Horse Show week, the workers walked away from their trams, bringing the city's main transport infrastructure to a halt. Murphy turned to the city's other employers and received wide-ranging support from them. Workers across the city found themselves locked out of their jobs. The ITGWU, for its part, boycotted the firms that had locked out their employees. Violence flared almost immediately and, on the first evening of the Lockout, as Larkin was addressing a gathering outside Liberty Hall, he burned a proclamation banning a planned meeting in Sackville Street. A warrant was issued for Larkin's arrest and riots broke out throughout the city. The police baton-charged the rioters, leaving one man dead and another mortally wounded.

On 31 August matters came to a head. Although the meeting was no longer proceeding as planned, Larkin had decided to give his address. In disguise, he made his way to a window in the Imperial Hotel (now Clery's) and addressed a crowd made up, for the most part, of peaceful citizens out for a Sunday walk through the capital city. The Dublin Metropolitan Police (DMP), having arrested Larkin, baton-charged the crowd. In a very short time some six hundred people were injured. Riots spread throughout the city and police damage to people and property was widespread. Soon the day became known as 'Bloody Sunday'. The Lockout continued throughout September. Dublin Corporation demanded an inquiry into police brutality. Jacob's biscuit company closed part of their factory in a dispute with the ITGWU. Two tenement buildings in Church Street collapsed, injuring many and killing seven people, including a 17-year-old boy who had just been locked out of his job at Jacob's. The Lockout spread to some 20,000 workers and their dependants.

Nationalist opinion was divided on the Lockout. The IPP was generally opposed to the strike. Within Sinn Féin there was a wide range of views among the diverse rank and file membership, and Arthur Griffith tried to find a middle route to avoid offending either side – promoting the Irish–Ireland line while condemning socialism as a foreign ideology.[50]

Among advanced nationalists such as Éamonn there was considerable sympathy for the workers. Patrick Pearse, in October 1913, wrote in his 'From a Hermitage' column in the IRB newspaper *Irish Freedom* that:

> I would like to put some of our well-fed citizens in the shoes of our hungry citizens, just for an experiment … I would ask those who know that a man can live and thrive, can house, feed, clothe and educate a large family on a pound a week to try the experiment themselves.[51]

Among the IRB senior ranks there were mixed views. Some, like Seán MacDiarmada, believed that trade unionism was a dangerous distraction from the main task of ridding Ireland of the British.[52] Bulmer Hobson took a 'friendly but neutral attitude' and recommended to a general meeting of the IRB that, since it supported all Irish citizens regardless of class, it should not intervene on the side of the workers. Sean O'Casey left the IRB in disgust at this attitude, regarding it as a betrayal of the workers.[53] Others in the Brotherhood mixed sympathy with a pragmatic recognition that failure to support the workers would be a missed opportunity for the separatist cause.

Áine Ceannt later recalled that:

> In the summer of that year, 1913, the big sympathetic general strike occurred in Dublin. It was the biggest strike ever seen in Dublin and there were many casualties. This was the atmosphere when, in November 1913, Éamonn Ceannt received an invitation from The O'Rahilly to meet John (Eoin) MacNeill and others in Wynn's Hotel.[54]

The success of the Ulster Volunteers had led Bulmer Hobson and his colleagues in the IRB to believe that the time would soon be ready to start an Irish Volunteer movement in Dublin. By October 1913, Hobson had gained the agreement of the IRB Supreme Council and been deputed to progress the plan on its behalf.[55] The IRB saw the establishment of the Irish Volunteers as the opportunity to respond in kind.

With the patience of even moderate nationalists wearing thin, Hobson's first task in getting the Irish Volunteers off the ground was to find a respected figurehead who would encourage cross-party support for a movement that, behind

the scenes, could be led by their much more radical counterparts in the IRB. Hobson persuaded The O'Rahilly to
approach Eoin MacNeill to chair the first meeting on 11
November in Wynn's Hotel. MacNeill was one of the founders of the Gaelic League and a Professor of Early and Medi-
eval Irish History at UCD. He had recently written an article
for the League newspaper, *An Claidheamh Soluis,* which was
now edited by The O'Rahilly, entitled 'The North Began',
advocating the formation of a national volunteer force along
the lines of the Ulster Volunteers.[56]

Éamonn was involved in the establishment of the Irish
Volunteers from an early stage. A week after MacNeill's article was published, he accompanied Hobson to a meeting
with Piaras Béaslaí, a member of the IRB who was also a
journalist, at Béaslaí's office in the *Evening Herald*. They told
him that MacNeill had agreed to attend a meeting at Wynn's
Hotel to discuss the possibility of starting a body of Irish
Volunteers and they asked him to attend. Béaslaí agreed and
later arranged with Seán MacDiarmada to attend the meeting together.[57]

Éamonn's Corporation colleague Sean Fitzgibbon remembered talking to Éamonn before the meeting. Fitzgibbon was
Chairman of the Central Branch of Sinn Féin.[58] Éamonn
had forwarded an invitation to Fitzgibbon with the question '*!!!An dtiochfadh tú?* EC' (Are you coming?) Fitzgibbon
responded '*Tiochfad!!!*' (I'm coming!!!)[59] Their excitement

was palpable. They agreed to meet up outside their offices in Dublin Corporation at 5pm before heading off to the meeting.

Bulmer Hobson and The O'Rahilly had issued invitations to a small group of men from across the political spectrum, although Hobson himself stayed away from the meeting for fear that his reputation as an extremist would prove a deterrent to others. The O'Rahilly later named the men and their affiliations as: Eoin MacNeill (non-IRB); Patrick Pearse (non-IRB); Seán MacDiarmada (IRB); Éamonn Ceannt (IRB); W J Ryan (non-IRB); Sean Fitzgibbon (non-IRB); James A Deakin (IRB); Piaras Béaslaí (IRB); and Joseph Campbell (non-IRB). The O'Rahilly thought that DP Moran had also been invited, but he had not turned up. Ryan, Deakin and Campbell subsequently dropped out.[60]

Out of this Provisional Committee, MacNeill, Pearse, The O'Rahilly, Béaslaí and Éamonn were also prominent members of the Gaelic League. The O'Rahilly, Éamonn and Sean Fitzgibbon were Sinn Féin Party members. Éamonn later recorded that, at the meeting, 'It was unanimously decided, come what may, to establish the Volunteers.'[61] The meeting also discussed the advisability of increasing the size of the committee to include suitable members from across a wider political spectrum, including the IPP. By the time of the second meeting, on 14 November, only three days later, the attendance had increased to thirty members. Twelve were

IRB, four were members of the IPP, four were members of the Ancient Order of Hibernians (AOH) and ten were not affiliated (including MacNeill, Pearse, Roger Casement, Thomas MacDonagh and Joseph Plunkett).[62]

In the intervening days, the ITGWU had decided to establish its own workers' militia. The Lockout was continuing to devastate life across the city. Áine Ceannt later recalled that when Éamonn returned from the meeting on 11 November, he had found the fire brigade trying to put out a fire in the premises beside their home. The Ceannt family thus experienced at first hand some of the devastating effects of the strike: six hundred tons of hay had been set alight in a malicious fire there because, 'the carters were on strike and the owner of the hay was a master carrier'.[63]

A few days later, James Connolly and Jim Larkin, on the latter's release from prison, announced the formation of the Irish Citizen Army to protect workers caught up in the ongoing Lockout from the excesses of the Dublin Metropolitan Police. By Easter 1916, the fortunes of the two new militias would become forever intertwined.

Éamonn reported that the Irish Volunteer movement

> … was publicly launched on Tuesday, 25 November, in the Rotunda Rink, Dublin, amidst great enthusiasm. The speakers included PH Pearse, Alderman Kelly [a Sinn Féin member of Dublin Corporation], and Luke O'Toole [Secretary of the GAA] … The object was the establishment of

a Volunteer force to defend the rights and liberties of the whole people of Ireland.[64]

The meeting in the Rotunda Rink was attended by thousands of people. Áine remembered that the numbers attending were so great that

... overflow meetings were addressed by Séan MacDiarmada and others. There was a special platform reserved for the ladies. The number of men attending was quite unexpected and it was evident that the physical force movement appealed to the manhood of Ireland, where the more constitutional movement of Sinn Féin, although revolutionary in character, did not make the same appeal. John [Eoin] MacNeill appeared on the platform and opened the meeting with the following words, '*Tosnuighimid anois, in ainm Dé.*' Then he said, 'We will begin now, in the Name of God.' All went well, and the various speakers were enthusiastically received until Mr Larry Kettle stood up to speak. He was a member of the Provisional Committee of the Volunteers but owing to the general strike in Dublin, his father, a farmer, happened to be involved in the dispute with his workers and some of the audience objected to Mr Kettle. A few shots were fired but there was really no panic and Captain White [Captain James Robert 'Jack' White, who was one of the co-founders of the Irish Citizen Army] went on to the platform and addressed the meeting. It had been agreed that members of the most advanced party, who might come under the notice of Dublin Castle, should not be prominent at the meeting, so Éamonn Ceannt, Sean Fitzgibbon and others did not address the meeting.'[65]

The deliberately broad-based philosophy of the Volunteers commanded the hoped-for broad-based support. The group's manifesto, written by Eoin MacNeill, stressed that it was a citizen army, the duty of which was to safeguard the rights of all of the people of Ireland. The Volunteers were to be defensive and protective, never contemplating aggression or domination. In the long term, it was envisaged that they would form, 'a prominent element in the National life under a National Government' – effectively a national army. At last Éamonn had an 'Irish army' that, with a clear conscience, he felt he could join. Had he been blessed with foresight, however, he might have done well to remember the first of his youthful objections to an army career: 'Because the paths to glory lead but to the grave.'[66]

Out of some seven thousand estimated to have attended that night, over three thousand men enrolled immediately. Éamonn's membership card, initialled by Eoin MacNeill, was dated 1 December 1913. He was assigned to Company A, 4th Battalion, No. 109. The card shows that before the end of the year he attended Volunteer meetings on 1, 8 and 15 December.[67]

On 17 December Éamonn addressed a meeting of Volunteer recruits in Camden Row. He told them that the Provisional Committee had decided to divide the city into four battalion areas: the 1st and 2nd Battalions were to be on the north side of the city, while the 3rd and 4th were to be on the south side.[68]

The Volunteers lost no time in organising and setting up drilling practice. The effect was not lost on the politicians in Westminster, and on 4 December, having ignored the preparations of the Ulster Volunteers for nearly a year, the Westminster Government prohibited the importation of arms and ammunition into Ireland.

From the start, the IRB set out to infiltrate their members into positions of influence in the new organisation.[69] Leading IRB men, such as Éamonn, were also expected to ensure that IRB members among the rank and file of the Volunteers understood their lines of command. A dual command structure for IRB members was put in place from the outset and would remain in place until Easter 1916. Éamonn swore Liam Tannam, a young colleague in Dublin Corporation, into the IRB in July 1915. Tannam later recalled being informed that 'in the event of conflicting orders I was to take the orders of my next superior officer who was a member of the IRB as against the orders of any other officer. As far as I can remember it was Éamonn Ceannt who gave me these orders.'[70]

That year, during his appearance at Ronán's Christmas

party, 'Santa' had a lot on his mind. Éamonn's brother Michael noticed that he didn't seem to be as merry as of old, as if he had aged greatly. In his speech to the children he wished them well, 'in a neat verse', and finished by referring to the New Year and the coming of Home Rule, as well as to the Suffragettes. Michael recorded in his diary: 'Poor old Santa, shall we ever see him at "The Farm" again? He seemed done up and out of form.'[71]

Éamonn had a lot on his mind, indeed. He was a member of the secret IRB, in spite of the Catholic Church's disapproval; he had started to break ranks publicly with Douglas Hyde and some of his old friends in the Gaelic League; he had acted as public spokesman for the Sinn Féin Party while deploring the party's attitude to the ITGWU and the working class; and he had become a founder member of the Irish Volunteers.

Chapter Six

• • • • • •

1914–1915

A True Irish Volunteer

The year 1914 was a turning point – not just for Éamonn but also for Ireland, the continent of Europe and ultimately the geopolitical world order.[1]

Early in January 1914, the Lockout came to an end.[2] Although initially supportive, the British unions had failed to come out in solidarity and, without their help, the workers could not hold out any longer. The ITGWU bitterly decided that it had no option but to end the strike. The employers appeared to have won the battle over union membership, though once back at work the employees eventually began to return to the union in large numbers, and in the end, the employers could not risk another confrontation. In the meantime, what Éamonn had called the 'mirage' of Home Rule was becoming ever more illusory. By the end of 1913, after a summer of consultations, the reality was becoming clear: the Home Rule Bill could only be enacted if Ulster was excluded.[3]

Once the politicians had accepted the principle, the Unionists capitalised on their position of strength. Political influence apart, by now the Ulster Volunteers had 80,000 members. They were well officered and organised. There were only about 23,000 British Army troops on the island of Ireland. On St Patrick's Day, 17 March, the Cabinet made secret plans to use the military to contain the threat posed by the Ulster Volunteers. The British Army in Ireland had other plans. On 20 March, the vast majority of officers based in the Curragh military camp told their superiors that they would prefer to be dismissed rather than carry out active military operations against Ulster. In his book *Fatal Path: British Government and Irish Revolution 1910–1922*, Ronan Fanning highlighted the critical importance of this episode: 'An elite corps of British Army officers had revolted against the Irish policy of the democratically elected Government.'[4] It was unprecedented. The crisis deepened when, on the night of Friday, 24 April, the Ulster Volunteers, openly and with no opposition from the police, landed 25,000 rifles and 3 million rounds of ammunition, sourced from Germany, into Larne, Donaghadee and Bangor.

By the start of 1914, some 10,000 men had joined the Irish Volunteers and the numbers continued to grow. In the organisation's newspaper, *The Irish Volunteer*, Éamonn described these early months:

Drill began immediately. Halls were engaged; ex army men volunteered their services; a proper system of recording attendances etc., was devised, and the halls became models of orderly work carried out with perfect seriousness and the utmost decorum.[5]

The organisation grew quickly, as did the expectations of the recruits.

Éamonn, in full 'propaganda' mode, continued to write articles for *The Irish Volunteer*. On 7 February, he wrote an allegorical piece, 'The Volunteer Giant, what will he be like?' Describing the movement as a baby born in the back room of a house in Dublin who was introduced to the public on 25 November, Éamonn claimed that:

From that hour it was clear he was no ordinary baby … I see my baby grow, grow, grow. His voice resounds from hill to hill … He buckles on his sword that glistens in the sunlight. The tramp of his feet shakes the land, and he looks the Hope and Hero of Ireland … Will he fight?

Éamonn hoped that the Volunteers wouldn't have to fight. He advised them to 'be skilled in the art of war so that there may be no war … Be simple, be efficient, be noble and the world of Ireland is yours.'

On a lighter note, the newspaper also carried helpful advertisements for Volunteer recruits:

Riflemen!

Your eyesight is most important.

If you do not see the target cards clearly

call on me.

I will test your eyes free.

Volunteer Field Glasses and Telescopes.

E J Kearney, Sight Testing Optician,

26-27 Essex Quay, Dublin.

McQuillan's of 35-36 Capel Street urged Volunteers who wanted to look smart and ensure a good shave before going to a drill or march to buy a good razor from them.[6]

In the culture of glorified militarism that pervaded Europe in the early decades of the twentieth century, a suitably military appearance was vitally important for the credibility of the Volunteers. Early in 1914, Éamonn was appointed to the uniform sub-committee, which deliberated on everything from hats to belt buckles, and from kilts to puttee leggings.[7]

A William Royce wrote an article in *The Irish Volunteer* pleading for the kilt. Mr Royce rejected 'silly' proposals to revert to the tricorn hat and long skirted coat of the 1782 Volunteers. This left him with only two choices – a uniform drafted upon modern lines or a kilt, which would be 'in keeping with our needs and certainly with the spirit of a national civilization'. He opted for the kilt.[8]

Éamonn, the Gaelic revivalist who had happily marched through Rome in an eleventh-century piper's costume, took a more practical approach to the provision of a uniform for 'a force such as ours, which is not now, and never may be, State aided'. The boy who had grown up in drafty Constabulary barracks had very firm views on the practicality of cloth – tweed, frieze and serge all had their disadvantages. The brother of the well-travelled Sergeant Kent of the Royal Dublin Fusiliers also had very decided views on colour. He dismissed, out of hand, those misguided souls who thought khaki couldn't be beaten for its invisibility. This was fine, said Éamonn, for the tropics, 'where dust and mud are brown, and rocks and vegetation are of similar hue', but impractical for the grass and earth and mud and dust of Ireland. As for the kilt, he noted Mr Royce's argument that the kilt had been credited with keeping British soldiers from getting enteric fever (typhoid) while in South Africa. However, said Éamonn, Ireland was not South Africa, 'and enteric fever is not prevalent in our island. But rheumatism *is* prevalent, and the kilt is an obvious cause of rheumatism.' He also pointed out its unsuitability for horsemen and those riding bicycles. For Éamonn the knock-out blow, however, was the cost, which, he believed, would be unacceptably high.[9]

In their manifesto the Volunteers had promised that there would be opportunities for women to contribute to the movement. Áine Ceannt, having attended the inaugural meeting, was as enthusiastic as Éamonn about the new movement and was anxious to play her own part. She soon had an opportunity. On 2 April 1914, the inaugural meeting of Cumann na mBan took place in Wynn's Hotel. Cumann na mBan was an auxiliary organisation for the Irish Volunteers, which, unlike the Irish Citizen Army, did not allow women to join. Áine immediately joined the Central Branch – the first to be established. Her sister Lily also became a member.

As for the Volunteers themselves, the drilling and the uniforms only took them so far. Following the Larne gun running in April, the Ulster Volunteers had plenty of arms and ammunition. The quality may have been a different matter but their counterparts in the south did not know this. The Irish Volunteers felt emasculated; as the number of recruits accelerated, the lack of arms became an increasing concern. The urgent priority was to raise the necessary cash.

Meanwhile, in Westminster the path of Home Rule continued along its bumpy way. By March, the principle of excluding part of Ulster had been quietly conceded – even, reluctantly, by John Redmond on behalf of the IPP. The issues outstanding were the terms of the exclusion. Offered first three years and then six years, the Ulster Unionists

Left: Éamonn Ceannt's father, Royal Irish Constabulary (RIC) Head Constable James Kent.

Right: Éamonn Ceannt's mother, Johanna Kent.

Above: The former RIC barracks at Ballymoe, County Galway, where James Kent was stationed.

Below: The plaque above the door reads, 'According to local knowledge, Commandant Éamonn T. Ceannt was born in this building on the 21st of September, 1881. Signatory of the Proclamation of the Republic and one of the leaders of the 1916 Rising. Don't surrender until victorious.'

Do réir seárcais an ceancair rugaṡ an
Ceannṗorc Éamonn T. Ceannc.
san Áras seo 21 Meán Fómair. 1881.
Siniceoir ar Forógra na Poblácca
agus duine de luċc ceannais
Éirí Amaċ 1916.

Ní géilleaṡ go buaṡ.

C. Sexton. W. J. Redmond. O'C. Sullivan. C. Reddin. E. McCarron. E. T. Kent. C. P. Curran. H. Maher
T. Dillon. J. Duffy. J. O'Reilly. J. White. M. Moylan.
M. J. Reid. C. Smith. T. Sheridan.

Above: Éamonn (ET Kent, back row, third from right) with classmates at CBS North Richmond Street, Dublin, c. 1896.

Left: The headquarters of the Gaelic League, where Éamonn and Áine (insert) became acquainted.

Éamonn was a founding member of the Dublin Pipers' Club
(Cumann na bPíobairí).

Above: Éamonn (third from left, seated) as the blind piper in Douglas Hyde's play *Casadh an tSúgáin*.

Above: 'Mé Féin' – a self-portrait from 1909.

The Kent family.
Back row (l–r):
William, Richard,
Michael, Éamonn,
Áine (née Brennan).
Front row (l–r):
James Patrick,
Elizabeth (née
Cummins), James
Snr, Nell Casey (née
Kent), Jack Casey.

Dublin Municipal Officers' Association menu card, 1909.

rejected both, holding out for permanent or indefinite exclusion. The next question was the area to be excluded. Carson suggested in a private meeting with Prime Minister Asquith that his more extreme followers would prefer it limited to six counties rather than the whole province of Ulster which, given its religious demographic, might ultimately revert to a Home Rule parliament in Dublin.[10]

Although not apparent to the man in the street, the intransigence of the Ulster Unionists – supported by the Tory Opposition in Westminster – together with an army in Ireland refusing to carry out the policy of the democratically elected government, had created a situation that threatened the system of British parliamentary democracy at its core.[11]

On 24 May the House of Commons passed the Home Rule Bill and, on 8 July, an Amending Bill was passed in the Lords, providing for the temporary exclusion of Ulster from the workings of the future Act: the number of counties, and whether exclusion was to be temporary or permanent, remained to be negotiated.

Back in Ireland, John Redmond had begun to notice the success of the Irish Volunteers, many of whom were either constitutional nationalists, supporters of the IPP, or members of the AOH.[12] Unbeknownst to the IRB element on the Provisional Executive Committee, Eoin MacNeill, Colonel Maurice Moore[13] and Roger Casement had made some approaches to Redmond with a view to securing his support. Bulmer Hobson later recalled that, although he knew nothing about the approaches, which were made in a personal capacity, MacNeill undoubtedly 'thought it important that the new Volunteers should have the benediction of the country's leader [Redmond], or at least that it should not have his opposition'.[14]

Éamonn seems to have been unaware of these political overtures and, early the following month, on 9 June, he told a meeting in Dundalk, attended by over two thousand people, that:

> The business of the hour was to arm the Volunteers and not to sow dissention amongst them. There would be no 'Curragh' meetings in their ranks. Their men were not to be seduced from their allegiance. The Irish Volunteers were above party politics, and they would not allow their unity to be broken by the application of any political test.[15]

Éamonn was quickly proved wrong about the influence of party politics. On the following day, 10 June, John Redmond issued a pre-emptive statement supporting the Volunteers, but demanding that twenty-five of his own IPP nominees be allowed onto the Provisional Committee.[16] This was the same number as the existing committee, which already included a number of IPP supporters. If the Committee was not prepared to agree to his terms, he threatened to establish a rival volunteer movement. Hobson later recalled that the ultimatum came as a 'bombshell' to the Provisional Committee.[17]

Éamonn and the other members of the Provisional Committee faced a difficult choice: accept Redmond's nominees and lose control of the Volunteers; reject them and face a catastrophic split in the organisation; or resign.[18]

Although the Supreme Council of the IRB privately ordered its members to oppose it, the Provisional Committee of the Irish Volunteers reluctantly decided to accede to Redmond's demand. Áine Ceannt recalled that:

> On 16 June 1914, the Provisional Committee met. At this meeting, the twenty-five nominees were accepted, but nine dissented from this. They were Éamonn Ceannt, M J Judge,[19] Con Colbert, John (Sean) Fitzgibbon, Edward Martyn, PH Pearse, Seán MacDiarmada, Piaras Béaslaí and Liam Mellows.

Not all of the IRB members on the Provisional Committee dissented. Joseph Plunkett worried that resistance to Redmond would destroy the movement.[20] So too did Bulmer Hobson, who was convinced that the 'lesser evil' would be to accept Redmond's nominees on the committee, 'knowing that effective control was and would remain, in the hands of the officers who were already appointed, the majority of whom were members of the IRB'.[21] One of those officers was Éamonn, whose talents as a bookkeeper had been put to good use by the Provisional Committee. Pearse, although he had voted with the minority and signed his name to the dissentients' letter, saw the merit in remaining in the movement. By so doing they could, he believed, 'be watchful to checkmate any attempt on Redmond's part to prevent us from arming. This is the real danger.'[22]

Hobson wanted to avoid dissention for another reason. Certain members of the Provisional Committee, among them Hobson, MacNeill and Casement, with a loan of money from a group of English-based supporters including Alice Stopford Green and Mary Spring Rice, had arranged for a secret shipment of arms for the Irish Volunteers. In May, Darrell Figgis, an Anglo-Irish journalist, and Erskine Childers, a former British soldier and a clerk of the House of Commons, had bought rifles and ammunition in Germany. By the time of the crisis on the Irish Volunteer Provisional Committee, they were already en route from Germany, and arrangements were being made to land them in Ireland. At this critical moment a split could indeed have proved fatal to the success of the venture. The split in the Irish Volunteers was avoided, for the immediate future.

The IRB leadership, particularly Tom Clarke and Seán MacDiarmada, regarded Hobson's stance (i.e. accepting Redmond's nominees) as an unpardonable betrayal. After a showdown, Hobson resigned from the Supreme Council of the IRB and the editorship of *Irish Freedom* but retained his position as Chairman of the Dublin Centre's Board and on the Leinster Executive. His relationship with Clarke and MacDiarmada never recovered.

Hobson's prediction that it would be possible to 'work around' Redmond's nominees, however, proved correct. The expanded Provisional Committee was now composed of fifty-two members. The sheer number was unmanageable and the partisan wrangling made decision-making impossible. The essential decisions were about money and arms, and they were still tightly controlled by MacNeill and The O'Rahilly, who was the Treasurer. Éamonn, using his skills as a bookkeeper, assisted The O'Rahilly. Together they kept the books in perfect order but managed to conceal the arms transaction from the Redmondites on the Committee.[23]

Few, if any, of the rank-and-file members of the Volunteers had any idea of the difficulties on the Provisional Committee. The inclusion of Redmond's nominees had had the effect of strengthening the movement among the members by bringing recruits from the most unlikely places, including many former British Army officers and soldiers. The organisation of the Volunteers continued apace.

The Provisional Committee had, from the start, made it clear that the Irish Volunteers would be a democratic organisation and that the election of officers would ultimately be a matter for the members. On 29 June, Éamonn was unanimously elected Captain of the 4th Battalion, Company A. The chairman of the meeting, William O'Neill NT, in congratulating the company remarked that, 'although some present might differ from Éamonn Ceannt in their political views they all respected him as a true Irish Volunteer'.[24] The battalion had about eight hundred men in four companies, A to D.[25] The headquarters of the battalion was a disused mill at Larkfield, Kimmage, which was owned by Count George Noble Plunkett, the father of Joseph Plunkett. It was two storeys high and housed a drill hall and a miniature rifle range. Adjacent to the building was a field suitable for outdoor drills and other exercises.[26]

While all of this activity was going on in the public gaze, Éamonn continued to work behind the scenes with other dissenting members of the Provisional Committee to secure funding for arms and ammunition for the Volunteers. Towards the middle of July, Pearse wrote to Joseph McGarrity of the IRB's sister organisation in the United States, Clan na Gael, appealing for arms and ammunition as a matter of urgency. 'We want this request to take precedence of any request that may have been made by MacNeill or by anyone else … The men with whom I am acting more immediately in this are Sean McDiarmada [MacDiarmada], Kent [Ceannt] and [Sean] Fitzgibbon.'[27]

Towards the end of July, the guns which Darrell Figgis and Erskine Childers had bought in Germany were due to arrive in Ireland in a number of private yachts. One of the yachts, the *Asgard*, belonged to Erskine Childers; the other, the *Kelpie*, belonged to Conor O'Brien, a cousin of Mary Spring Rice.[28] The arms cargo from the *Kelpie* was transferred off the coast to another yacht, the *Chotah*, which belonged to the Dublin surgeon Sir Thomas Myles.

The plan was to secretly land the arms from the *Chotah* near Wicklow while the *Asgard* would sail boldly into Howth harbour in full daylight to gain publicity for their arrival. Bulmer Hobson had rationalised that, although the amount and quality of the arms and ammunition was not very impressive, the Volunteers could attract more funds for the organisation by getting the maximum publicity for their arrival.

Hobson was the overall organiser and Éamonn was involved in both events. Éamonn's friend Sean Fitzgibbon, who was responsible for the Wicklow landing, had decided that Kil-coole was the best location in Wicklow for a secret landing.

The date set for the Kilcoole landing was Saturday, 25 July. Éamonn was adjudicating a piping competition at the Oireachtas of the Gaelic League when he got word that the boat had been delayed and the landing deferred for a week. Accounts of the subsequent events differ slightly. Áine recalled that since the pickup cars were already in place in Wicklow, the Volunteers 'had to utilise them and go joy riding round the countryside so as not to evoke suspicion'.[29] Some of the Volunteers involved thought the event was a clever rumour deliberately put about to put the police off the scent.[30]

The following day, Sunday, 26 July, Hobson's plan for the Howth landing was put into effect. The 4th Battalion, with Éamonn in charge, met in Kimmage for an early-morning parade before marching across the city to join about eight hundred of their fellow Volunteers in the Irish Citizen Army grounds in Croyden Park, Clontarf, for the march to Howth.[31] The Volunteers had been holding route marches on several of the previous Sundays and the police no longer paid them much attention. Other Volunteers, who were mainly IRB members, travelled out to Howth by taxi. They had been instructed to invite lady friends for an outing at the seaside. The Volunteers arrived in Howth just as the *Asgard* sailed into view.

The bemused Sunday-morning crowd looked on as the Coastguard officers who tried to intervene were tied to a post.[32] While the Volunteers unloaded the cargo, Éamonn's 4th Battalion was last to arrive at the pier. Éamonn retrieved some long wooden batons from a cart. He distributed them to his men and stationed them at the start of the pier to prevent anyone other than Volunteers from gaining access.[33] One Volunteer recalled that a police sergeant and constable tried to gain access but were turned back by Éamonn, who 'laughed at them saying: "In the name of the Republic you will not be admitted until this little operation is over." Then they went away and the next thing we saw was rocket signals from the Police Barracks.'[34]

As those closest to the *Asgard* had started offloading the precious cargo, Volunteer Joseph O'Connor relieved Éamonn to allow him and his men to collect their rifles from the yacht. Some of the ammunition, which was very heavy, was loaded into the taxis, presumably to the surprise of the ladies who were left to find their own way home. The rest was loaded onto a cart brought by the boys of Na Fianna. The Volunteers shouldered the unloaded rifles for the march back to Dublin.

The 4th Battalion was at the rear of the parade back to the city so did not know what was happening when it came to a halt just past Raheny. Some of the men took the opportunity to eat the sandwiches they had brought with them.[35] Then word spread that the British military were blocking the road ahead – this turned out actually to be two tramloads of policemen who dismounted but did not stop the parade.[36] The march continued as far as the junction of the Howth and Malahide roads at Clontarf, where they were met by a group of soldiers from the Scottish Borderers. With them was Assistant Commissioner William Harrell of the Dublin Metropolitan Police. Harrell stopped the Volunteers and demanded that they give up their rifles. While Hobson, Darrell Figgis and Thomas MacDonagh kept Harrell talking, the rest of the Volunteers were ordered to disperse with the rifles into the surrounding streets and fields. One Volunteer recalled Éamonn "'moseying" around from one fellow to another saying, "Get your rifles away. Get across the wall and into Croydon Park."'[37]

As the Volunteers were faced by soldiers with fixed bayonets, there was a brief scuffle when the police, ignoring Harrell's orders, charged the Volunteers. There was considerable confusion and ranks were broken. During this incident, one of the members of the Provisional Committee, M J Judge, received a gash from a bayonet.[38] One member of Éamonn's A Company was wounded, though not seriously.[39] Áine Ceannt later recalled being told that:

> Many of the men were being bayonetted and Éamonn Ceannt fired from his Mauser and injured one soldier, Lance Corporal Finney, in the ankle. This caused the soldiers to turn and run, as Darrell Figgis said it was the first time in his life he saw the British soldiers running away.[40]

One Volunteer later recalled Éamonn, prior to this incident, stopping the ammunition cart, which was being transported by members of Na Fianna. He demanded that they let him have some ammunition and said that he was not going to be unarmed.[41] Éamonn was not the only Volunteer to use his small arms and to attempt to get ammunition. A member of Na Fianna said later that they 'had a stiff time keeping off the Volunteers who were clamouring for ammunition from the trek-cart'.[42] Another recalled that when the Scottish Borderers moved up, 'I saw Commandants Éamonn Ceannt and Thomas MacDonagh in front; both officers knelt down; Ceannt rested his Mauser pistol on Thomas MacDonagh's shoulder and opened fire.'[43]

As the talks continued, the men at the front of the parade passed their rifles to the men at the back, who scattered to nearby houses, gardens and fields. Some weapons were stowed in the taxis used earlier, which returned to the city by circuitous routes.[44] In all, the soldiers seized only nineteen rifles and, when Colonel Maurice Moore of the Irish Volunteers went to Dublin Castle a few days later to demand their return, they were handed back to him.[45]

The rest of the unwieldy rifles had to be retrieved from their hiding places across the north side of the city. Days later, Volunteers were still trying to retrieve them. One of Éamonn's men, Volunteer James J Burke, was wounded during the gunrunning. He received 'a bayonet in the left side, just under the heart'. Éamonn came to see him as he recovered in bed and, Burke recalled later, 'he smilingly unrolled a package which he had brought with him, gave me a Howth gun and said, "That may be of use to you later on."' Shortly afterwards, Burke was promoted to Company Adjutant.[46]

With the Volunteers dispersed, the British Army soldiers and police made their way back into their barracks. Word of the landings had reached the city, and as the soldiers marched from Sackville Street and down Bachelor's Walk towards the Royal Barracks (now the National Museum, Collins Barracks), they were greeted by a jeering crowd and pelted with stones and rotten fruit. In the mêlée the soldiers fired. Three people, Mary Duffy, Patrick Quinn and James Brennan, were killed. Many others were injured. A Royal Commission of Enquiry later found that the shootings had been unwarranted.

The massacre on Bachelor's Walk, as it quickly came to be called, was a publicity disaster for the British Army. By an equal and opposite reaction, the Howth gunrunning had been a major publicity success for the Irish Volunteers.

The funeral of the Bachelor's Walk victims, on 28 July, which was attended by thousands of Dubliners, presented the Irish Volunteers with another public-relations opportunity. The Volunteers mustered with bandoliers, belts and haversacks. Some shouldered their rifles. Éamonn marched immediately behind the third hearse together with The O'Rahilly, Colonel Moore, Laurence Kettle, Sean Fitzgibbon and other members of the Provisional Committee. At Beresford Place, the band of the ITGWU joined the cortège playing Chopin's funeral march. The funeral Masses took place in the Pro-Cathedral.[47]

The following weekend, the yacht *Chotah*, carrying the balance of the guns and ammunition, was due to make its delayed entry to Kilcoole. Sean Fitzgibbon and others travelled down in a charabanc and a number of motorcars on the pretense of going on an excursion. Éamonn arrived in Kilcoole by car with Seán MacDiarmada. Another car brought Sean T O'Kelly, Cathal Brugha and MJ Buckley, who was the City Engineer in Dublin Corporation. The party also included Bulmer Hobson. Others followed by bicycle, motorcycle and train.

After an altercation with a couple of RIC men, the rifles were rowed ashore from the yacht and loaded onto the charabanc with the Volunteers perched on top.[48] The back axel of the charabanc broke as they got to Little Bray and the Volunteers had to hide the arms and ammunition in nearby houses until a message could be sent to St Enda's in Rathfarnham, where a number of cars were waiting to offload the charabanc. Liam Mellows, the messenger, reached St Enda's on his motorcycle at approximately 3.30am and the cars drove quickly – 'thirty miles per hour across Ticknock' – to collect the stranded weapons.[49] Eventually the rifles and ammunition were rushed off to various places of safety throughout the city.

Within days of the Kilcoole gun-running, events on the European Continent had reached crisis point. The assassination by a Bosnian Serb nationalist of the heir to the Austro-Hungarian Empire, Franz Ferdinand, and his wife in Sarajevo a month earlier had sparked a domino effect of alliances and counter-alliances between the great powers of Europe. Austria declared war on Serbia, Germany declared war on Russia, then on France. On Monday, 3 August, Germany invaded Belgium. On the same day John Redmond, in the House of Commons, asked the House to leave the defence of Ireland in the hands of the Irish Volunteers. The following day, 4 August, Britain declared war on Germany.

The announcement of war had a range of consequences for the Irish situation.

As Britain mobilised its reservists, young men rushed to join up and 'do their bit' before the war's end – which was expected to come by Christmas – denied them the opportunity. Even the politicians were caught up in the euphoria. The historian Charles Townshend has pointed out that:

> For the Liberal Cabinet, the onrush of war was a heady experience, and not least because it instantly pushed the Irish problem from the centre of the political stage to the remote background. In July, Ireland was on the point of overwhelming the bulwarks of the British constitution; the failure of the last ditch efforts to negotiate a Home Rule compromise in the Buckingham Palace talks, and the deadly affray on Bachelor's Walk, led some to think the unthinkable – the possibility of civil war. In August, Ireland suddenly became almost invisible.[50]

For the IRB, the announcement of war was welcome. Sean T O'Kelly later recalled:

> I think I can say with truth that the announcement that war had begun in Europe was welcomed with real joy, certainly by the men of the IRB. Their feeling generally was that now their time had come. The opportunity for which they had hoped and prayed for so long was now theirs, and it was, they felt, up to them to see that they were ready and willing to make the fullest possible use of that opportunity so as to win complete independence for Ireland.[51]

The political parties in Westminster, long divided by the Irish question, now found themselves united in the face of a common enemy, imperial Germany and its allies. The influence of the IPP on the political arithmetic of Westminster disappeared. John Redmond agreed to the suspension of Home Rule for the duration of the war, in return for which Prime Minister Asquith agreed to suspend partition – the exclusion of Ulster.

The Third Home Rule Bill, accompanied by the Suspensory Bill, went through the House of Commons on 18 September. The Bill, now entitled the Government of Ireland Act 1914, received royal assent the same day. Even though the Prime Minister had assured them that Ulster would not be coerced into any form of Home Rule, the

Irish Unionists walked out of the Commons *en bloc*. If that party failed to recognise what, according to Ronan Fanning 'was in reality a victory',[52] the Irish Parliamentary Party and their supporters failed to recognise the limitations of their apparent success. Stirring congratulatory messages came from home and abroad on the passing of the Act. The Mayor of New York, Mr JP Mitchel, a grandson of the Young Ire-lander John Mitchel, sent his congratulations on this great 'Charter of Liberty'.[53] At home, supporters of the United Irish League in county councils, urban district councils and Volunteer units throughout the country sent messages of congratulations and support.[54]

Even before the outbreak of war Redmond had sug-gested that British troops be withdrawn from Ireland, leav-ing the Irish Volunteers to defend their shores, and freeing British soldiers up to take part in the European war. During September, tensions on the Provisional Committee of the Irish Volunteers about their wartime role reached breaking point. At a meeting on 9 September, Pearse recommended that, during the war, the actions of the Volunteers should be confined to defending Ireland and securing the ports to prevent food shortages. He had heard a rumour that some members of the committee were in talks with the War Office to hand over the Irish Volunteers to the Eng-lish. An altercation broke out and reports of the meeting suggested that revolvers had been drawn.[55] Éamonn wrote to the *Irish Independent* some days later refuting this suggestion. He reported that:

> I was present during the whole of the meeting referred to, and neither I nor any member associated with me either used, or drew, or threatened to draw, or use a revolver or other firearm of any kind whatsoever. Neither did I personally see any person produce a firearm or any other weapon.[56]

By the time the letter was published, the dispute on the Provisional Committee had been overtaken by events.

During an address to an open-air meeting in Woodenbridge, County Wicklow, on Sunday, 20 August, Redmond committed the Volunteers to active participation in the war itself. He said:

> The interests of Ireland – of the whole of Ireland – are at stake in this war. This war is undertaken in the defence of the highest principles of religion and morality and right, and it would be a disgrace for ever to our country and a reproach to her manhood and a denial of the lessons of her history if young Ireland confined their efforts to remaining at home to defend the shores of Ireland from an unlikely invasion, and to shrinking from the duty of proving on the field of battle that gallantry and courage which has distinguished our race all through its history. I say to you, therefore, your duty is twofold. I am glad to see such magnificent

material for soldiers around me, and I say to you: 'Go on drilling and make yourself efficient for the Work, and then account yourselves as men, not only for Ireland itself, but wherever the fighting line extends, in defence of right, of freedom, and religion in this war.'

It has been suggested that Redmond's objective was to discourage the British Government from extending conscription to Ireland by facilitating a high level of voluntary recruitment.[57] In the wave of martial euphoria that greeted the war, the speech, allied to an intensive recruitment effort and a wave of sympathy for 'little Catholic Belgium', had a galvanising effect. In the first six months of the war, 50,000 Irish men enlisted in the British Army and another 25,000 followed them in the next six months. Approximately half of all of the recruits came from the Irish Volunteers and the Ulster Volunteers.[58] One of the recruits later recalled that 'the number of men who went away was colossal'. They left Dublin Bay in mail boats and liners escorted by destroyers, with troops packed everywhere:

> From stem to stern … All the other ships in the harbour would blow their sirens while everybody sang 'Rule Britannia' … and 'God save the King' … There was hardly a family in Dublin that was not affected, with the exception of the extreme Nationalists, and even these were affected in some cases.[59]

In the face of Redmond's declaration at Woodenbridge, the Provisional Committee of the Irish Volunteers faced a new crisis. Even for Eoin MacNeill and the moderate separatists on the committee, Redmond had taken a step too far. On 24 September, MacNeill and the majority of the founding members released a statement – a 'Minority Manifesto' – to the press, accusing Redmond, whose nominees they had accepted as a 'lesser evil' three months previously, of announcing 'a policy and programme for the Irish Volunteers fundamentally at variance with their own published and accepted aims and pledges'. They accused him of 'declaring it to be the duty of the Irish Volunteers to take foreign service under a government which is not Irish', and of doing this without consulting the committee, the Volunteers themselves, or the people of Ireland. They declared that he was no longer entitled to any place in the Irish Volunteers and that his nominees were no longer members of the committee.[60] Éamonn was one of the signatories to the statement.[61]

The split that many had feared now took place. Two rival Volunteer organisations came into being. The original founders of the movement retained the name The Irish Volunteers – frequently erroneously referred to by the authorities as the Sinn Féin Volunteers[62] – while Redmond's followers became The National Volunteers. The effect of the split was immediate and traumatic. Only ten percent of the members of the movement stayed with The Irish Volunteers. The remaining ninety percent were loyal to Redmond.

The *Irish Independent* printed a long report of the Volunteer districts that had gone with Redmond. Included among them was Company A, 4th Battalion – Éamonn's battalion. It reported that:

> After the latter's drill last night at Larkfield, Kimmage, Mr Éamonn Ceannt read the recent minority manifesto, and then asked those who adhered to it to fall out: of about seventy men present, some fifteen left the hall.[63]

Volunteer George Irvine, Captain of B Company, 4th Battalion, later recorded that out of his complement of approximately 130 men, the split left him with about fifty.[64]

Over time, the impact of the split, combined with the attrition from wartime recruitment, proved equally damaging to the National Volunteers. The military men who had been their instructors immediately reenlisted in the British Army. Many of the rank-and-file Volunteers followed them by enlisting too. Over time, the IPP began to lose interest in the National Volunteers. Without the ideological passion that continued to drive the much smaller Irish Volunteers, the numbers in the National Volunteers continued to decline.

Cumann na mBan, the women's auxiliary movement, also split along similar lines. The Central Branch, of which Áine was a member, was reduced from about two hundred members to about two dozen. Those who sided with Áine and the Irish Volunteers included her sister Lily and Kathleen Clarke, wife of Tom.[65]

From the point of view of the advanced nationalists in the Irish Volunteer movement, the loss of men who were not ideologically committed to the separatist cause was not – at least in hindsight – a disaster. One member of Éamonn's A Company, 4th Battalion later recalled that:

> It was at this stage that A Company commenced to become an efficient military unit. The officers were no longer burdened with the handling of a large body of men, many of whom were strangers to them, and for the first time felt that they had the full confidence of the men. In consequence the officers were accepted by the men as leaders in a movement that had a serious purpose and personal associations were formed which were invaluable to efficiency and esprit de corps.[66]

Over time, the numbers in both the Irish Volunteers and their counterparts in Cumann na mBan began slowly to increase again.

As far as the IRB leaders were concerned, Redmond's stance cleared the air. Even before the split in the Irish Volunteers, possibly on 9 September, two weeks earlier, representatives of the advanced nationalist movement, including the IRB, Sinn Féin and the Labour movement, had organised a meeting to consider the new situation brought about by the war.[67, 68]

Relationships between these groups had long been strained, but the international situation had changed that.[69] The meeting agreed to make a joint effort to secure Irish independence before the end of the war, to do everything possible to fight recruitment and conscription into the British Army, and to resist the British forcibly if they attempted to disarm the Volunteers.[70]

The trade-union activist William O'Brien recalled that it was at this meeting that the Irish Neutrality League was established, with James Connolly as President. One of its objectives was to prevent employers from coercing their employees to enlist.[71] While the organisation was suppressed not long after by Dublin Castle, the concern was valid. In the absence of conscription, employers were being urged to provide incentives for their employees to join the army. Civil servants who enlisted were entitled to full pay, to have their military service counted towards their pensions, and to have their jobs kept open for them – assuming they survived the war. Dublin Corporation was less enthusiastic and only provided half-pay, and then at the Corporation's own discretion. Firms such as Guinness also provided half-pay and promised to hold open the jobs for recruits.[72]

On 24 September, the same day as the publication of the Irish Volunteers' Minority Manifesto, Prime Minister Herbert Asquith visited Ireland on a recruitment drive. His visit was part of a tour around Britain and Ireland and he had already spoken in London and Edinburgh; a meeting in Cardiff was to follow. He gave a speech at the Mansion House in Dublin, sharing a platform with the Lord Lieutenant, Lord Aberdeen; the Chief Secretary for Ireland, Mr Augustine Birrell; Lord Meath, a prominent Conservative member of the House of Lords; and John Redmond. Asquith later recalled that the huge audience in Dublin was unanimously enthusiastic. The Irish Volunteers made various attempts to disrupt the meeting, including an abortive plan to fuse the lights, but these came to little in the face of a strong security presence.[73]

Éamonn had long been a vocal and determined opponent of any British Army enlistment campaign and was now intent on warning members of the Irish Volunteers not to believe the propaganda that was appearing all around them. Writing in *The Irish Volunteer* on 10 October, he claimed that 'the story is now being circulated that there is no real desire on the part of Home Rule MPs to get Irishmen into the English army'. On the contrary, he asserted, 'the Mansion House meeting showed that a deep-laid plot existed for the purpose of entrapping the Volunteers into a Help-the-Empire League'. He contrasted this attitude to that of his fellow founders of the Irish Volunteers who

> … stand for the independence of the force under its own freely elected Executive or an Irish Parliament representative of the whole people of Ireland. The [Redmond] nominees

stand for a Volunteer force under the control of Lord Kitchener of Omdurman.[74]

A week later he followed up this article with another on the subject 'Kitchener of Omdurman'. At the time, Kitchener, as Secretary of State for War, was in charge of recruiting a massive volunteer British Army. One Irish Volunteer recalled later that, 'Nearly every dead wall in the city had an enormous outsize picture of Kitchener's forbidding countenance pointing a huge forefinger at us with the single pronoun in huge capitals: YOU!'[75] Éamonn contrasted the arrangements under which the defence forces of South Africa, Australia and Canada agreed to support the English Crown – 'out of gratitude for the protection afforded by England's army and more especially, England's navy' – with the plans of Asquith and Redmond for Ireland which were, he said:

> … to hand over the Irish Volunteers to the British War Office. Ireland is not to have the status of a British colony. Ireland, deprived of its native Parliament, is asked to hand over its native defence forces to the control of the British War Office under Earl Kitchener.

An outraged Éamonn condemned Lord Kitchener in particular for his actions some years previously where he conducted an unrelenting and bloody campaign against Arab tribes, 'who had the audacity to take up arms in the Soudan in defence of their miserable rights and liberties'.[76] Now,

Éamonn said, the leopard had changed his spots and 'today the victor of Omdurman appeals to the Irish slaves, through the mouths of Redmond, Devlin and Nugent to help him in their present war for the defence of small nationalities, for the upholding of honour, religion and truth'.[77] The *Irish Volunteer* itself constantly reminded its readers that, contrary to Kitchener's ubiquitous recruitment campaign, it was not 'little Catholic Belgium' that needed help – 'The Small Nation that needs YOUR help is Ireland.'

On 25 October, the first Convention of the Irish Volunteers was held in the Abbey Theatre. In keeping with the original democratic manifesto of the Irish Volunteers, the 160 delegates elected a new Executive Committee, which, together with representatives from each of the thirty-two counties and nine provincial towns, formed a General Council. The General Council was to be the new governing body of the movement.[78] Éamonn was unanimously reappointed to the Executive Committee, together with the other members of the original Provisional Committee who had signed the manifesto expelling Redmond's nominees.[79] Following the convention, the Executive Committee met and appointed officers who would be responsible for the day-to-day operations of the movement. MacNeill had already been re-elected President and The O'Rahilly, Treasurer. Éamonn was now elected Financial Secretary.[80] In this position Éamonn became responsible for keeping the accounts and making the scarce funds stretch to cover the movement's main priorities – or at least satisfy their most pressing creditors. Among these were the outstanding bills from a number of irate taxi drivers who were still waiting to be paid for bringing Volunteers out to Howth and later returning some of the rifles and ammunition to the city.[81]

Shortly after the convention, Éamonn was again writing in *The Irish Volunteer.* He addressed the many Volunteers who, he claimed, were still neutral and in doubt as to the real issues. The issue, he assured them, was not one of personal loyalty to John Redmond for his past services to the Home Rule campaign. It was a matter of which policies would best serve Ireland. He stated that it was a false argument that loyalty to Britain would lead to genuine Home Rule after the war was over. He claimed that England had never 'redressed an Irish grievance before the Irish people had made clear their deter-mination to take the law into their own hands'. Citing the Land War, Catholic Emancipation, and the disestablishment of the Church of England as earlier examples, he concluded that 'the placing of Home Rule in its present comparatively satisfactory position is due immediately, if not primarily, to the silent threat of the Irish Volunteers'.

Slowly but surely the Irish Volunteer network began to regenerate. The process was accelerated by a reversal in senti-ment towards enlistment in the British Army as the lists of war dead began to appear and the wounded began to return to Ireland. It was becoming clear that the war would not be over by Christmas.

For those remaining at home in Ireland, the impact of the war was also making itself felt. In the first budget after the outbreak of war, in November 1914, income tax was doubled. While unpopular among the wealthy and the middle classes, this affected only those earning over £160 a year, and excluded many skilled workers, lower paid white-collar workers, and the poor. Everyone, however, was affected by the increase in duties on staples such as tea, porter, strong ale and stout.[82]

In the meantime, the Irish Volunteers were benefiting from an influx of money which had begun to arrive from the United States following the Howth gunrunning. An instalment of £2,000 from America in November had been spent on rifles, which could now be openly purchased. Battalions were urged to arm themselves and to learn how to use their weapons. A booklet entitled *Rifles* was prepared and others on *Rifle Ranges* and *Musketry Practice* were in preparation. The series were made available 'in handy and attractive form at 2*d*. each'.[83] Individual battalions found ways to raise funds for themselves. Éamonn composed a song to the tune of the German national anthem, 'Deutschland Über Alles'; entitled 'Ireland Over All', it was sold and the small profit was donated to the 4th Battalion, Irish Volunteers.[84]

The Irish Volunteers were openly proceeding with the

reorganisation of the new, smaller group. Éamonn attended a meeting of the Central Executive on 2 December, which was chaired by Pearse. Pearse submitted a scheme for the establishment of a headquarters general staff, and a draft scheme for the military organisation of the company and the battalion. This military organisation scheme reflected the Irish Volunteers' opposition to the recruitment campaign for the British Army and, in the event that it came to it, conscription. The plan was to resist any such imposition.[85] MacNeill was appointed Chief of Staff of the Headquarters General Staff; Pearse was appointed Director of Military Organisation; The O'Rahilly, Director of Arms; MacDonagh, Director of Training; Plunkett, Director of Military Operations; Hobson, Quartermaster. The following year Éamonn joined the Headquarters Staff as Director of Communications.

The scheme of military organisation formed the Irish Volunteers in Dublin city into four battalions. Éamonn, in the capacity of Acting Commandant, commanded the 4th Battalion. Edward Daly, Tom Clarke's brother-in-law, commanded the 1st Battalion. Thomas MacDonagh commanded the 2nd Battalion and Éamon de Valera commanded the 3rd. Pearse, Plunkett, The O'Rahilly and Hobson were commandants on the Headquarters Staff.[86]

At this time the objective of the moderates on the Executive Committee of the Irish Volunteers, including MacNeill, Hobson and Fitzgibbon, was to arm and organise a large body of Irish men for the defence of Ireland so that, by the end of the war, when joined by the disillusioned ex-soldiers who had fought in the British Army for the rights of other small nations, they would be in a position of strength to demand Irish independence.[87]

The provision of arms remained an urgent priority. Under the auspices of the Provisional Committee an 'advance fund' had been established with 'loans from friends who may be willing to advance sums of not less than £5'.[88] Where possible, Volunteers were also expected to purchase their own arms, and an advertisement in *The Irish Volunteer* Christmas edition helpfully pointed out that ideal Christmas presents for Volunteers could include revolvers at 14*s.* 6*d.*; B.S.A. air guns for 40*s.*, and, for those anxious to give a particularly generous gift, a new Lee-Enfield magazine rifle with protected sights, complete with bayonet, could be purchased for the splendid value of £5 5*s.*[89]

With the outbreak of war, some senior members of the IRB, in particular Tom Clarke and Seán MacDiarmada, had already started planning for an insurrection in Ireland. Their plans were kept secret even from some of their colleagues, including Bulmer Hobson, who remained committed to the IRB constitution, which forbade an insurrection against Britain without the support of a majority of the Irish people.

From then on, Éamonn and a number of other senior Irish Volunteers, who were also members of the more radical wing of the IRB, played a dual role. Initially discussions about a Dublin rising took place within a 'shadowy advisory committee comprised of Irish Volunteer commandants and vice-commandants who were also IRB members'.[90] Clarke was not happy with the outcome and the committee was allowed to lapse.

Although the depth of his involvement in the IRB until this time remains unclear, there is no doubt that by the end of 1914, Éamonn was firmly established in the IRB inner circle. In October, just before the Irish Volunteer convention, Pearse told his contacts in Clan na Gael, the IRB's sister organisation in the US, that Éamonn was one of those who could be relied upon to make sure that monies for arms got into the 'right' hands. The others he named were Clarke, MacDiarmada, Hobson, and himself. He said he had no doubts about the honesty of others such as MacNeill and The O'Rahilly, but warned that 'they are not in or of our counsels and that they are not pledged to strike, if the chance comes, for the complete thing'.[91]

Clan na Gael, for its own part, had been meeting with the German Ambassador in the still-neutral United States since August 1914 to seek German support for an armed revolt in Ireland. Roger Casement, a retired British consular official, who was also a Gaelic Leaguer, a member of Sinn Féin and a founder member of the Irish Volunteers, was in the US at the time and offered himself as an intermediary. He travelled to Germany with funding from the Clan. His mission was to seek German support for Irish independence, to secure a shipment of arms and to establish an Irish brigade from among British prisoners of war in Germany. Before the end of 1914, he did achieve some broad statements of support from the Germans, together with permission to found a brigade and a promise to provide arms and ammunition.

As the year 1915 opened, the prospects for peace were further away than ever. January saw the first Zeppelin raids in Great Britain, bringing civilian populations into the firing line for the first time. In the Atlantic, German submarines began to attack merchant vessels. In April, clouds of poison gas spread a new and terrifying threat among the troops trapped in the trenches. Two weeks later a German U-boat torpedoed the Cunard liner, the *Lusitania*. She sank approximately eleven miles off the Old Head of Kinsale, County Cork, with a loss of 1,200 lives.

The Irish soldiers on the front line in Europe and beyond were taking a severe battering. In April, the 2nd Battalion of the Royal Dublin Fusiliers had suffered heavy casualties following the second Battle of Ypres. Throughout April and May, reinforced with an influx of new recruits, it suffered further casualties in a series of gas and artillery attacks at Mousetrap Farm (St Julien). Between 25 April and 25 May, the battalion war diary recorded the following losses: 24 officers and 103 other ranks killed; two officers and 1,094 other ranks missing; 14 officers and 291 other ranks wounded – resulting in a total loss to the battalion of 1,528 men. Many others would die of illnesses related to their wounds and to the gas attacks following their return to Ireland.[92]

In addition to the decimation of the 2nd Battalion on the Western Front, the 1st Battalion, on 25 April, lost 569 men in the ill-fated Gallipoli landings in the Dardanelles.[93] Since at that time the majority of the men involved were Dubliners born and bred, it has correctly been suggested that 'the grief inflicted on the people of Dublin during those early months of 1915 must have been shattering'.[94]

In Westminster, the Irish question had been completely eclipsed by the exigencies of the war. In May 1915, a wartime coalition Government was formed between the Liberals and the Conservatives. Although no longer holding the balance of power, Redmond was asked to join the Cabinet, but he declined Asquith's invitation. The Irish Unionist Sir Edward Carson, the implacable enemy of Home Rule, became Attorney General.[95]

The second war budget introduced the same month by the new coalition Government doubled the duty on beer and whiskey, and was deeply unpopular in Ireland. Although a mass protest meeting was held in the Phoenix Park, the impotence of the IPP in the face of the new political environment had become clear for all to see.[96] Recruitment of Irishmen into the British Army, which had amounted to

43,000 between August and December 1914, began to taper off steeply. Between January 1915 and April 1916 there were only 12,000 recruits.[97]

In contrast, the number of recruits to the Irish Volunteers began to pick up in early 1915, albeit from a low base. Éamonn was kept busy visiting the companies in his 4th Battalion and following up the visits with a conference of his officers. On 16 January *The Irish Volunteer* urged other acting-commandants to follow Captain Ceannt's example and, 'get similarly busy'.[98] In early February, Éamonn met with his company and other officers for special fieldwork. They discussed the defence of their HQ in Kimmage, a scheme for cycle scouting, the best sniper vantage points and the best method of advancing under cover. They then cycled to Templeogue and Balrothery for a series of open-air lectures and discussions.[99]

Éamonn was clearly an innovative officer and, in the middle of February, *The Irish Volunteer* again congratulated him on a 'new and valuable departure' whereby ten men of each company in the 4th Battalion bivouacked in Kimmage for a weekend. 'Special drill, a Céilidhe and church parade were features.'[100] Around the same time Thomas MacDonagh, Director of Training, was setting out an eight-week training programme for the Volunteers that incorporated many of the initiatives already instituted by Éamonn.[101]

On 3 February Éamonn chaired the meeting of the Central Executive during which the form of field kit necessary for each Irish Volunteer was agreed. The kit included clothes, arms and equipment, first-aid equipment and sundries including matches, spare bootlaces, scissors, needles and safety pins. Officers were expected to carry a pistol or revolver, one hundred rounds of ammunition, a whistle, notebook, watch, compass, field glasses and a map of the district, and were responsible for ensuring that suitable sleeping arrangements, eg. blankets or sleeping bags, were available for their men.[102]

During February, Éamonn recorded in his notebook the decision of the Executive Committee to form a mutual Insurance Society to be known as An Cumann Cosanta, The Irish Volunteer Insurance Society. The object of the society, which was based on an idea which Bulmer Hobson had formulated many years previously, was, 'to insure its members against possible loss of the means of livelihood consequent on their connections with the Irish National Movement and in particular with the Irish Volunteers.'[103] Michael O'Hanrahan was appointed Secretary and Organiser, under Bulmer Hobson's direction.[104]

Although in many ways Éamonn's involvement in the Irish Volunteers, and to an even greater extent in the IRB, suggests that he was a risk taker, he was always meticulous about mitigating his more risky activities whenever possible. For a long time he kept his membership of and activities within the IRB secret, even from Áine. Even though his own employment in Dublin Corporation was relatively secure, he would have fully supported the principles underlying An Cumann Cosanta and had already taken out personal life assurance policies in favour of Áine and Rónán. In 1914 he paid annual premiums of £4 4s. 4d. and £3 9s. respectively for each of them.[105]

At a meeting of the Executive Committee on 10 March 1915, the formal appointments under Pearse's Scheme of Military Organisation were made, and December's acting appointments were confirmed. Éamonn, who had been Acting Commandant with the rank of captain, was confirmed as Commandant of the 4th Battalion. The Vice-Commandant was Lieutenant Cathal Brugha. The other Dublin battalion commandants whose appointments were confirmed were Edward Daly, 1st Battalion; Thomas MacDonagh, 2nd Battalion; and Éamon de Valera, 3rd Battalion.[106] A short time afterwards, the Dublin battalions were formed into a brigade under the command of Thomas MacDonagh.[107] Of the four new commandants, Éamonn was already a member of the IRB and Edward Daly, who was a brother-in-law of Tom Clarke, had recently joined.[108] Thomas MacDonagh, who was a tutor to and close friend of Joseph Plunkett, joined the IRB in April 1915. Éamon de Valera also joined later in the year. On 13 March 1915 Pearse met with the four Dublin battalion commandants to discuss the feasibility of an insurrection the following September. The four shared his belief that England's wartime difficulty was Ireland's opportunity

– that the time to stage an armed insurrection was before the war's end.

As the year progressed, Éamonn remained busy with his Volunteer duties. He gave his battalion a 'Visual Training Lecture' based around the South Dublin Union (SDU) – a workhouse on the grounds of the present-day St James's Hospital and later the site of Éamonn's actions during Easter Week 1916 – as well as a 'Street Fighting Lecture', which contained details of how to prepare a house for occupation; how to establish communications trenches; and the effect on morale of being attacked by artillery.[109]

The high point of the year for many members of the renascent Irish Volunteers was the Easter manoeuvres, which took place in early April. With Pearse in overall charge as Brigade Commandant General, the exercise, which did not prove very successful due to the inexperience of both officers and men, involved:

> The sudden mobilisation of the four Dublin battalions and of the auxiliary Fingal Brigade, constituting the Dublin Brigade: the attack and defence of a position in North County Dublin; and the despatch of a flying column to a point south of Dublin.[110]

Éamonn's 4th Battalion was ordered to mobilise about a mile northwest of Phibsborough Roman Catholic Church. The battalion split into two groups with 'a strong cycle corps' preceding the main body. After the exercise the troops rallied in Finglas.[111]

During the war, the Gaelic League continued its cultural activities and, although Éamonn was no longer active on the Coiste Gnótha, he remained involved. In May, he adjudicated for the piping competitions at the Feis Ceoil. The organisers of the Feis were acutely aware of the tragic events happening in the wider world. *An Claidheamh Soluis* reported that, while it was 'impossible to escape from the pervading atmosphere of sorrow that is over all civilised countries today', the organisers had reluctantly agreed to go ahead with just the competitions and to hold only one concert – for the prizewinners. Arrangements were in train to hold the Oireachtas and the Árd Fheis of the League in Dundalk at the end of July.

The IRB members in the League used the occasion of the Árd Fheis to fundamentally change the constitution of the organisation. Seán MacDiarmada had, some months previously, tried to persuade his IRB colleague Sean T O'Kelly to sponsor an amendment to the League constitution to include the overtly political aim of 'winning the freedom of Ireland' as one of the League's objectives. Although O'Kelly refused, the Keating Branch, of which MacDiarmada was a member, sponsored the amendment. In spite of Hyde's objections, the amendment was placed before the Árd Fheis and carried. [112]

At the same time, the IRB had been covertly using its

authority among members within the League to influence the elections to the Coiste Gnótha. When the elections took place, the new committee included among its number many committed IRB members such as Sean T O'Kelly, Piaras Béaslaí, Thomas Ashe and Seán MacDiarmada who, at the time, was in prison for sedition.[113] Douglas Hyde immediately resigned as President, followed shortly afterwards by a number of his supporters. Eoin MacNeill replaced him. By 1915, the balance of power had passed irrevocably into the hands of those whose interest was primarily in politics, not the Irish language.

At the same time as some of their associates were covertly securing the politicisation of the Gaelic League during its Árd Fheis in Dundalk, Éamonn and his IRB colleagues among the Irish Volunteers were helping to stage-manage a much more public event in Dublin. Jeremiah O'Donovan Rossa, a veteran Fenian, had died in the United States on 29 June. Tom Clarke, in consultation with his old American colleagues in Clan na Gael, saw an opportunity to return O'Donovan Rossa's remains to Ireland for a high-profile national funeral that would publicise the separatist cause. Complex and detailed arrangements were put in place for the funeral. Thomas MacDonagh, as General Officer Commanding and Chief Marshal, had overall responsibility for the arrangements. Éamonn was a member of the Publicity Committee, as well as the Officer Commanding the Dublin

Brigade of the Irish Volunteers. Éamonn's wife, Áine, was one of the Cumann na mBan representatives.[114]

Archbishop William Walsh agreed to allow O'Donovan Rossa's remains to lie in state in the Pro-Cathedral from 27 to 31 July, during which time tens of thousands of Dubliners – the committed and the merely curious – passed to pay their respects. The funeral took place on Sunday, 1 August. Crowds thronged the streets to watch the Irish and National Volunteers, the Irish Citizen Army and Na Fianna, as well as representatives of Sinn Féin and the GAA, march out to Glasnevin Cemetery in an unprecedented display of national unity.

Tom Clarke had asked Pearse to deliver the now-famous graveside oration with instructions to: 'Make it hot as hell, throw all discretion to the winds.'[115] Pearse took the advice to heart and delivered a memorable speech:

> They think they have pacified Ireland. They think they have purchased half of us and intimidated the other half. They think they have foreseen everything, think that they have provided against everything; but the fools, the fools, the fools! – they have left us our Fenian dead, and while Ireland holds these graves, Ireland unfree shall never be at peace.

During that summer of 1915 Éamonn, Áine and Rónán stayed for about a month with the Thornton family in Spiddal, County Galway. Micheál Ó Droighneáin (Thornton), the son of the host family, was a founder member of the Irish Volunteers in Galway and had joined the IRB in 1910. Éamonn was constantly aware that he was being followed and his activities monitored by the police, yet he addressed a meeting of Micheál's IRB circle to encourage them in their work. One day, Ó Droighneáin received a message that the RIC sergeant at Spiddal was talking to his superiors in Galway about someone they were shadowing. He later recalled, 'Presuming that they were referring to Ceannt, we decided that neither he nor I would sleep in the house that night. So we kept watch all night but nobody came to bother us.' [116]

Throughout the summer, Éamonn was very active in directing his battalion of the Irish Volunteers. Regular battalion meetings took place, as did a series of test mobilisations. During July the 4th Battalion organised an *aeridheacht* in Larkfield before a 'fairly large' attendance. The Celtic Glee Singers contributed choruses and there was a series of recitals and songs. The Fintan Lalor Pipe Band played a number of marches and Éamonn contributed a few selections on the pipes. There were Irish dances and violin recitals. A company of the Irish Volunteers, under Éamonn, gave a drill exhibition. The proceedings ended with the singing of 'A Nation Once Again'.[117]

Éamonn was also active in meeting members of the estranged National Volunteers to encourage them to return to the fold. National Volunteer Laurence Nugent later recalled that, not long after the funeral of O'Donovan Rossa, Éamonn addressed a meeting of the National Volunteers and assured them that 'there was a possibility of a large consignment of rifles and ammunition being landed in the country. Probably a lot more than the Irish Volunteers would be able to use.' He asked them if they would take part in any action decided upon for the freedom of the country, telling them that they would probably be compelled to strike soon. Nugent said that 'every man promptly agreed' and that the details of the meeting were kept secret until 1916. He also recalled that around the same time Éamonn addressed the Dún Laoghaire battalion with the same encouraging results.[118]

During August, Éamonn was appointed to the Headquarters Staff of the Irish Volunteers as Director of Communications.[119] The need for a secure network of communications between the executive and the battalions, and between the battalion and company commanders and their troops at local level, was heightened by the close scrutiny under which the Dublin Castle authorities had placed the Volunteers, as well as those who were prominent in Sinn Féin and the independence movement in general.[120] In this context, the Irish Volunteers had been officially described as, 'constituting a danger to the defence of the Realm'.[121] In addition to the police monitoring, the Post Office was known to be closely watching the correspondence of members of the independence movement.

Letters addressed in the Irish language were also frequently delayed or not delivered at all.

The Volunteers decided to set up their own postal system and during the remainder of the year Éamonn was occupied with its establishment. It was a responsibility for which he was well suited, as it required detailed planning, careful organisation and ongoing control. Collection points in the Dublin district included Tom Clarke's shop at 75a Parnell Street. The cost, based on the normal postal service, was a penny for each letter or postcard, with circulars in open envelopes at a halfpenny each. As an interim measure in the early days of the arrangement, the Volunteer Post reserved the right to repost letters in the ordinary post offices, and warned that letters which must not be so reposted should be clearly marked 'By Hand Only'.[122] After Éamonn had identified trustworthy contacts in companies of the Irish Volunteers, the service was extended to other parts of the country. This involved detailed maps of collection and delivery addresses as well as the identification of reliable messengers to carry the post. Ideally the messengers were required to have motorcycles, sidecars or bicycles at their disposal and to travel in pairs. Messenger Receipt Books were printed and distributed.

The exercise was not without its difficulties. The Naas Company reported that:

Two young, rather enthusiastic cyclists were dispatched to

Kildare and reported back as follows: 'Left Naas at 11.25am. Owing to trouble with one bike, walked 2.5 miles into Newbridge, delay 40 Minutes.'

When they reached their destination, the contact was not at home so they left the parcel with 'the woman in charge of the house with instructions to deliver it the moment he returned'.[123]

Micheál Ó Droighneáin later recalled that during the Ceannt family's summer visit to Spiddal, Éamonn spoke to him many times about the Rising that was coming and 'before he left us he had arranged in code the message which he would send to me when the Rising was about to take place'. Éamonn had undertaken to write to Ó Droighneáin an ordinary letter, in Irish, in which he would mention a date three days *after* the date agreed for the Rising – 'for instance, if he had mentioned 25th, the Rising would commence on the 22nd'. Ó Droighneáin also recalled that Pearse had visited him at Coláiste Chonnacht in Spiddal where he was teaching during August. Pearse 'spent two whole hours walking up and down between the College and the entrance gate, taking about the coming Rising'.[124]

Both Éamonn and Pearse were well positioned to know the plans for a Rising. During the early summer of 1915, the executive of the IRB had established a secret Military Committee charged with drawing up a plan for a Rising. It was composed of Éamonn, Pearse and Plunkett: a Corporation clerk, a schoolteacher and a poet – none of them had military experience.

Éamonn's outstanding competence was probably his organisational rather than military talent. He was a man who could be relied upon to get things done, unlike either Pearse or Plunkett, neither of whom was known for their administrative abilities. JJ 'Ginger' O'Connell, the Chief Inspections Officer for the Irish Volunteers, once recalled that meetings of the military HQ staff of the Irish Volunteers tended to degenerate into rambling discussions unless the 'business-like' Ceannt was presiding.[125] Mortimer O'Connell, a customs officer who was a Volunteer and member of the IRB, described Éamonn's role on the Military Council as 'a very active capable man but never appeared in the public eye but who was, of course, a great worker behind the scenes'.[126]

The plan for a Rising was based on an original idea drawn up by Joseph Plunkett who had been refining it since his appointment as Director of Military Operations for the Irish Volunteers.[127] Plunkett travelled to Germany, clandestinely and by a circuitous route, between March and early June 1915, where he met up with Roger Casement to negotiate a draft agreement for the purchase of arms for the Volunteers. He participated in Casement's attempts to recruit an Irish Brigade, but he appears, correctly, to have realised that it had little chance of success.[128] By early June, however, Plunkett believed that he had succeeded in coming to satisfactory terms with the Germans regarding an arms shipment. The IRB would pay for a cargo of arms that would be sent to Ireland by the Germans on a date to be confirmed, but expected to be some time around Easter 1916. The agreement also envisaged that a small force of officers and men would accompany the arms. Leaving Casement in Germany, Plunkett returned to Ireland in July to report to his colleagues on the Military Committee.[129]

During March 1915, while Plunkett and Casement were in Germany, Sean T O'Kelly was dispatched to the United States by Clarke and MacDiarmada to notify their Clan na Gael colleagues about the projected Rising. He was told no date, but was given to understand that detailed plans had been put in place for the seizure and occupation of Dublin city by the Irish Volunteers. He was told that the Military Committee were working out options for the rest of the country and that details would be forwarded to the United States at a later date. He was also told to ask the Clan for as much money as they could provide to help arm the Irish Volunteers. O'Kelly himself later recalled that he had no knowledge of Plunkett's trip to Germany and had received no instructions about discussing with the Clan any plans relating to Germany or German association with the Rising. During his visit, however, O'Kelly guessed that they were aware of it and that John Devoy, in particular, was in informal discussions with German contacts.[130]

With Clarke and MacDiarmada effectively running the show following a reorganisation of the Supreme Council[131], the IRB formally adopted a policy of insurrection despite the reservations of Patrick McCartan[132] and Bulmer Hobson. Pearse's biographer Ruth Dudley Edwards has suggested that it was at a meeting in September that 'the Military Committee became the Military Council, and its numbers were increased to five by the addition of Clarke and MacDiarmada'.[133] The decision had apparently been taken to launch a rebellion within the following six months.[134]

With German arms in prospect following Plunkett's mission, Pearse sent Diarmuid Lynch to Cork and Kerry to scout for suitable landing places.[135] Joseph Plunkett, although visibly suffering from tuberculosis, prepared to travel to the United States to inform Clan na Gael of the German agreement. He carried coded papers of the detailed plans in a hollowed-out walking stick prepared by his brother Jack.[136]

Frustratingly, little or no evidence survives of Éamonn's activities on the Military Council of the IRB. It is reasonable to assume that he took part in the discussions on the military plan, but no evidence survives. Éamonn, who was meticulous about keeping every cheque stub and business paper regarding his private life, was equally meticulous about maintaining the secrecy of the Military Council. On top of his busy schedule with the 4th Battalion, he was certainly involved in briefing local Irish Volunteer officers who were members of the IRB on the general outlines of the plan, as he had briefed Micheál Ó Droighneáin in Spiddal. During Easter week 1916 these arrangements were carried out to the letter.[137]

He was also starting to alert his own men about the possibility of action. One of the members of A Company recalled later that in November 1915, during a route march to the Pine Forest (in the Dublin mountains), Éamonn lined up the whole battalion and told them that he had heard them singing the chorus of the Volunteer's marching song (later the national anthem of the Republic of Ireland) 'Amhrán na bhFiann' which includes the phrase, 'Soldiers are we,/whose lives are pledged to Ireland,/Some have come from a land beyond the sea.' This led him to tell them:

'Well, the time is not far distant when [you] will have to shame that boast or prove it true.' He then stressed that we were to obey every mobilisation order promptly as from this day on. 'Any such order may be the serious one. I myself do not know when that order may come, but I do know that it cannot be far distant. We have organised a fund in America to look after the wives and dependants of those who will go down and each man is to hand in the names of his dependants to his Company Captain immediately. Prepare yourselves for the day and put your souls in order.'[138]

The Second Annual Convention of the Irish Volunteers was held in the Abbey Theatre on Sunday, 31 October 1915. Éamonn and the other members of the Headquarters Staff were reappointed to their old positions and, in his capacity as Director of Communications, Éamonn reported that, 'numerous lines of communication between Dublin and the provinces had been established'.[139]

Although the stealthy presence of the IRB members was stronger than ever, with fourteen IRB out of the twenty members on the executive, Eoin MacNeill remained in charge and the *Declaration of Policy of the Irish Volunteers* remained the same. In spite of the secret plans of the IRB Military Council, there was no change to the original mandate 'to defend the Irish Nation and to resist any attempt to force the men of Ireland into military service under any Government until a free National Government is empowered by the Irish people themselves to deal with it'.[140]

• • • • • • •

Chapter Seven

January–April 1916

Preparing for the Rising

As the year 1916 started, the Great War continued una-
bated across the globe. On the European Western Front,
four million men were bogged down in opposing trenches.
The lists of dead soldiers in the newspapers and the constant
shiploads of casualties arriving home from the front were a
stark indicator of the human cost of the war. In January the
Westminster Government decided to introduce conscription because of the urgent need to replace the mounting
losses of the hitherto volunteer army, and the Military Service Act passed into law on 27 January. For the first time
in the modern era, British men were compelled by their
government to fight for their country. The Act introduced
conscription for all single men between the ages of eighteen and forty-one in Great Britain, with a small number of
exemptions. The Act did not apply to Ireland, but many were
convinced that it was just a matter of time. Redmond's Irish

Parliamentary Party appeared to many to be impotent in the face of this threat, and even some Roman Catholic bishops publicly criticised the party for its position on recruitment.

The growing fear of conscription in Ireland as well as disillusionment with the progress of the war was welcome news for the radical nationalist movement.[1] In the IRB, Thomas Clarke and Seán MacDiarmada also became increasingly convinced that the Germans and their allies could win the war.[2] The Irish Volunteers, under Eoin Mac-Neill's leadership, remained committed to the principle of the defence of Ireland but began to accept that an offensive strategy might become necessary to resist any attempt to force the men of Ireland into military service. Behind the apparently united front of the Irish Volunteers, however, there was a deepening rift. Some senior Volunteers, including Bulmer Hobson and Ginger O'Connell, believed that, in the event that it was necessary to go on the offensive, any plan embarked upon should have a realistic chance of military success and probably be based on an extended campaign of guerrilla or hedge fighting across the whole island of Ireland. On the other hand, Éamonn, together with Pearse and Punkett, was already secretly committed to an offensive before the war's end. Although no copies of their military plan survive, many attempts have been made to 'reverse-engineer' it based on surviving evidence, testimony of participants and actual events.[3]

The key elements of the plan appear to assume that the British Army would be distracted by the expected offensives on the Western Front and that a supply of arms, paid for by supporters in the United States and provided by the Germans, could be landed successfully in the south of Ireland at the same time as the outbreak of the Rising. The Rising itself would be a set piece battle in Dublin based around a number of fortified strategic locations. They expected that the government administration would remain paralysed into inaction long enough for the country to rise up in support of the daring nature of the Rising. There were plans for a ring of opposition around the capital city, providing cover, if necessary, for a fighting retreat to the country.

The IRB Military Council was not alone in organising itself for pre-emptive action. The Irish Citizen Army was also preparing for a fight. James Connolly had published a series of articles during the previous summer on 'Insurrection and Warfare', and had travelled the country giving talks on street fighting.[4] Relationships between the ICA and the Irish Volunteers had long been strained, although their joint participation in the funeral of O'Donovan Rossa represented a significant *rapprochement*. Both the Irish Volunteers and the IRB, however, were deeply concerned at the prospect of any pre-emptive – and, they feared, ultimately futile – action by the tiny ICA.

In January 1916 matters began to come to a head. Towards the middle of the month, the Irish Volunteers became so concerned at the rumours emerging from the ICA that Eoin MacNeill, alerted to the danger by Bulmer Hobson, and accompanied by Patrick Pearse, arranged to meet with James Connolly in the headquarters of the Irish Volunteers. Connolly told them that he wanted to take immediate action by seizing selected buildings in Dublin, which would encourage the country to rise in response. MacNeill made it clear to him that the ICA could not rely on support from the Irish Volunteers, since he saw no possibility of military success. Unable to come to an agreement, MacNeill left the meeting while Pearse stayed on to talk to Connolly. MacNeill later recalled that Pearse told him that he had 'succeeded with Connolly'.[5]

The exact meaning of Pearse's report is open to a number of interpretations. MacNeill appears to have been reassured that Connolly – and indeed Pearse himself – had been brought around to his point of view. He wrote to Pearse and received further assurances that no pre-emptive action was on the cards. Unknown to MacNeill, however, on Sunday, 16 January, the Supreme Council of the IRB met at Clontarf Town Hall and approved Seán MacDiarmada's motion: 'We fight at the earliest date possible.' Even they were not told that the Military Council had already agreed on the date of the Rising: 23 April – Easter Sunday. Terrified of the betrayal that had foiled so many Irish nationalist uprisings in the past, the Military Council was determined to preserve the secrecy of their plans – even from the highest elected body in their own organisation.[6]

During early 1916, the Military Council continued to meet secretly. Some of the meetings took place in Éamonn's house in Dolphin's Barn. The plans for the Rising were such a closely guarded secret that even Áine was not aware of what was being plotted from her living room. She recalled meeting the members only once and remembered the group to include Clarke, MacDiarmada and Pearse. She thought that Plunkett was there also.

Later in the month, around payday in the Corporation, Áine remarked jokingly to Éamonn that he should give her some money 'before the rebellion starts'. Éamonn replied, 'It may start sooner than you think,' continuing, 'James Connolly has disappeared.' Áine later recalled that he insisted, 'We can't let the Citizen Army go out alone; if they go out we must go with them.'[7]

On Wednesday, 19 January, James Connolly left Liberty Hall at lunchtime without telling his colleagues where he was going. He did not reappear until the following Saturday evening, provoking alarm among his closest colleagues that he had been kidnapped either by the British authorities or by the leadership of the Irish Volunteers. There is no defini- tive account of what actually happened during this period and Connolly refused to say.[8] The evidence suggests that he was collected in a rented car by two members of the IRB

Military Council. Geraldine Plunkett Dillon, Joseph Plunkett's sister, believed that the two were Seán MacDiarmada and Éamonn Ceannt.[9] They drove to an empty house in Dolphin's Barn and met with other members of the Military Council there.

At some stage during the days of Connolly's absence, a separate meeting took place between Michael Mallin, Connolly's second-in-command, and members of the Military Council – probably Seán MacDiarmada and Éamonn.[10] Mallin had been travelling the countryside looking for Connolly and threatened that the ICA would take action if Connolly were not released at a certain time. According to Frank Robbins, an ICA man who talked to Mallin about this meeting shortly before the Rising, Éamonn sarcastically retorted, 'What could your small number do in such a situation?' This prompted Mallin to reply, 'We can fight and we can die, and it will be to our glory and your shame if such does take place.' Pearse is reported to have responded by banging on the table and saying that he, for one, was with them.[11] Mallin's biographer Brian Hughes concluded that, while this may have been a 'somewhat glossy version of the events', there may have been some truth in it.[12]

The outcome of the meeting between the Military Council and Connolly was by no means certain. Geraldine Plunkett Dillon recalled that her brother Joseph had told her that Connolly had been very angry at first, which led to long hours of plain speaking.[13] According to Áine, Éamonn had instructed his officers to report to their house; when he returned there, it would be either to give them orders for ordinary manoeuvres, 'if the situation has cleared, or alternatively to take their places for the fight'. He returned to the house at 10.30pm, dismissed the waiting officers and told Áine that Connolly had reappeared.[14] George Irvine of B Company recalled later that Éamonn had intimated that, having called the officers together, he didn't want to mention the problem with the ICA since it was now solved. Instead he went over some battalion business, read out the words of a song he had composed – 'Ireland Over All' – and dismissed the meeting.[15]

Whatever the exact sequence of events, it is clear that the representatives of the Military Council had informed Connolly of their plans for an uprising the following Easter and that Connolly had, at least provisionally, committed himself and the Irish Citizen Army to work together with them towards that end. Connolly was present at the next meeting of the Military Council in the Ceannt house and 'was a member of that body from that day forward'.[16]

The general attitude of distrust between the ICA and their new IRB allies took a while to dissipate. Mallin had been hurt by the 'sneering way' in which Éamonn questioned the fighting potential of the ICA, but Éamonn's response was probably symptomatic of the deep concern that all of the members of the Military Council felt at the prospect of their careful plans being pre-empted by a 'forlorn hope' uprising of the Irish Citizen Army. The prospect of dying for their country was also clearly at the forefront of everyone's mind. While there is no evidence that Éamonn subscribed to the doctrine of blood-sacrifice written about so eloquently by Pearse, Plunkett, MacDonagh and even Connolly, Éamonn was clearly preparing, in his usual business-like way, for the possibility of death.

On 7 January 1916, he wrote a draft will in the back of a small notebook:

In case of my death I leave all my possessions present and future to my wife; failing her to my brother Richard in trust for my son Rónán; failing my son Rónán, then to Miss Lily Brennan, my sister-in-law.

Éamonn Ceannt
(Edw. T. Kent)
7th January 1916[17]

Éamonn's multifaceted role as a member of the Military Council, Director of Communications for the Irish Volunteers, and Commandant of the 4th Battalion placed him at the heart of the complex series of events that would unfold over the following months. All of this work had to be done during his lunch hours, evenings and weekends since his job in Dublin Corporation kept him fully occupied during office hours.

His position as Director of Communications on the Headquarters Staff of the Irish Volunteers provided him with ideal cover for the work he was to carry out of alerting IRB members among the senior staff of the Irish Volunteers to their roles in the upcoming Rising, and in facilitating the distribution of arms and ammunition. The Rising was being organised in plain sight under cover of the publicly announced manoeuvres planned by the Irish Volunteers for Easter 1916. This enabled messages to be sent to the various country Brigades of the Volunteers as to the positions they were to occupy during the manoeuvres.

Some time in late February or early March, Éamonn asked Garry Byrne, First Lieutenant of C Company, 4th Battalion, whether, in the case of a fight, he would be prepared to go down to the country – Éamonn explained that they wanted men to take charge of operations there. Byrne opted at the time to stay in the city. Éamonn asked him again about a month before the Rising and told him 'that it was decided that he should go'. Byrne then, 'more or less agreed'. Following subsequent briefings from Pearse and MacDiarmada, Byrne travelled to Kells, County Meath, where he made contact with Donal O'Hannigan and some of the local Volunteers.[18] O'Hannigan himself was also a member of C Company and had been travelling around the south of Ireland distributing small arms and inspecting centres.[19]

The Military Council was making plans to land the German arms in Fenit, near Tralee, County Kerry. From there they would be distributed around the south and west of the country. On 6 March, Éamonn told IRB man Michael Staines, then Quartermaster of the Dublin Brigade, that the Headquarters Staff had 'instructed' him to tell Staines to give up his day job and take over as Quartermaster General from The O'Rahilly. Éamonn said that this was because the latter 'was opposed to the Rising'. Staines later recalled that O'Rahilly didn't demur, and he took up his new position on 16 March. His responsibilities included buying lamps and, on the instructions of Seán MacDiarmada, a marquee to provide shelter for the men who would be engaged in the Tralee landing. Staines also recalled sending arms and ammunition for Liam Mellows in Galway and Terence MacSwiney in Cork.[20]

Éamonn was particularly close to Liam Mellows, who was a member of Na Fianna and the Irish Volunteers, as well as of the IRB. During 1915 Mellows had been appointed to command the Irish Volunteers in south Galway. His activities had brought him to the attention of the authorities and he had been arrested under the Defence of the Realm Act. He was placed initially in Arbour Hill Barracks prior to being deported to England. His absence was a blow to the plans for the Rising. Éamonn asked Áine to call to his mother each day on the latter's return from visiting Liam in Arbour Hill, and to check whether he had been deported. Following his deportation, he lived with relatives in England until shortly before the Rising in April.[21]

In addition to allocating duties to senior IRB members in Volunteer companies throughout the country, Éamonn was also actively engaged in recruiting new IRB members. Henry Murray, of A Company, 4th Battalion, later recalled being approached by Éamonn towards the end of 1915. Éamonn said he assumed Murray understood that the Irish Volunteers:

> Might at any time have to face a serious situation and that it might be necessary to carry on the organisation under-ground. He stated that it was considered desirable therefore to invite officers and men who were regarded as dependable to become members of the Secret organisation. Éamonn Ceannt enquired if I had any conscientious scruples in the matter and, on my replying that I had not, he invited me to attend at his private residence where I was sworn in by him.[22]

Éamonn's recruitment technique was not always as formal as that recalled by Henry Murray. Michael Lynch was a colleague of Éamonn's in Dublin Corporation and a member of B Company, 4th Battalion. He had previously been co-opted by Éamonn to help him copy routes onto tracing paper for use by couriers using the Volunteer Post. He later wondered whether this had been some kind of test of his loyalty to the cause when Éamonn asked him to join what he called 'the inner organisation' that was behind the Volunteers. Éamonn told him, without actually divulging the date of the Rising, that 'sooner or later it would mean a fight against the British'. After a few days thinking it over, Lynch agreed, and one day, very early in 1916, Éamonn administered the IRB oath to him at the junction of Grantham Street and Heytesbury Street in Dublin. Lynch recalled that Éamonn told him he didn't need to raise his right hand – just remove it from the handlebars of his bicycle![23]

Apart from his Irish Volunteer 'headquarters' tasks, Éamonn had a busy schedule of duties as Commandant of the 4th Battalion. The battalion now had six companies, A to F.[24] Although there was a clear delegation of powers and responsibilities to the senior officers, Éamonn took his position as overall commandant very seriously. The battalion was busy during the early months of 1916, training and organising, and gathering arms and equipment. Éamonn regularly visited the companies, most of which were training in the Plunkett home in Larkfield.[25] He also took part in the frequent field exercises. One of these exercises was later recalled by Laurence O'Brien, an Irishman who had been working in the civil service in England until the threat of conscription led to his return to Ireland in early February 1916. He joined C Company and later recalled a battalion exercise during which they paraded 'with full field kit, field kitchens and 12 hours rations'. They marched to Glendhu in the Dublin Mountains, only to find it covered in snow – thus making operations difficult![26]

One of the main events for the battalion as a whole took place on St Patrick's Day, 17 March 1916. The sight of armed Irish Volunteers on manoeuvres was a frequent spectacle, particularly around the capital city. To a significant extent this lulled the authorities into a false sense of security, while at the same time enabling them publicly to suggest that the political situation in Ireland remained stable and peaceful.

On St Patrick's Day, the Irish Volunteers, together with members of the Irish Citizen Army and Cumann na mBan, mobilised 1,400 members in Dublin city and a further 4,500 in the provinces in a dramatic display of strength. The Dublin Brigade assembled in St Michael's and St John's Church on Essex Quay (now Smock Alley Theatre), for a special military Mass at nine o'clock in the morning. Áine later recalled that:

On this occasion the honour of serving the Mass and of providing the guard of honour for presenting arms at the Elevation was given to the 4th Battalion under Commandant Ceannt. The Volunteers, with rifles and fixed bayonets, swung into College Green from Sackville Street and formed a hollow square.[27]

Éamonn was on the platform when MacNeill, as Chief of Staff, took the salute and the brigade took over the centre of the city. It occupied Dame Street from City Hall to the Bank of Ireland for over an hour.[28] After the inspection, the 4th Battalion marched in formation back to Dolphin's Barn. Éamonn addressed them, after which they sang 'The Soldier's Song' and, dismissed, returned to their homes.[29]

Under cover of the public display by the Volunteers, the Military Council was continuing with its own plans. In his capacity as a member of the IRB Military Council, Éamonn was responsible for reconnoitring the locations chosen by the Military Council for their designated garrison areas during the planned Rising. The area to which the 4th Battalion was assigned was the South Dublin Union (SDU), which was very close to Éamonn and Áine's home in Dolphin's Barn. The SDU, now the site of St James's Hospital, was one of the city's two workhouses and occupied a large site overlooking Kingsbridge railway station (now Heuston Station), which provided access for British troops arriving from the south and west of the country. It also controlled the routes to the city centre from Richmond Barracks (now St Michael's Estate, Inchicore), Islandbridge Barracks (latterly Clancy Barracks) and the headquarters of the British military at the Royal Hospital Kilmainham.

Early in 1916 Éamonn asked Harry Nichols to prepare drawings and get some prints of the SDU. Nichols was a

Lieutenant in the 4th Battalion, with responsibility for engineering. He did as Éamonn requested and later recalled, 'He did not say what it was for and I didn't ask him.'[30] In the week before the Rising, Éamonn himself, accompanied by Áine, visited the Union; Miss Annie Mannion, Assistant Matron, later recalled that they had visited her to collect a toy gramophone for Rónán, who was ill. During the visit, Éamonn said he wanted to see the grounds. Mr Dooley, who was a ward master, took him through the garden infirmary. Éamonn 'walked around and examined the views'.[31]

During the same week, Éamonn asked William T Cosgrave, the Sinn Féin Councillor and then a Lieutenant in B Company, 4th Battalion, to arrange for them to visit the Guinness brewery near the South Dublin Union. Cosgrave's family home and business was across the road from the Union and he knew the area well. Éamonn was surprised at the size of the brewery site and remarked only that the barrels might be useful as barricades.[32] On another occasion he was to tell his officers that the Guinness brewery had been dismissed as a suitable site because it was impossible to garrison and had no food.[33] The corollary of this assessment may suggest the reason why the South Dublin Union was chosen as the final site, even though, from a purely humanitarian viewpoint, given the presence of many ill and infirm residents, the choice is difficult to defend. Apart from the strategic location already cited, it was militarily ideal from a number of other perspectives. High walls surrounded it, enclosing what was effectively a small town, which made it relatively easy to defend. It was laid out in a myriad of small alleyways and culs-de-sac, surrounded by high buildings, making it ideal for troops trained, as the 4th Battalion was, in street fighting – particularly against troops sketchily trained for trench warfare. Finally, it was well provisioned and even had its own bakery.[34]

Éamonn also got John Styles, who acted as his courier and who was the proud owner of a motorcycle and sidecar, to drive him down to the Curragh military camp one Sunday. While there, Éamonn took notes on the surroundings, drew a map of the camp and marked in the railway line and bridges around Newbridge.[35] Closer to home, Éamonn and Patrick Pearse ordered Michael Staines, the Quarter-master General, to survey Islandbridge Barracks on the south side of the Liffey. Helped by a soldier, Staines gained entry to the barracks and was able to sketch all of the important buildings.[36]

Throughout these months Éamonn and his colleagues on the Military Council were living a dangerous double life. Convinced that they had the best interests of their countrymen and women at heart, they were determined to maintain the secrecy of their plans for a Rising. That meant the details had to be kept secret not only from the authorities in Dublin Castle but also from their colleagues on the Irish Volunteer Headquarters Staff, who were beginning to suspect that they were attempting, in contravention of the constitution and defensive policy of Irish Volunteers, to draw them into an unwinnable insurrection. Even after Pearse had assured MacNeill in January, following the meeting with Connolly, that no pre-emptive strike was planned, Bulmer Hobson, Ginger O'Connell and others correctly remained sceptical.

On Wednesday, 5 April, Hobson persuaded MacNeill to call a special all-day meeting in MacNeill's home near Rathfarnham. Éamonn attended the meeting together with MacNeill, Hobson, Pearse, The O'Rahilly, MacDonagh and O'Connell. Plunkett's ill health prevented him from attending. Once again, Pearse denied that there was any intention to draw the Irish Volunteers into an insurrection. Once again, to Hobson's disgust, MacNeill accepted their reassurances. He did, however, prepare an order specifying that all non-routine orders would, in future, require his countersignature. All in attendance at the meeting agreed.[37]

The following Saturday, 8 April, Pearse, in his capacity as Director of Military Organisation, publicly announced details of the Irish Volunteers' Easter mobilisation, to take place over the coming holiday weekend. This subterfuge, of hiding the plans for the Rising in plain sight, was effective. The announcement came as little surprise to either the

Volunteers or the authorities, since similar training exercises had taken place the previous year and the recent St Patrick's Day manoeuvres had passed peacefully. There was, however, a rising sense of expectation among both Volunteers and the Castle authorities that *something* was in the wind.

Although, at its most senior level, Dublin Castle was still pursuing a policy of crisis avoidance, a number of options to deal with any threat were under secret consideration. They included internment, the incarceration of Tom Clarke under the terms of his previous sentence, and even the banning of certain manoeuvres. Although each in turn was dismissed, the Inspector General of the RIC, Sir Neville Chamberlain, warned against allowing an organisation so hostile to British interests to grow in strength and armaments. He urged the Chief Secretary, Augustine Birrell, and his Deputy, Matthew Nathan, to consider arresting the Volunteer leaders, whom he described as a pro-German 'pack of rebels who would revolt and proclaim their independence in the event of any favourable opportunity'.[38] His advice was not heeded, although he was closer to the truth than anyone outside the close confines of the Military Council could guess.

On Sunday, 9 April, following a confused series of communications between Clan na Gael in the United States and the military authorities in Germany, a consignment of arms was loaded aboard a steamer, the *Aud,* in Lübeck, Germany, bound for the coast of Kerry. The confusion had arisen over the date on which the arms were to be landed. The Military Council feared that if they arrived before Easter Sunday, the plans for the Rising would be revealed and the element of surprise lost. As it turned out, the element of surprise was already lost. British naval intelligence had broken the code between Germany and the United States and, on 18 April, they intercepted a message from the Military Council demanding that the arms be landed in Kerry no earlier than the night of Easter Sunday, 23 April.[39] In happy ignorance that the British Navy was tracking the *Aud*, the Military Council accelerated their final plans for the Rising.

In the weeks immediately before Easter, Éamonn and the other battalion commandants in the Volunteers and the ICA began cautiously alerting their senior staff to the likelihood of action. A number of the officers of the 4th Battalion later recalled that Éamonn had gathered them near Tallaght on a Sunday a week or two before the Rising. Christopher Byrne recalled that 'he as much as told us the Rising was coming off. He did not tell us definitely that it was coming off but he gave us a few hints about it'.[40] Edward O'Neill recalled that Éamonn took a crowd of them out beyond Blessington one Sunday and sat them on a wall around him. 'He told us what to prepare for and said, "Get guns and ammunition, honest if you can, but get them."'[41]

Around the same time, key Volunteers began to reappear

in Dublin while others disappeared on secret orders. Liam
Mellows, selected to play a key role in the Rising in the
west of Ireland, was still under deportation in England, staying in a relative's home, and the Military Council wanted
to get him back to Ireland as soon as possible. Around 15
April, Éamonn arranged for his courier, John Styles, to
help Mellows's brother, Barney, to travel to England to visit
him. On the day of Barney Mellows's departure, Éamonn
was having lunch with Seán MacDiarmada and Michael
Staines, the Quartermaster General, when Styles reported
that he had put Barney on the train. Éamonn explained to
his companions that everything was going as planned and
that Styles was 'one of my boys'. Styles recalled that Mac-
Diarmada was very excited at the news.[42] Once Barney
reached Liam in England, the brothers swapped clothes
and Liam returned to Ireland using a ticket that Barney
had provided. Barney took his brother's place in England
until suspicion had died down, before eventually returning
to Ireland. Éamonn asked Áine to prepare a bed for Liam
Mellows on the night of his arrival in Ireland, but her hos-
pitality was not required since Mellows was given a bed by
another sympathiser.[43]

Donal O'Hannigan was another Volunteer and IRB man
who was sent to the country to take charge of the Rising – in
his case to the north east. O'Hannigan had initially received
his instructions from Tom Clarke about three weeks before

the Rising. He later recalled that on Tuesday, 11 April, he met with Pearse in St Enda's, and Pearse instructed him to mobilise the local Volunteers at Tara on Easter Sunday and to read the Proclamation before moving on to form part of a ring around Dublin city. The objective of the ring was to prevent any attack on the city from the rear; to prevent reinforcements from reaching the city; to maintain a supply of food for the Volunteers and the people in the city; and, most important, to hold a line of retreat open in case it was necessary for the Volunteers to leave the city. O'Hannigan received his final instructions from the Military Council at a meeting which took place in Éamonn's house on Friday, 14 April, at 8pm. In addition to Éamonn, Tom Clarke (who was in the chair), Patrick Pearse, Seán MacDiarmada, Thomas MacDonagh, Joseph Plunkett and James Connolly attended the meeting. Éamonn's Vice-Commandant, Cathal Brugha, guarded the door. O'Hannigan reported that progress was very satisfactory but expressed his concerns that Tara was an inconvenient place for the mobilisation. Pearse explained that Tara was 'all important' for historical reasons. As he left the meeting, the Council were all in 'very good spirits and laughing and talking with each other'. Éamonn walked O'Hannigan to the gate and warned him to be careful not to get himself arrested.[44]

HOLY WEEK 1916

Palm Sunday

The week started well. On Palm Sunday, 16 April, the Dublin Volunteers held route marches and 'they all came back full of enthusiasm'.[45] That evening, however, at a Cumann na mBan concert in 41 Parnell Square, Bulmer Hobson publicly voiced his concerns at the actions of Éamonn and his colleagues on the Military Council. Speaking in guarded language to avoid alerting the authorities, he warned the many Volunteers attending the concert of the dangers of 'being drawn into precipitate action, which could only have the effect of bringing the movement to an end'. He concluded by asserting that 'no man had the right to risk the fortunes of the country in order to create for himself a niche in history'.[46] Hobson believed that the vast majority of Volunteers agreed with himself and Eoin MacNeill that the Volunteers should only resort to physical force – and then guerrilla tactics only – if and when they were attacked or the existence of the Volunteers was threatened. Most of those in attendance at the concert probably failed to fully appreciate his guarded nuances. But it did not take long for Hobson's words to reach MacDiarmada, who vowed to put a stop to 'this bloody fellow'.[47]

Monday, 17 April

At the start of the week, Éamonn returned home from a meeting and told Áine that they had been discussing the posts that they would hold in an Irish government, 'when the fight was over'.[48] This was probably the meeting held in the restaurant belonging to John and Jennie Wyse Power in Henry Street when the Military Council also discussed the Proclamation of the Republic, which had been drafted by Pearse, with input from Connolly and MacDonagh.[49] It is also likely that the Military Council decided at this meeting to kidnap Hobson in the light of his outburst the previous night.[50]

Éamonn was pleased that he had been chosen as Minister for War. He thought that either Pearse or MacDonagh had been chosen for Minister for Education. When Áine asked him about de Valera, he replied that he expected 'to go down in the fight', while MacDonagh expected to come through, 'as he always falls on his feet'.

Áine, who was still ignorant of the precise plans for the Rising and of the fact that it was offensive rather than defensive in nature, asked Éamonn how long the fighting would last. He replied, 'If we last more than a month we will have won.' Had she been more suspicious she might have wondered about Éamonn's response to her next query. She passed him an invitation that they had received to a *céilidhe* being organised by B Company, 4th Battalion, for the Sunday after

Easter, 30 April. Áine was looking forward to it but Éamonn merely said, 'Perhaps.' That morning Éamonn told Áine that he was taking a week's holidays from his work in Dublin Corporation, as he 'did not wish to be caught like a rat in a trap'.[51]

Later that day they visited St Enda's where Áine was surprised to see Liam Mellows, safely returned from England and disguised as a priest. That night she accompanied his mother to St Enda's to say goodbye to her son before he left for Galway. Éamonn had arranged for Mellows to travel by motorcycle and sidecar to the west. On the way through Ballinasloe, his driver was startled to discover that his clerical passenger had a large .45 revolver between his knees! He delivered his passenger safely to his colleagues in Galway.[52]

Tuesday, 18 April

The following day, Tuesday, Éamonn asked Áine for directions to Mount Pleasant Square where he wanted to meet up with Sean Fitzgibbon before Fitzgibbon left for Limerick in preparation for meeting the arms from Germany. Fitzgibbon was one of the moderate Volunteers who allied himself with MacNeill and Hobson. As they had walked together to their offices in Dublin Corporation the previous Saturday, Éamonn asked him to do a job for the Volunteers – to land guns from Germany in Limerick and Kerry. Since he had successfully organised the Kilcoole arms landing in

1914, Fitzgibbon was happy to do so. He asked Éamonn whether MacNeill knew about the plan. Éamonn told him he didn't but that Pearse would be telling him the following day. When Fitzgibbon visited Pearse on Palm Sunday evening, Pearse assured him that MacNeill both knew and agreed. Fitzgibbon later discovered that this statement was completely untrue. There seems little doubt but that it suited Éamonn and his colleagues to have Fitzgibbon usefully occupied outside the capital and out of contact with Mac-Neill. A similar deception was being attempted on Ginger O'Connell, another of MacNeill's allies. O'Connell was the Volunteer Chief of Inspections and one of the best military minds in the organisation. He was asked to lead the Volunteers in South East Leinster. [53]

When Éamonn returned from seeing Fitzgibbon off, he told Áine about a secret document that the highly respected Alderman Tom Kelly would read at a meeting of Dublin Corporation the following day. A sympathetic official in Dublin Castle had purportedly leaked this, the so-called 'Castle Document'. It set out a plan of action for the military to conduct a wide range of repressive actions, including the suppression of the Volunteers and the arrest of its entire leadership. Áine always maintained that Éamonn never doubted 'the genuineness of this document',[54] nor did Seán MacDiarmada who, a few hours before his execution, told his priest that 'it was an absolutely genuine document'.[55] It is now widely accepted that the document, while based on a real contingency plan for the military to deal with disruption arising in the event of conscription, was a version edited – or at least selectively decoded – by Joseph Plunkett, and that the timing of the leak was carefully planned to win over Mac-Neill and his allies.[56]

MacNeill was certainly convinced, and that evening he showed it to Hobson and asked him to circulate copies. Hobson had doubts about the genuineness of the document, but MacNeill assured him that he himself had no doubts. MacNeill convened an emergency meeting of the Executive of the Volunteers that night. It took place in the home of The O'Rahilly rather than in Volunteer Headquarters for fear that the entire leadership of the Volunteers would be arrested en masse.[57]

Before he and Áine went to sleep that night, Éamonn 'took out his Mauser pistol and placed it beside his bed ready for use'. 'We are living in stirring times,' he told her, and, 'if we live through this night we will have drawn first blood.'[58]

Spy Wednesday, 19 April

Wednesday was 'an exceptionally wet day', and Áine was kept busy buying stores for Éamonn's knapsack in preparation for what she still believed was just another set of Easter manoeuvres. Elsewhere, it appeared as if Eoin MacNeill had at last been convinced of the need for action. For weeks he had been vacillating between his long-held belief that any pre-emptive action should be defensive with a reasonable chance of success, and reluctant support for action if it could be shown that there was a valid and rational reason. The Castle Document appeared to provide just such a justification. MacNeill issued a general order for all units to be prepared to engage in defensive measures to preserve the arms and organisation of the Volunteers.[59] Alderman Tom Kelly duly read the Castle Document into the record of Dublin Corporation. This enabled it to be widely reported in the newspapers, thus avoiding the censors.

During the evening, the Military Council finally informed Volunteer commandants who were to be involved in the Rising of the exact date – Sunday, 23 April – and time – 6.30pm in Dublin and 7pm in the country. Coded messages were issued. MacDiarmada briefed Diarmuid Lynch over lunch and Tom Clarke informed young Ned Daly, his brother-in-law. James Connolly briefed the officers of the Irish Citizen Army.[60] Éamonn, meanwhile, called over to the house of Frank Fahy and his wife, Anna, in Island-bridge, where Liam Mellows had hidden out before he left for Galway, and asked Anna Fahy to take an important and urgent message to Athenry the following day, Holy Thursday. Anna later discovered that the message detailed the orders for the Rising in Galway.[61]

All of the leaders were terrified that the military would

start to round them up, bringing their plans to naught. As a result, Éamonn later told Patrick Egan, recently promoted to 1st Lieutenant, C Company, to keep Wellington (later Griffith) Barracks (now the site of Griffith College) under observation throughout the night and to report any signs of military activity. Egan cycled slowly around the area all night, but there was no activity to report.[62]

Holy Thursday, 20 April

Áine remembered Holy Thursday as 'a busy day in Volunteer circles' and that 'the leaders were endeavouring to induce John [Eoin] MacNeill to agree to the coming fight, and it had taken some persuasion'.[63] This was something of an understatement. Throughout the day a series of events convinced Hobson that his suspicions that MacNeill was being manipulated were true. That evening Hobson met with Ginger O'Connell. Unlike Fitzgibbon, who had taken Pearse at his word that MacNeill was on side and had headed off happily to meet the German arms in Limerick, O'Connell had been more sceptical of his orders to take command of the Volunteers in South Leinster. He decided to confirm the orders with Hobson. Hobson's worst fears that an insurrection was imminent were now confirmed. He also discovered from O'Connell and Eimar O'Duffy that Pearse had issued orders to mobilise the Volunteers for manoeuvres on Easter Sunday. They went to see MacNeill and together they roused Pearse from his bed in St Enda's.[64] For the first time, Pearse admitted to MacNeill that a Rising was planned, that the Volunteers would be under the control of the IRB and that he, MacNeill, was powerless to prevent it.[65] MacNeill returned home to Woodtown House, near Rathfarnham, and wrote out a series of orders including one cancelling all special orders issued by Pearse and declaring that only he, or his successor as Chief of Staff, would issue all future special orders.

Throughout the evening of Holy Thursday, a constant stream of couriers called to the Ceannt house in Dolphin's Barn en route to the country with instructions for the Rising.[66]

Good Friday, 21 April

With the prospect of their carefully laid plans unravelling before their eyes, Seán MacDiarmada took action early on Good Friday morning. Followed closely by Pearse and Mac-Donagh, he called out to MacNeill's house to make one last effort to get him on side. MacDiarmada finally revealed their trump card – that a German arms shipment was due to land imminently. MacNeill, who still apparently believed the Castle Document was genuine and that the Volunteers were in danger of being suppressed and disarmed, capitulated and agreed to join them, even though he was still in ignorance of what their plans actually were. He sent a message to Hobson and placed on hold the orders that he had written the previous evening.

Believing that MacNeill was at last on side, the Military Council was concerned that Hobson, as a senior IRB man, could still throw a spanner in their plans. They now saw him, not the vacillating MacNeill, as their greatest internal threat. As they walked back from a meeting in MacNeill's house during the week, Thomas MacDonagh told Éamonn that, 'Bulmer Hobson is the evil genius of the Volunteers and if we could separate John MacNeill from his influence all would be well.'[67] Éamonn was of the same mind. The previous weekend he had told Seamus O'Connor: 'Hobson has been an obstacle in our path. He is opposed to an insurrection. He is perfectly honest, he is not a traitor but it would be better that he were as then we could shoot him.'[68] James Connolly felt equally strongly that Hobson must be silenced – he had suggested that he be chloroformed for the duration of the Rising![69] During the afternoon of Good Friday, Hobson was lured to a spurious meeting of the Leinster Executive of the IRB, at Martin Conlon's house at 76 Cabra Road, where he was detained until after the Rising had started.

Meanwhile, over breakfast that Good Friday morning, Áine drew Éamonn's attention to a report in the newspaper of the mysterious arrival of a collapsible boat off Kerry and the arrest of a strange man.[70]

At midday, while they ate lunch in the Red Bank restaurant, Seán MacDiarmada handed Diarmuid Lynch, his colleague on the IRB Supreme Council, sketches of the Four Courts, Jacob's biscuit factory, the South Dublin Union and Boland's mills. He asked Lynch to deliver them into the hands of the various battalion commandants. Lynch delivered the plans of the South Dublin Union to Éamonn in his Dublin Corporation office off Lord Edward Street.[71]

During the afternoon, Éamonn and Áine attended their Good Friday devotions. A Volunteer entered the church and looked around until he spotted Éamonn, to whom he whispered something, then left. By this time, news from Kerry was filtering through to Dublin. The three men who had been dispatched by Tom Clarke to signal to the German arms shipment had drowned; their car drove into a river in the darkness.[72]

The mounting scale of the disaster was not yet clear, however, and plans for the Rising continued throughout the day. Pearse arranged for grenades and bombs that had been made in St Enda's to be transported to the city.[73] While Éamonn was attending his Easter devotions, his courier, John Styles, was, on Éamonn's orders, gathering together the ammunition that had been assembled around the city during the preceding weeks. Éamonn ordered him to deliver it to a grocer's shop facing the South Dublin Union; Styles believed the owner of the shop was related to Volunteer Lieutenant William Cosgrave.[74] At the same time, Seamus Kenny, the 4th Battalion Quartermaster, was delivering hand grenades out of an old cab to a number of different locations including the South Dublin Union and Watkin's Distillery. Kenny was terrified that the explosives would detonate as he drove around the city. He went to Confession as soon as he had delivered the last of them.[75]

That evening after tea, Éamonn and Áine went for a walk in the fine weather. But it was no innocent stroll, as far as Éamonn was concerned. The Magazine Fort, an ammunition store for the British Army in the Phoenix Park, which was their destination, was scheduled to be one of the first locations attacked during the Rising. The plan, agreed at a meeting of the Military Council in Clontarf Town Hall on Palm Sunday, was for a group of Na Fianna boys to approach it in the guise of a football training exercise before overcoming the guard and stealing the ammunition.[76] On the evening of Good Friday, Éamonn and Áine sat with their backs to the fort. Áine noticed that there was a continuous stream of lorries leaving it. Éamonn remarked, 'You can almost over-organise things.' Áine later learned that the lorries had probably been removing the ammunition from the store.[77]

All of the leaders slept away from home that night.

Easter Saturday, 22 April

Very early on Easter Saturday morning, the news of Roger Casement's arrest – for he was the strange man of Áine's

newspaper reports – reached Liberty Hall from the Volunteers in Kerry. Connolly summoned an emergency meeting
of the Military Council. By early afternoon, worse news followed. The British Navy had captured the *Aud* and her captain had scuttled her, along with the arms and ammunition,
within sight of Queenstown (Cobh) harbour.[78]

The Military Council had no intention of revealing this set-
back to MacNeill but, during the afternoon, The O'Rahilly,
Sean Fitzgibbon and Colm O'Lochlainn had tracked Mac-
Neill down at his home. Fitzgibbon and O'Lochlainn had
met up on their return from Limerick and Kerry respectively
and brought the devastating news. They also told MacNeill
that the Castle Document was, according to O'Lochlainn
– who had been involved in printing the transcript of the
document in Plunkett's home in Larkfield – a forgery. And,
finally, they had come to realise that Hobson had probably
been kidnapped by the IRB.[79]

After hearing the news, MacNeill again confronted Pearse
in St Enda's. This time Pearse made no attempt to evade the
truth. In O'Lochlainn's account of the meeting on the steps
of St Enda's, Pearse told MacNeill: 'We have used you and
your name and influence for what it was worth. You can issue
what orders you like now, the men won't obey you.' MacNeill
replied that he would act in accordance with his conscience
and told Pearse that if he had anything further to say, he
could meet him at 9pm in the house of his friend Dr Seamus

O'Kelly in Rathgar Road.[80]

While the confrontation with MacNeill was coming to a head, Éamonn and Áine were out of the city. Éamonn had decided to visit a friend in Dalkey, from whom he wanted to borrow a set of field glasses. On the way out in the tram, Éamonn whispered to Áine that the man who had been arrested in Kerry was Roger Casement. Éamonn was on edge and, although they stayed in Dalkey for lunch, he insisted on being back in the city by 4pm.

It was that evening, about 6pm, that Éamonn told Áine for the first time about their plans for a Rising the following day. 'He said they would strike the following day and his head-quarters would be the South Dublin Union,' she recalled. He added:

> There are rumours of a secret session of the British par-liament … and that means either peace with the Liberals in power, or conscription. We Volunteers, an armed body, could not let this opportunity pass without striking a blow while England is at war. We would be a disgrace to our generation. So we strike tomorrow at 6 o'clock. I shall not sleep at home tonight in case of accidents but will stay with John Doherty at James' Terrace.

Áine asked Éamonn whether the men knew what was planned and he assured her that the Volunteers, and certainly his battalion, had been warned repeatedly that some day 'they would go out not to return'. He explained that they had not been told the exact day in case they 'thronged the Churches for confession', thereby alerting the authorities. After breaking this news to Áine, Éamonn finished his tea, wrote two letters to his brothers Michael and Richard, and went to confession. [81]

The letter to Michael, which was sent by the Volunteer Post, did not reach him until Easter Sunday afternoon. With barely suppressed excitement, Éamonn wrote:

> To Master Michael and family with best Easter wishes. All well here – on the defensive. If the friends of the small nationalities should decide on interfering with our Inspections tomorrow I would advise you to make yourselves scarce. Your own house is the safest place from 4 p.m., our hour of assembly, until such time as the danger of an attack is passed which would be about 7. Come what may, we are ready.
>
> Éamonn Ceannt
22/4/1916[82]

Éamonn, apparently still unaware of Pearse's earlier confrontation with MacNeill, left home for John Doherty's at about 10pm and Áine broke the news of the Rising to her sister Lily, who was a fellow member of Cumann na mBan.

The emergency meeting convened by MacNeill started at 9pm in Dr Seamus O'Kelly's house in Rathgar. Members of the Central Executive and the Headquarters Staff of the Volunteers attended, as did Arthur Griffith, Sean T O'Kelly, Liam O'Briain and Eimar O'Duffy. Thomas MacDonagh, who had been alerted by Pearse, arrived around 11pm. MacDonagh did his best to get MacNeill back on their side. Sean T O'Kelly later recalled that MacDonagh insisted MacNeill had been fully informed of the arrangements and that it was no time to back down on what he had already agreed. He told MacNeill that the Volunteers had greater faith, confidence and trust in Pearse than in him.[83]

Ultimately, however, it was too late. He failed to convince MacNeill who, at last, realised that he had been fed a series of half-truths and was facing a mutiny among his senior officers. Liam O'Briain later recalled MacNeill saying that he had been left completely in the dark, only finding things out gradually and by accident. MacNeill said that he now believed 'that the enterprise was madness, would mean a slaughter of unarmed men and that he felt it to be his bounden duty to try and stop it'.[84] With help from Arthur Griffith, he drafted an order cancelling the Volunteer manoeuvres planned for the following day, Easter Sunday:

> Volunteers completely deceived. All orders for special action are hereby cancelled, and on no account will action be taken.

> Eoin MacNeill, Chief of Staff

He dispatched senior staff officers to take the message to Volunteer units throughout the country and made his own way to the offices of the *Irish Independent* just in time to arrange for its publication on Easter Sunday morning.

When Padraig O'Keefe, an IRB member present at the meeting, realised what was happening, he slipped away to alert Éamonn's Vice-Commandant, Cathal Brugha, who lived nearby. Brugha rushed around and tried, unsuccessfully, to prevent the countermanding order being circulated.[85]

Easter Sunday, 23 April

After Éamonn had left to spend the night in Doherty's, Áine went to bed around midnight only to be woken by someone knocking on the hall door at about 2am on Easter Sunday morning. It was Cathal Brugha, calling out in Irish and looking for Éamonn. Áine sent him to Doherty's. Sean T O'Kelly was on his way home from Seamus O'Kelly's house a short time later when he met with Éamonn and Cathal Brugha. They walked together while Éamonn asked O'Kelly to explain what had happened at the meeting. O'Kelly later recalled that when Éamonn heard what MacNeill had done, he denounced him fiercely and said that if he had full authority, MacNeill should be shot. Both Éamonn and Brugha were very upset and Éamonn made his way to Hardwicke Street where MacDiarmada had been spending the night. He found MacDonagh there too, briefing MacDiarmada on what had happened. When Kathleen Clarke came by with a message shortly afterwards, she found a group of the leaders huddled together in semi-darkness by the light of flashlights.[86]

Éamonn returned home and told an astonished Áine: 'MacNeill has ruined us, he has stopped the Rising ... The countermanding order is in the hands of the paper. I am off now to see if anything can be done.' For the rest of the night he searched frantically around the city for his fellow conspirators. At Liberty Hall, where James Connolly was sleeping, the guard refused to wake him. Slightly reassured that Connolly would not be sleeping if the rumours were true, Éamonn continued on down Abbey Street to the Metropole Hotel beside the GPO, where Joseph Plunkett was staying. He had no better luck there. Plunkett had left instructions not to be woken until 9am as he was sick. Disheartened, Éamonn returned home to Dolphin's Barn at about 5am, where Áine made him some hot milk and persuaded him to sleep. As he lay down, the Angelus bell was striking 6am and he told Áine, 'If I sleep now, I would sleep on dynamite.' At 7am a courier arrived with a letter from Liberty Hall summoning Éamonn to a meeting.[87] Áine decided not to waken him, as she 'expected he would have serious decisions to make during the coming day'. She left the letter beside the bed where he would see it when he woke. At approximately 8.30am, Seamus Murphy, Captain of A Company, 4th Battalion, called and insisted on seeing Éamonn on an important matter. Áine reluctantly woke Éamonn, who found the letter from Connolly beside his bed. Having disposed quickly of Seamus's query, Éamonn jumped on his bicycle without breakfast – or even his shirt collar and tie – and pedalled off frantically for Liberty Hall.[88]

In Liberty Hall, where the Proclamation was being printed, the members of the Military Council began to assemble around Connolly – first MacDiarmada, then Clarke and MacDonagh, followed by the frail Plunkett. Éamonn arrived shortly afterwards, followed by Pearse. James Connolly's daughter, Nora, cooked them breakfast while they read MacNeill's countermanding notice in the newspaper. They were devastated at the turn of events.[89] Clarke, the last to learn of MacNeill's countermanding order, called it 'the blackest and greatest treachery'.[90]

The historians Michael T Foy and Brian Barton have described the subsequent meeting of the Military Council in Room Number Seven of Liberty Hall as follows:

> Despite all the turmoil the Military Council methodically examined its options. For the first time a body that hitherto had been Clarke and MacDiarmada's instrument now became a genuine War Cabinet, a forum for argument and dissent in which members like Ceannt and MacDonagh at

last found their own independent voices as they negotiated a way out of the blind alley into which MacNeill appeared to have driven them.[91]

The meeting went on throughout the morning. Eventually, over the objections of Tom Clarke, who wanted to proceed with the original plan, the decision was taken to postpone the Rising until noon the following day, Easter Monday. The first step was to send out a notice confirming that the Easter Sunday manoeuvres were indeed cancelled. Later that day, Pearse issued secret orders to the Volunteers to mobilise again the following day.

The Ceannt home at Dolphin's Barn was besieged with callers throughout the morning as members of Éamonn's battalion looked for instructions in the face of MacNeill's countermanding order. Con Colbert had been staying for safety with his friend Christopher Byrne on the Saturday night and, like many others, had read the notice in the newspapers on his way home from Mass. Together with Christy and Larry Murtagh, they were among those crowding Áine's drawing room, with bicycles stacked four abreast on the railings outside.[92]

This was the sight that met the astonished eyes of Éamonn's brother Michael when he arrived by tram with their sister, Nell, at Dolphin Terrace. Michael and Nell, like the vast majority of Dublin citizens, knew nothing about the planned Rising. Éamonn's letters to Michael and Dick were still making their slow way through the Volunteer Post. In the meantime, they were preoccupied with sad news of their own. Their sister-in-law, Liz Kent, wife of retired RIC Constable JP Kent, in Stratford-on-Slaney, County Wicklow, had died at 8am that morning, just days after giving birth to their first child. Michael and Nell had called to Éamonn's house to see if he or Áine would join them on a visit of condolence to their bereaved brother.

It was soon clear that Éamonn and Áine were otherwise occupied. Áine explained that there was something too important on. Michael looked at the 'mere boys' in the drawing room and said to himself: 'Look what's going to free Ireland!' Later he would 'marvel that those same boys would create such a stir in Dublin as would make England tremble and send a thrill through millions of hearts the world over'. While Michael and Nell waited in the back room, Éamonn arrived in the hall. Someone gave a command and, recorded Michael: 'Apparently they all stood to attention for poor Commandant Éamonn.' Michael later recalled that: 'All thro' this I had the feeling that the whole thing was just a jest: that they were boys playing at being soldiers. At the same time I dreaded the result as for some time past they had been "trailing their coat" on the ground for someone to walk on it and generally they were "looking for a fight".' Although Éamonn was shocked at the news about his sister-in-law's death, he didn't delay and went on about his business. Michael thought that he seemed 'in great good humour'.[93]

Éamonn had instructed his men not to leave the city and to stay available at short notice. For some of them, the day 'passed off in a kind of subdued disappointment and anxiety as to what might happen next.'[94] That afternoon after lunch, Éamonn and Áine got the tram out to Howth where Éamonn stood silently at the end of the pier on which the famous Howth rifles had been landed just two years previously. After they returned home and had their tea, Éamonn told Áine he needed to use the drawing room. Áine lit the fire and left him. Later he gave her a bundle of mobilisation orders to fill out, telling her that they planned to strike the following day, Easter Monday, and the orders should specify mobilisation at 11am in Emerald Square, near Cork Street. Once the mobilisation orders were written, Áine went around to Dan McCarthy's house, where Éamonn's couriers were having a bit of a singsong while awaiting their instructions.

Éamonn slept at home that night. It was a small mercy for which he thanked Eoin MacNeill. He believed, with considerable justification, that not only was MacNeill lulled into a false sense of security, but so also were the British authorities.[95]

Later that night, returning from his visit of condolence to Stratford, Michael Kent drafted a letter appealing to Éamonn to give up the Volunteers. Michael recalled later that he believed there was 'sure to be trouble', and 'like the vast majority of the Irish people, I believed physical force against England with her Super-Dreadnoughts (which could blow up Dublin city from 9–10 miles out to sea), would be utter madness'. He later acknowledged that he hadn't appreciated the strength of Éamonn's feelings for the Volunteer movement. He wrote in his diary: 'Once they got the guns and ammunition and there was even a small chance of striking back England for her ferocious wrongs to Ireland, wild horses would not pull him back.'[96]

Chapter Eight

Easter Week

24–30 April 1916: The South Dublin Union

Easter Monday, 24 April

The confusion of orders and counter-orders was to prove disastrous for the plans of the Military Council. Even under the best of circumstances, the secret arrangements for the insurrection relied on a tiny number of people, most of whom only discovered their own part of the plan late in the day. MacNeill's countermanding order, followed by Pearse's confirmation that the Sunday manoeuvres were cancelled, followed yet later by mobilisation orders for Easter Monday, made it virtually impossible to ensure a full turn-out.

On the other hand, the confusion, following on from the arrest of Roger Casement and the sinking of the *Aud*, served to validate the authorities in Dublin Castle in their 'live and let live' attitude to the Volunteers. In spite of the contingency plans in the Castle Document, their greatest fear, even in the face of intelligence to the contrary, had been that any attempt to suppress the Volunteers would be the spark that would ignite an insurrection.

With MacNeill's countermanding order appearing in the Sunday papers and the German arms at the bottom of Queenstown harbour, the authorities relaxed their guard completely. The Chief Secretary, Augustine Birrell, decided to spend Easter in London. So too did the senior military officer, Major General LB Friend. Most of the army officer corps who were billeted in Dublin happily travelled to Fairyhouse racecourse on Easter Monday for a day at the races.

Uniquely, the Lord Lieutenant, Viscount Wimborne, was not convinced that all was secure, and urged that Liberty Hall be raided and the ringleaders be rounded up immediately. The Under Secretary, Sir Matthew Nathan, played for time, unwilling to take action without the authorisation of the Chief Secretary, who was in London. By the time the authorisation arrived it was too late. The Rising had already started.

Éamonn and Áine got up early on a gloriously sunny Easter Monday morning and before long there was a constant stream of Volunteers arriving at the house. Liam O'Flaherty and Ciaran Kenny had arrived after 6am Mass in Mount Argus and were busy writing up the last few mobilisation orders. Éamonn left the house at 7am, saying that he was going to a meeting in Liberty Hall (where the other leaders were gathering). He was back by 8.30am.[1]

Áine's sister Lily had received no mobilisation orders from her branch of Cumann na mBan, so she decided to attach herself to Éamonn's 4th Battalion. She gathered up her equipment – rations for twenty-four hours, bandages and first-aid equipment, a towel, soap, comb and scissors – into her nephew Rónán's schoolbag. Finally she added a copybook, pencil and a prayerbook and, strapping a waterproof onto her bicycle, 'rode joyously down Cork Street'.[2]

Éamonn was also gathering up his own equipment – he had a large bag of ammunition as well as his overcoat and bicycle. While Áine helped him to adjust his Sam Browne uniform belt, she asked him again how long he expected the fight to continue. He replied:

> If we last a month they – the British – will come to terms. We have sent out messages throughout the country, but as the men have already received at least two other orders, it is hard to know what may happen. I have made sure of Galway, where the finest men in Ireland are. My message to Mellows is 'Dublin is now in action!'

However, he added, 'We will put our trust in God.'

Turning to ten-year-old Rónán, Éamonn kissed his son and said, '*Beannacht leat, a Rónáin,*' to which the child replied, '*Beannacht leat, a Dhaide*'. Éamonn asked him to promise to look after his mother, which he did, and father and son parted forever. Áine wanted to go to Emerald Square to see Éamonn off but he asked her not to. They embraced, Áine wished him 'God speed', and Éamonn was on his way.[3]

Éamonn had dispatched his mobilisation orders on Easter Sunday night, but many failed to reach their destinations in time for Volunteers to arrive in Emerald Square by the deadline of 11am. Peadar Doyle was the first to arrive. With only a policeman on his beat for company, Peadar spent a half-hour unhappily parading around the square, 'in a semi military uniform, fully armed and 500 rounds of ammunition etc'.[4] Lieutenant William Cosgrave had heard of the mobilisation from his brothers and cycled to his battalion headquarters at Larkfield only to find it empty. He was redirected to Emerald Square and arrived just in time for departure.[5]

By 11.30am about a hundred Volunteers had assembled – well below the battalion complement of seven hundred. The battalion moved off shortly before noon, followed by various stragglers. When Henry Murray arrived with a group from Larkfield at 12.15pm, he found the main party had left, and that 'a very hostile crowd of civilians had gathered'. Subjected to 'very hostile verbal abuse', he eventually discovered the route that the battalion had taken.[6]

The battalion was heading for the South Dublin Union located between St James's Street and the old Main Line of the Grand Canal at Rialto. This ended at Grand Canal

Harbour off James's Street close to a smaller harbour at Guinness's brewery.[7] A short time before the Rising, Éamonn had described 'with enthusiasm' to Captain Seamus Murphy, A Company, 'how from the South Dublin Union we could control or stop the troops entering the city from Richmond Barracks [Inchicore].' He had also explained that by occupying Marrowbone Lane distillery they 'would control the situation [because] if the troops attempted to use any by-road, such as Cork Street, they could be seen from the end of Marrowbone Lane. Also it overlooked the back of the South Dublin Union.'[8]

Irrespective of its strategic location and the attempts made to shield the inmates of the workhouse throughout the following week, it is difficult to understand the choice of the site given the potential for collateral civilian damage. The South Dublin Union was one of two very large workhouses in Dublin which housed the city's destitute, infirm and insane. It occupied a site of approximately fifty acres on the west side of Dublin city, and, at the start of April 1916, it had 3,264 inmates and a large staff of doctors, nurses, orderlies, kitchen staff, bakers and other ancillary workers. The inmates included 585 able-bodied men; 738 able-bodied women; 904 aged and infirm men; 581 aged and infirm women; 331 children aged between five and nine years; 71 children between two and five years; and 54 infants less than two years of age.[9] The site included a number of buildings – several hospitals, an infirmary, living quarters and two churches (one Roman Catholic and one Church of Ireland), offices and a bakery. The buildings were laid out in a complex pattern of streets, alleys, culs-de-sac, courtyards and several acres of open fields known as McCaffrey's estate, the Orchard Fields and the Master's Field. The whole site was surrounded by high stone walls.

Along the way the battalion divided into a number of smaller groupings. Most of A Company, under Captain Seamus Murphy, made their way to Jameson's distillery in Marrowbone Lane; C Company, under Captain Thomas McCarthy, to Roe's distillery in Mount Brown; and F Company, under Captain Con Colbert, to Watkin's brewery in Ardee Street.

Éamonn entered the Union first, together with Captain George Irvine of B Company and a small group of Volunteers riding bicycles. They approached the back gate from Brookfield Road, Rialto, pushed past the astonished gate-keeper, tied him up and gagged him, and cut the telephone wires.[10] Éamonn instructed Captain Irvine and a small group of Volunteers to get into position in the huts opposite the gate and to barricade it.[11] He then led the rest of the company across the site to the front entrance of the Union on St James's Street, where Vice-Commandant Cathal Brugha had ordered Volunteers Michael Lynch, Paddy Maloney and James Foran to 'charge that gate and keep it open'.[12]

They held the gate open to admit the rest of the battalion led by Cathal Brugha, William T Cosgrave, First Lieutenant B Company, and Captain Douglas ffrench Mullen of D Company.[13] A cartload of tools and bombs arrived shortly afterwards. The Volunteers sent the horse away, emptied out the contents of the cart, and used it as a barricade. Volunteer Peadar Doyle was ordered to command some of the nearby inmates to help him remove the ammunition and equipment from the cart at the gate to the new headquarters. Since he had no idea how to order them to do it, he pragmatically offered them a 'price for the job'. They happily took the offer and had the ammunition moved within ten minutes.[14]

Across the road, Captain Tom McCarthy of C Company, with a party of twenty Volunteers, occupied Roe's distillery.

Éamonn initially set up his headquarters in the buildings near the entrance gate. Lieutenant Gerald Murray, with a small group of Volunteers, including James Foran and Michael Lynch, remained to occupy and fortify the boardroom, which was directly above the main gate. Having allowed some people who wanted to leave to depart,[15] they barricaded the main gate.[16]

Sometime later, Éamonn, Cathal Brugha and William Cosgrave were sending dispatches to the outpost at Marrowbone Lane and to Jacob's factory. Cosgrave, who knew the area well, realised that they were in a vulnerable position. He recommended that Éamonn move his headquarters to the Nurses' Home, 'a three-storey stone structure in a commanding position'.[17] The night nurses, who were asleep when the Nurses' Home was occupied, were escorted to another building where they remained in relative safety for the rest of the week.

The arrival of the 4th Battalion at the South Dublin Union was timed to coincide, at midday, with the storming of the General Post Office (GPO) on Sackville Street, led by James Connolly and the Irish Citizen Army – who had marched down from Liberty Hall – and by Patrick Pearse, leading the 4th Battalion's E Company, which had mobilised at Beresford Place. They were met with a muted response from the bemused but astonished bank-holiday clientele, who were busy buying stamps and sending telegrams. Elsewhere, equally amazed Dubliners saw similar scenes in the Four Courts, Jacob's biscuit factory, Boland's bakery and St Stephen's Green. Another group, under ICA man Sean Connolly, headed for Dublin Castle and City Hall, beside the offices of Dublin Corporation where Éamonn had been working until just a few days previously.[18]

As the main body of Éamonn's 4th Battalion entered the gates of the South Dublin Union, they heard the sound of a military band carried on the wind from the nearby Richmond Barracks in Inchicore. Éamonn remarked to the Volunteer beside him that, 'They do not yet know.' As he spoke, the music petered out and Éamonn realised that news of the Rising had reached the barracks, and the Volunteers could expect an early reaction.[19]

Éamonn's plans to occupy the complex had been conceived in the expectation that his battalion would be at full strength and that he would have several hundred men at his disposal. With the battalion severely understrength, and with A, C and F companies spread out in the outlying sites, he now found himself with fewer than sixty-five men under his command in the fifty-acre Union site.[20] Even in these disheartening circumstances, he was, apparently, in excellent form. When Volunteer Thomas Doyle arrived with a dispatch from F Company, Éamonn was 'so excited he couldn't write' and had to get his staff orderly, Peadar Doyle, to write the reply for him. Thomas Doyle also recalled that Éamonn had told his men that the Rising had the Pope's blessing and that he expected the whole country to be out under arms shortly. [21]

Ever conscious of his men's spiritual needs, Éamonn made arrangements for Father Dillon, a priest who was visiting the Union, to hear the Confession of any Volunteer who wanted it. He also asked William Murphy, the Union storekeeper, for supplies, particularly of corned beef or bacon. Murphy told him he could not provide the meat but could let him have any other supplies, such as tea, sugar, condensed milk etc. Éamonn handed him a written order for the provisions.

Throughout the next week, Murphy, with the agreement of the Volunteers, managed to get supplies to the various departments of the institution, wearing a white coat and carrying a white flag mounted on a broom.[22]

After reviewing the survey maps of the site with Cathal Brugha, Éamonn deployed the rest of his men – one team to the far side of McCaffrey's estate, another to the upper edge of the estate, along the rear wall of the Nurses' Home. Another small team of an officer and five men were sent to guard the wall along the canal at the rear of the Union, and Captain Douglas ffrench Mullen and his men occupied Hospital 2-3.

When armed men rushed around the complex, the staff and inmates were initially mystified. No doubt some of them thought it was a repeat of the Irish Volunteer manoeuvres to which the city had become accustomed. One nun asked Volunteer Peadar Doyle, as he entered the convent on the Union site, whether he had come to read the gas meters. Doyle 'politely but quickly replied, "No, Sister, but we are in a hurry".'[23]

The resident medical practitioner, Dr McNamara, was not so naïve. He became understandably agitated and tried to stop the Volunteers who were barricading the entrance gate. Lieutenant Gerald Murray told him to calm himself, but Dr McNamara ignored him and reached for a telephone. Murray shouted, 'Stop that man, he is telephoning to the enemy.' Finding himself at the point of a bayonet, Dr McNamara reluctantly replaced the receiver.[24] Before long, inmates were being moved to places of relative safety and Red Cross flags were draped from the windows of the buildings occupied by inmates and staff.[25]

In the meantime, Éamonn had been correct in realising that word of the Rising had reached Richmond Barracks. Before long, the men that Éamonn had sent to the far side of McCaffrey's estate, near Mount Brown, could see a column of soldiers from the Royal Irish Regiment heading in their direction. The regiment was stationed at Richmond Barracks and had received a telephone message informing them that 'Sinn Féiners' had occupied the GPO and ordering them to march down to Dublin Castle.[26] Their route took them past the South Dublin Union and the Volunteers that Éamonn had posted at the Mount Brown/Brookfield Road edge of McCaffrey's estate. The regiment included raw recruits recently arrived from County Tipperary as well as seasoned veterans of the Western Front.[27] Having allowed the small advance party to pass, the Volunteers opened fire on the second tranche of soldiers. The soldiers were soon returning fire, and in the firefight that followed, Volunteer John Owens was mortally wounded and two other Volunteers were hurt. Reinforcements quickly arrived from Richmond Barracks and prepared to attack the Volunteers in the South Dublin Union in force.

Lieutenant RL Owens and his adjutant, Captain Roche Kelly, of the Royal Irish Regiment, sent a team of men from the regiment to take up firing positions on the roof of the Royal Hospital Kilmainham, which overlooked McCaffrey's Fields. Using an automatic machine gun, they were able to provide covering fire for the men preparing to directly attack the Union.

Volunteer Lieutenant William O'Brien realised quickly that his troops were now in an impossible position against a much larger force. He ordered his men to retreat across the fields towards the front gate. They came under heavy fire as they tried to find shelter across the undulating fields, and Volunteer Richard O'Reilly was shot and killed. A number of other Volunteers were wounded as they dodged the bullets and, some time later, Vice-Commandant Cathal Brugha sent James Coughlan and William McDowell, together with a couple of inmates, to help rescue them from the field.[28]

As O'Brien and his men retreated, the Rialto gate, defended by Captain Irvine and his men, also came under attack. The hut in which the Volunteers were sheltering was soon riddled with ricocheting bullets. The invalids in the building to the rear of the hut fell to the floor, terrified of the gunfire. Volunteer John Traynor, aged seventeen, was fatally wounded. Captain Irvine sent Lieutenant Sean McGlynn across the Union site to ask for orders from Éamonn. Éamonn ordered the unit to retire towards the convent. McGlynn managed to make his way back to the Nurses' Home but encountered 'withering fire' and remembered later that 'the spokes were shot out of my bicycle'.[29] Captain Irvine didn't believe he could get the rest of his men through safely, and the Volunteers at the Rialto gate were effectively cut off from the rest of the battalion.[30]

The British forces were unable to get through the gate at the Rialto entrance until Lieutenant Alan Ramsey, a twenty-six-year-old veteran of the Western Front, found a small wooden door that his men were able to dismantle. As they rushed through the door, Lieutenant Ramsey was fatally wounded. Following a short truce to allow his men to collect his body, his captain, Alfred Ernest Warmington, also a veteran, led another charge through the gate before being shot dead himself. His men retreated and another truce allowed them to collect his body. The fighting continued but the position of the Volunteers was becoming impossible. After a desperate fight, during which the British soldiers broke down their barricade with a large iron lawnmower, Volunteer Captain Irvine realised that they could hold out no longer. He asked his men whether they should surrender and they reluctantly agreed.[31] Captain Irvine, Jimmy Morrissey, Willie Corrigan, Sean Dowling and James Burke were taken to Kilmainham police station, while the wounded Paddy Morrissey was taken to hospital – a few days later, in spite of his shattered leg, Morrissey escaped in a milk cart. He was never formally arrested.[32]

While British troops were breaching the Rialto gate to the Union, another squad of Royal Irish Regiment soldiers was coming under sniper fire from the Volunteers in Marrowbone Lane distillery as they made their way to the small entrance along the bank of the Grand Canal. Eventually, having sustained heavy casualties, they forced the gate open and entered the grounds of the Union. As the Volunteers defending the gate retreated towards Hospital 2-3, Volunteers Brendan Donelan (aged eighteen) and James Quinn were mortally wounded.

The walls of the Union had now been breached to the west and south, and Éamonn's Volunteers were restricted to the buildings surrounding the main gate at St James's Street. Intense fighting took place in the labyrinthine alleys, roads and culs-de-sac around Hospital 2-3 with the Volunteers on the upper floors taking aim at British soldiers, who soon lost their bearings in the unfamiliar terrain. Before long, however, the troops had entered the hospital and gun battles took place along the corridors and in the wards.

In the meantime, Éamonn, faced with conflicting and confused messages from his beleaguered outposts, had set out to reconnoitre the situation for himself and was very nearly captured by the advancing British troops. Together with another Volunteer, who had bumped into him as he tried to help a badly wounded man, he retreated into a blind cul-de-sac which separated the Protestant Hospital from the Catholic Women's Hospital. Trapped, they were trying to force their way through a heavy wooden gate when they were rescued by an inmate who gave them a ladder with which they were able to climb the wall of the Protestant Hospital. Discovering that they hadn't been followed, Éamonn went into the hospital and sent help to the wounded Volunteer. He and his unwounded companion covered their uniforms with some old canvas and prepared to break cover in an attempt to get back to his headquarters. Unexpectedly, a nun opened a gate, giving them access to the rear of the Catholic Women's Hospital, and they were able to retreat under cover of fire from the Volunteers on the upper floors.[33]

One of the nurses in Hospital 2-3 was less fortunate. Nurse Margaret Keogh had decided to stay with her patients, and when the British troops advanced through the building, Volunteers Jim Kenny and Dan McCarthy opened fire on them before trying to escape from the ground floor. Nurse Keogh, who was on an upper floor, apparently thought the way was now clear to return to the lower floor. As she came down the stairs in full uniform, the British soldiers, taken by surprise, fired, and she was killed instantly. Volunteer Dan McCarthy had been wounded as he tried to escape and was carried to one of the wards where the chronic patients were sheltering from the firefight.[34]

As dusk approached, Éamonn gathered together his senior officers – Brugha, Cosgrave, ffrench Mullen, McGlynn, O'Briain and Byrne – in the Nurses' Home and studied a large map by the light of electric torches. Éamonn's staff orderly, Peadar Doyle, was making tea by the fireplace. Volunteer James Coughlan was on sentry duty outside when Éamonn told him to come in for a cup of tea. Coughlan recalled later that he found Éamonn in exceedingly cheerful spirits. Éamonn told them that he had sent a message to the officer in charge of the British forces asking for a temporary truce to allow both sides to collect their dead. The message came back to say that negotiations were impossible since all of their (British) officers were dead. When tea was finished, Éamonn assembled his entire remaining garrison, with the exception of the sentries, in the room and produced a copy of the Proclamation. When he had read it aloud, he explained to them the circumstances that had led up to the Rising. Coughlan recalled being told that:

The Volunteer Executive had information that the British Government were about to hold a secret session of Parliament to discuss negotiating a peace settlement with Germany; that a solemn military alliance between this country and Germany had been signed on our behalf by Roger Casement and on Germany's behalf by the Kaiser; that the object of the Rising was to establish Ireland's position as a belligerent nation taking part in the Great War, and thus be entitled to representation at the forthcoming Peace Conference. He [Éamonn] explained that MacNeill's cancellation of the mobilisation orders for Easter Sunday was due to the capture of Casement, the loss of some arms expected from Germany, and the obvious knowledge by the British of our intention to revolt. He stated that the Volunteer Executive had considered the British authorities' reaction to the cancellation of the mobilisation, and a majority had decided that sooner than have each individual Volunteer resisting arrest in his own home, thereby endangering the lives of his womenfolk (as he was pledged not to surrender his arms without a fight), it would be better to proceed with the original plan as far as possible, and so the Rising was re-ordered for Easter Monday.[35]

The Volunteers posted sentries, recited the rosary and settled down for the night. After a day of unaccustomed fighting and dodging bullets, the Volunteers in the Nurses' Home were exhausted and on edge. The strain on the men was so great that sentries had to be relieved every hour.[36]

While the battle was raging in the South Dublin Union and at the other sites chosen by the Military Council throughout Dublin, in England the Prime Minister, Herbert Asquith, had spent Easter in his country home, where he was preparing for an important Commons debate on conscription. He didn't arrive back to Downing Street until midnight on Easter Monday night. On being informed of the Rising, he took it calmly and went to bed.[37]

For ordinary Dubliners, the fine Easter bank holiday had turned into an unnerving day. Soon after Éamonn's departure, Áine had left home with her young son and her distracted mother, who made all kinds of excuses about 'not being ready'. Áine took all the money she had in the world and all the perishable food she had in the house and she wore two dresses. They had made arrangements to stay with Caitlín, Cathal Brugha's wife, in her family home in Dartry because Éamonn expected their own home, not far from the South Dublin Union in Rialto, would be in the line of fire. Soon after she reached the Brugha's home, Caitlín's sister, Miss Kingston, arrived and reported that she had heard shots. They went out later to buy provisions and were disgusted to meet a Volunteer who, on his bicycle, was fleeing for his life.[38]

The rest of the Kent family, over in Drumcondra, were getting piecemeal news of events from neighbours and passers-by. When Michael saw a car whizzing past with a couple of armed Volunteers, his immediate thought was:

> that the Volunteers were mere boys: and most of the spectators (including myself) thought it was a terrible mad business, the general expression of those looking on being: 'Lord, if we thought they had the least chance wouldn't we all be in it.'

He was startled by the complete disappearance of the police from the streets and the almost complete absence of soldiers, 'except an odd one home on furlough from France'. The trams returned to their depots and, at about 3pm or 4pm, Michael saw a large body of cavalry passing the house. He learned afterwards that they were the Lancers who charged down Sackville Street in one of the first engagements of the week. They were now returning, chastened, to Marlborough Barracks. As the afternoon drew in, Michael had a good laugh at the expressions on the faces of the thirsty crowd returning from Fairyhouse Racecourse when they discovered that all the public houses were closed.[39]

Easter Tuesday, 25 April

Shortly before dawn on Easter Tuesday in the South Dublin Union, Lieutenant William Cosgrave was woken up by a sentry who thought he heard digging along the wall of a small yard beside the Nurses' Home. Cosgrave soon discovered that the 'trench' that the anxious sentry thought he had seen was a small path and the noise of 'digging' was just a window blind flapping in the wind.[40]

Another sentry was not so fortunate. Cosgrave's half-brother, Frank Burke, was a Section Commander in C Company. He had escaped the fighting in McCaffrey's estate the previous day but, early on Tuesday morning, he was shot dead by a British soldier in the hospital across from the

Nurses' Home. Burke had leaned across a window to light his cigarette from a match held by a fellow Volunteer named Fogarty. The tragedy unhinged Fogarty and, for the rest of the week, Éamonn ordered that he be kept out of harm's way – unarmed and supervised.[41] Éamonn later oversaw Frank Burke's burial party, under the protection of a Red Cross flag, in the field behind the Nurses' Home.

The occupants of the Union were not the only ones killed and wounded in the gunfire that was raking the site. A Mrs Heffernan, who lived across the street from the entrance to the Union, was killed in her home by a stray bullet. A visitor to Dublin from Belfast, Mr Halliday, was shot dead as he walked along the South Circular Road.[42]

Throughout the morning, the Volunteers in the Nurses' Home remained under fire from the British soldiers from their commanding position in the Royal Hospital Kilmainham. The Nurses' Home was exposed to attack, with windows to the front and rear and a large window above the staircase. Volunteer James Foran got his men to barricade the windows with books and ledgers.[43] In the meantime, Éamonn supervised the reinforcement of the front door. The Volunteers erected a barrier between the door and the porch entrance. Constructed of sandbags, stones, mattresses, bedsteads and furniture, the barrier reached almost to the ceiling, and created an effective second barricade a few yards behind the porch entrance. By the end of the day, with work started on a route to connect the building to the men holding out in the boardroom, the Volunteer garrison had turned the Nurses' Home into a defensible fortress.

During Tuesday, Éamonn received a dispatch from Michael Staines, the Quartermaster General, based in the GPO, to inquire whether he needed any ammunition or food. Éamonn reported back that they needed nothing.[44] It was certainly true that the garrison in the Nurses' Home was well supplied with food, although their ammunition stores were not plentiful. After the turmoil of Easter Monday, however, it was clear that the allocation of the available food among the garrison was becoming urgent. The men had been told to bring forty-eight hours' rations when they mobilised and these were now eaten. On the evening of Easter Monday Éamonn, under sniper fire from the British forces, had made his way alone to check on the men in the boardroom. He found them well supplied with tea and bread but otherwise running low on supplies. He later sent them a ham.[45]

On Tuesday evening, Éamonn appointed Peadar Doyle, his staff orderly, as Quartermaster in charge of all food supplies. They had plenty of food and water in the Union and Doyle recalled that, 'frequently small parcels of cooked food were thrown over the wall and messages of a friendly nature gave us the impression that there was a change of opinion in our favour in the city'.[46] The bakery in the Union continued to work throughout the week, with supplies being issued

THE STOLEN ADVERTISEMENT.

Below is a photograph of the streamer and poles erected by the United National Societies Committee, with the permission of the Dublin Corporation, to draw attention to the Independence Demonstration at Beresford Place on June 22nd—the day the King of England was crowned. This advertisement was stolen by the police, and is now in their possession in Dublin Castle. The fight is still on—whether the Dublin Corporation or Dublin Castle have control over the streets of Dublin. This photograph, with the other—the police removing the poles—can be had in postcard form. The poles and streamer at 6d. per dozen wholesale, and the other at 9d. per dozen wholesale, to be had from this office, from *Sinn Féin*, 49 Middle Abbey Street; the National Council, 6 Harcourt Street.

It was for selling these cards that Mr. Seamus O Dubhthaigh was arrested on Tuesday night—police spite.

Left: 'Deeds that won the Empire – The capture of the poles', *Irish Freedom*, July 1911.

Below: Sinn Féin anti-enlisting car, *Sinn Féin,* 24 May 1913.

THE SINN FEIN ANTI-ENLISTING CAR.

Commandant Éamonn Ceannt in the uniform of the Irish Volunteers.

e last time I saw Éamonn ... the night before he was executed

To Master Michael and family
with best Easter wishes. All
well here — on the defensive.
If the friends of the small
nationalities should decide on
interfering with our Inspections
to-morrow I would advise you
to make yourselves scarce. Your
own house is the safest place
from 4 p.m., our hour of
assembly, until such time as
the danger of an attack is passed
which would be about 7. Come
what may we are ready.

Éamonn Ceannt
22/4/1916

Above: A letter from Éamonn Ceannt to his brother Michael Kent, warning him about the Rising.

Right: A British soldier stands guard outside the GPO after the 1916 Rising.

Above & right:
The exterior and the internal staircase of the Nurses' Home, South Dublin Union.

Left: Major Sir Francis Fletcher Vane of the Royal Munster Fusiliers.

Below: South Dublin Union buildings to the left of the Nurses' Home.

BROTHERS IN ARMS

A pathetic tragedy is revealed in two deaths notices:

KENT—In memoriam. Eamonn (Edmund) Kent, executed in Kilmainham Jail, Monday, May 8, 1916. R.I.P.

KENT—April 24, 1917, Wm. L. Kent, eldest son of the late James Kent, 13 St. Alphonsus road, Drumcondra, R.I.P.

Eamonn Kent was one of the signatories to the Republican Proclamation issued on April 24, 1916. He was taken prisoner, tried by Field Court Martial, and was executed on the morning of Monday, May 8, 1916. On the same morning Cornelius Colbert, Michael Mallon, and J. J. Heaston were also executed.

Wm. L. Kent, who was killed in action in France on the anniversary of the Dublin Rebellion, was a brother to Eamonn. He was a colour-sergeant in the Royal Dublin Fusiliers, a most efficient non-com., and extremely popular with all ranks and with his numerous friends in Dublin and Naas, where he was stationed at the Depot during the rising.

EAMONN CEANNT
(Commandant of the South Dublin Area),
EXECUTED 8th MAY, 1916,
One of the Signatories of the "Irish Republic Proclamation."

Brothers in arms: news of the death of Company Sergeant Major William Kent of the Royal Dublin Fusiliers during the Battle of Arras reached his family on the first anniversary of Éamonn's death, 8 May 1917.

Gv RI

HE whom this scroll commemorates was numbered among those who, at the call of King and Country, left all that was dear to them, endured hardness, faced danger, and finally passed out of the sight of men by the path of duty and self-sacrifice, giving up their own lives that others might live in freedom. Let those who come after see to it that his name be not forgotten.

Coy. Serjt. Maj. William Luman Kent
Royal Dublin Fusiliers

Áine Ceannt.

Rónán Ceannt.

to the Volunteers, the British soldiers, the inmates and staff as well as local people who were cut off from their normal supplies.[47]

In spite of the occupation by the Volunteers and the British Army, the staff of the South Dublin Union continued to look after their charges. From the start, every effort was made to move inmates away from the most dangerous positions. Invalids still had to be fed, the injured and ill had to be nursed, and those who died in the fighting and of natural causes had to be buried. The Assistant Matron, Annie Mannion, had been visiting a friend in Belfast and reported back for duty on Easter Tuesday morning. She found the place in a state of panic and later recalled: 'We did not know what we were doing.' With the Volunteers confined to the Nurses' Home and the area around St James's Gate, she found that the British soldiers were, 'wandering around the hospital at a loose end rather than taking up any definite position'.[48]

There was a reason for the apparent hesitancy of the British soldiers. On the morning of Easter Tuesday, although Éamonn and his colleagues were not aware of it, the British forces that had successfully taken control of most of the site on Monday were withdrawn from within the walls of the Union. The regimental history records that, having occupied the Union for the night and the following morning, 'for some extraordinary reason, it was decided to evacuate the Union and concentrate at Kingsbridge station. This was done under protest.'[49] Part of the reason for the withdrawal of the British forces from inside the Union may have been the surprisingly small numbers available in Dublin on Easter Monday. It has been estimated that the total force amounted to no more than four hundred. They soon found themselves spread thinly across the city as the Volunteers took up their positions. Although Dublin Castle now seemed to be safe, there remained a concern about the security of the head-quarters of the army in the Royal Hospital Kilmainham.[50]

As far as the Volunteers in the South Dublin Union were concerned, however, the danger continued. Outside the walls of the Union, along St James's Street and from their vantage point in the Royal Hospital Kilmainham, the British forces kept Éamonn's Volunteers pinned down with machine-gun and sniper fire. The British troop positions were well entrenched. The soldiers in the building on St James's Street were particularly fortunate. The building belonged to Guinness's and the brewery's catering manager supplied the 150 troops who were garrisoned there with 1,500 meals through-out the week.[51]

By Tuesday, however, the situation from the British side had started to change. The first trainload of reinforcements arrived at Kingsbridge station at 2.15am on Tuesday morning. By 5.20am, the whole Curragh Mobile Column of 1,600 men had arrived, as had their Brigadier General, WHM Lowe. A further 1,000 men from the 25th Irish Reserve

Infantry Brigade followed shortly afterwards. General Friend left London and, travelling by destroyer overnight, arrived in Dublin at 9am. Reinforcements from England were soon dispatched for Kingstown (Dún Laoghaire).

With the civil authorities in disarray, the Lord Lieutenant declared martial law in Dublin. As Michael Kent had already observed, the Dublin Metropolitan Police were withdrawn from the street.

Brigadier General Lowe's strategy was to establish a central axis of communication running from Kingsbridge Station to the North Wall and Trinity College, followed by the cordoning off of the main rebel positions.[52] This is what was happening around the perimeter of the outpost at the South Dublin Union.

In their memoirs, the Volunteers in the South Dublin Union described the later part of Tuesday as 'uneventful'. In spite of the covering fire from the British troops, the Volunteers were able to walk about in the interior courtyard of the Nurses' Home.

That evening at about 8.30pm, Éamonn sent Volunteers Liam O'Flaherty and Sean Murphy out of the Union by a small wicket gate at the rear of the Nurses' Home. He ordered them to make contact with Captain Tom McCarthy and his men in Roe's distillery in Mount Brown, approximately one hundred yards from the main St James's Gate to the Union. They found the distillery deserted except for a caretaker who told them that the Volunteers had left because they had no provisions and were unable to hold the building.[53] It later emerged that a number of the men had made their way to Marrowbone Lane, where they joined Seamus Murphy's garrison.[54]

In fact, the small garrison under Captain McCarthy had run out of ammunition as well as provisions and, before they decided to leave the distillery, had made several dangerous but vain attempts to contact the garrison across the road in the South Dublin Union. Lieutenant Cosgrave later said that Captain Tom McCarthy was a painstaking, industrious, efficient and punctual officer, who never shirked any undertaking he was given. With an implicit criticism of Éamonn's leadership – or at least of Éamonn's choice of McCarthy for the post to which he was allocated – Cosgrave added that McCarthy 'would have served with distinction had he been under the immediate direction of a superior officer'.[55] After the Rising, an enquiry, headed up by Vice-Commandant Cathal Brugha and Captain Liam O'Brien, exonerated the garrison of all blame in leaving their post.[56]

By the end of the second day of the Rising, Dublin was rife with rumour. Michael Kent recalled that 'as the day advanced the rumours were spread of a great force of Germans coming ... It was said Cork was ablaze with the rebellion, also Galway, Dundalk etc., and that several transports from England with soldiers were sunk by German submarines.' The Kent family on the city's north side had absolutely no news of either Áine or Rónán, nor they could get any reliable information about their brother Éamonn's whereabouts. On Tuesday night both Michael and Richard Kent were picturing their brother 'lying stark and stiff in death somewhere'.[57]

Wednesday, 26 April

On the other side of the city, in the South Dublin Union, Éamonn was alive and well, although his future safety was by no means certain. By Wednesday, he was well entrenched in the Nurses' Home in the Union itself but had lost contact with all three of his outposts. In the outpost in Watkin's brewery, Ardee Street, Captain Con Colbert's company had seen little action since they had established themselves there on Easter Monday and, 'they had nothing to do except erect barricades'. They hadn't even seen any British troops. Unable to contact Éamonn, Colbert sent a message to the garrison in Jacob's and was instructed to take his entire company to Jameson's distillery in Marrowbone Lane to reinforce Captain Seamus Murphy and his garrison. Colbert's men left Ardee Street for Marrowbone Lane at dawn on Wednesday morning.[58]

The Marrowbone Lane garrison originally comprised Captain Seamus Murphy's A Company, together with a large contingent of women and girls from Cumann na mBan.

Among the Cumann na mBan contingent was Éamonn's sister-in-law Lily, who later recorded her excitement as the garrison arrived in the distillery on Easter Monday:

> I knew that the dream of my girlhood had come true. The history of Ireland; her songs; music; traditions seemed a surging force behind me, as I saw with pride the soldiers of Ireland prepare to fight again for their freedom and Oh! how glorious it was that we, girls, were by their side to help.[59]

In fact, for the first two days of the Rising, although Captain Seamus Murphy had efficiently garrisoned the building with sentries, organised a reserve supply of water, and arranged for the distribution of arms and ammunition, the only significant action was the continuous and highly effective fire that snipers on the upper floors of the distillery rained down upon the British soldiers who were trying to penetrate the Union by way of the rear gate along the canal.[60] Volunteer Christopher Byrne remembered, 'We were so free from fighting that Seamus Murphy, the O/C, suggested that we should have a sing-song – to keep the fellows' hearts up.'[61]

In Marrowbone Lane they could hear the noise of fighting in the city. Unlike the Union, where food was plentiful, Marrowbone Lane was, at least initially, on short rations. Lily O'Brennan later recalled, with the benefit of somewhat rose-tinted hindsight, that dry bread and black tea, 'seemed splendid fare when we remembered the courage and endurance of the Irish Volunteers around us'.[62] Other members of the garrison were more practical. A passing bread van was hijacked to replenish their supplies; some chickens were purloined from a passing messenger; and a young man leading cattle down the road found three of his animals forcibly sidetracked into the distillery where Robert Holland, an apprentice butcher, killed and butchered them. Holland, who was a sniper and a member of Na Fianna, was in no doubt about the eventual success of the Rising. As he settled down to sleep that night, he reflected that 'if all the garrisons were like ours, and we had no doubt that they were, we were doing very well indeed'.[63]

In both the South Dublin Union and Marrowbone Lane, although there was intermittent firing from the surrounding forces, Wednesday was the day of the calm before the storm. During the day, Lieutenant Cosgrave recalled that Éamonn was delighted to receive a dispatch from the GPO. The dispatch courier was Volunteer Peter Reynolds. He had been sent by Pearse with a dispatch for Cosgrave to be passed on to Éamonn. Reynolds dodged bullets on his motorcycle as he rode at speed to the Union, which was the furthest outpost from the GPO. The message was 'to say that there were 680 men "out" in Dublin, and that they were holding out successfully'.[64]

In the Union, Éamonn had received a reasonably accurate update on the rebellion from a sympathiser who called to him over the wall of the little yard. He gave Éamonn 'particulars of the enemy and told him he believed they were arranging a big attack' on Éamonn's position. He then threw a large piece of meat over the wall.

As the Volunteers gathered for prayers that evening Éamonn told them that the *Irish Times* – another useful donation that had been pitched over the wall to him during the day – was reporting that 'there was a Rebellion in Dublin but that the remainder of Ireland was normal'. Éamonn welcomed, at least, the earlier part of the description because, 'he and the Executive were afraid that it would be called a riot and treated as such. He was delighted at it being called a rebellion. We were acknowledged as soldiers. Our first victory was won.' [65]

In a sense, Éamonn was correct. The Government had indeed been hoping to portray the insurrection in the international media as a local riot. By Wednesday, however, the Lord Lieutenant, without consultation, had extended his declaration of martial law to the whole island of Ireland. Throughout the city, official notices informed citizens that their right to be tried by a jury, for offences contrary to the Defence of the Realm Regulations, had been revoked. Henceforth such offences would be tried by courts martial. [66]

The historian Fearghal McGarry has pointed out that the

decision to invoke martial law, 'ceded a propaganda success to the rebels ... [and] had the potential to alienate moderate nationalist opinion without providing meaningful additional powers'. When the Government, against the advice of the Chief Secretary, formally endorsed the imposition of martial law, even in the peaceful areas of the island of Ireland, it sanctioned the dominance of 'wartime political and military interests of English politicians and the British Army' over any local political concerns about the effect on Ireland.[67] It was a decision that would have far-reaching effects for the future of Ireland and, ultimately, the British Empire – and personally for Éamonn.

For the average Dublin citizen, martial law was more than an inconvenience. In addition to the destruction, gunfire, artillery and looting, the trams stopped and people couldn't get to work. Supplies of food and fuel were running ominously short.

At the same time, there were tentative signs of a change in attitude among Dubliners towards the Volunteers. The writer James Stephens, a friend of Thomas MacDonagh's, had initially encountered a mixture of responses towards the rebels, ranging from astonishment to hostility. By Wednesday, however, he had identified a belief that the Volunteers might hold out longer than anyone imagined to be possible: 'The insurrection having lasted three days, people are ready to conceive that it may last forever.' While this did not convey approval of the Volunteers' actions, it was, according to the historian Charles Townshend, the beginning of respect.[68]

The British military leaders, however, had no intention of letting the insurrection go on forever. The reports that Éamonn had received about a big attack were accurate. In the face of the weakness of the civil government, the British Army was preparing a full-scale military response to the Rising.

The reinforcements from England had arrived at Kingstown (Dún Laoghaire). By 10.35am on Wednesday, most of the men of the Sherwood Forester Regiment were on their way into the city, receiving, initially, a warm welcome from the well-to-do residents of Ballsbridge. The 2/5th and 2/6th battalions, taking the upper road, reached Kilmainham and Kingsbridge without incident, but the 2/7th and 2/8th battalions, making their way along the coast road through Ballsbridge towards the city, met with some of the most serious resistance of the week from the 3rd Battalion of Volunteers, a group of which was stationed at the canal crossing at Mount Street.[69] Elsewhere in the city, the HMS *Helga,* an armed fishery protection vessel, had moved up the Liffey during the morning and started firing eighteen-pound shells at Liberty Hall.[70]

Thursday, 27 April

On Thursday, a glorious spring day, the British brought their forces to bear on the rebel positions. Until then, Éamonn and his men in the South Dublin Union, together with the 3rd Battalion outpost at Mount Street Bridge, were the only ones to have seen significant combat.[71] That would all change as the British forces advanced towards the GPO with machine guns and artillery shells. Elsewhere in the city, the cordon established by the British forces began to tighten around the other Volunteer outposts.

In the South Dublin Union, the morning was quiet except for the ongoing sniper fire. Other than Éamonn's occasional sorties, there had been little connection between the Volunteers in the Nurses' Home and Lieutenant Gerald Murray's men in the boardroom.[72] By Thursday, determined to unite his small force, Éamonn decided to break a viable route through. With a small team of Volunteers, including Lieutenant Sean McGlynn, they spent much of the morning clearing a route from the Nurses' Home through the adjoining dormitory to the outpost in the boardroom. In the meantime, Volunteer James Foran and his colleagues were burrowing a route from the opposite direction.[73] When the two groups met at either side of a hole broken through the wall, each initially thought the other was the enemy. Lieutenant McGlynn gingerly put his head through only to find himself at 'the point of a big six-chamber revolver in the hands of Jim Foran'. He recalled with relief that, 'only that he being an old soldier and has [sic] used an old soldier's judgement I would have been "minus my head" today'.[74]

Vice-Commandant Cathal Brugha, with Lieutenant William Cosgrave, remained in charge of the Nurses' Home. Brugha was on an upper floor and Cosgrave on the ground floor.[75] Éamonn was gone about half an hour and the men in the Nurses' Home were just finishing their lunch, when Cosgrave shouted, 'Enemy attack – to your guns!'[76] Suddenly explosions shook the building, plaster fell from the ceiling and walls, and a dense cloud of dust enveloped the interior of the building. The windows in the back of the Nurses' Home came under sustained fire.

The reason for the renewed British assault on the South Dublin Union was to allow a wagonload of ammunition, and its escort of soldiers, to cross Rialto Bridge to reach the Royal Hospital Kilmainham. The ammunition and its escort had come under heavy sniper fire from the Volunteer garrison. Lieutenant Colonel Oates, the British commanding officer, sent for reinforcements. When they arrived, under Major Sir Francis Vane of the Royal Munster Fusiliers, Lieutenant Colonel Oates ordered an advance guard to 'occupy as much as possible of the South Dublin Union, with a view to distracting the enemy's attention whilst the transport crossed the bridge'.[77] Oates invited Major Vane, with his veteran troops, to assume command of the assault.[78] As these troops advanced across the Union grounds from the Rialto gate, they were reinforced by another group of soldiers who had forced their way into the grounds of the Union through the back gate by the canal, in spite of heavy fire from the Volunteers in Jameson's distillery.

Under the command of Major Vane, the assaulting troops advanced across the site through the narrow lanes and buildings towards the Nurses' Home, where they could see a 'rebel' flag flying from the roof. The British troops, who had been trained for trench warfare, were not familiar with urban warfare through a maze of buildings and little streets – which were often overlooked by snipers. Major Vane later wrote to his wife:

> Everything was bizarre on that day for we advanced through a convent where the nuns were all praying and expecting to be shot, poor creatures, then through the wards of imbeciles who were all shrieking – and through to one of poor old people. To get from one door to another was a gymnastic feat because you had to run the gauntlet of the snipers.[79]

It was an advance squad of the British forces, under the command of Lieutenant Monk Gibbon, which had alerted the Volunteers as they ate their lunch. Gibbon's men entered a small orchard at the rear of the Nurses' Home. Once spotted, they were soon under fire from the Volunteers at the rear windows of the home.

Throughout the afternoon, the small Volunteer garrison remaining in the Nurses' Home came under attack from all sides. British troops had forced their way through the wards to the left, and another group had entered the hospital building in front of the main entrance to the home. Finally, a small group had entered the bakehouse and courtyard between the boardroom and the Nurses' Home.

Major Vane later described the British assault to his wife:

> They had the most awful time, poor fellows. I thought I would never see one of them alive again – two were killed and two wounded. But in the wards it was a dreadful sight, the killed brought in and the wounded lying close up to the poor old paupers, who were, of course, shrieking with fear. I have never seen a more horrible sight and I have seen some. [80]

When the assault started, Volunteer James Coughlan took cover on the landing facing the front door of the Nurses' Home. Captain Douglas ffrench Mullen was on his left and Jack Doherty on his right. They opened fire on the Sherwood Foresters who were making a frontal assault on the building.

Realising that the troops' frontal assault was not succeeding, Captain 'Mickey' Martyn decided to approach the Nurses' Home from the left. His men bored through from the house next door only to find themselves trapped in a narrow space between the high barricade which the Volunteers had constructed below the main staircase and the front porch entrance to the Nurses' Home. Volunteer James Coughlan, under cover on the landing, had heard the noise of the tunnelling. He saw a khaki cap appear above the top of the barricade and whispered to Volunteer Captain ffrench

Mullen, who threw a grenade towards the barricade.

A long and bloody fight followed, with live grenades and homemade bombs being tossed across the barricade in both directions, and the Volunteers on the upper landing firing down on the British soldiers who were trapped beneath the barricade in the porch. In the meantime, the shooting continued from the orchard to the rear of the building and from the upper windows of the hospital facing the front of the Nurses' Home. Before long, the Nurses' Home was a scene of utter devastation.

As Cathal Brugha, who had been on the upper floor of the Nurses' Home, started down the stairs, a grenade, lobbed from the porch, hit him and he came under sustained fire. Ferociously wounded, he dragged himself into shelter. He sent Douglas ffrench Mullen to Cosgrave with the news that the British soldiers had entered the building and that the men were to retire from it. Cosgrave was sceptical, but obeyed orders.[81] They began to retreat towards the boardroom. Their route took them across the yard behind the Nurses' Home, through the paint shop, upstairs and into a dormitory.

In the meantime, Éamonn and his group were fighting their way back from the direction of the boardroom. After a firefight with some British soldiers, the two groups met in the dormitory where, behind a barricade of mattresses, they prepared to take their final stand.[82] Back in the Nurses' Home, Brugha was defending the building single-handedly.

In the dormitory, Cosgrave, who was still not convinced that the retreat from the Nurses' Home had been necessary, was telling Éamonn that he believed that the British had not penetrated the building and that they should return.[83] As they were talking, they heard Brugha taunting the British soldiers behind the barricade and singing 'God Save Ireland'. This, together with the fact that the firing was continuing, convinced Éamonn that Brugha was holding out. He led Volunteers Coughlan and Moore back to the Nurses' Home where they found Brugha directing an imaginary force of subordinates to confuse the British. He sat with his back to the wall and his 'Peter the Painter' revolver trained at the barricade.[84] Having sent Moore back for the rest of the Volunteers in the dormitory, Éamonn went down on one knee and embraced his wounded friend. The two men talked quietly in Irish together for a few minutes before Éamonn ordered Brugha to be moved to a position of relative safety to get medical help. His left foot, hip and leg were practically one mass of wounds.[85]

Éamonn quickly organised his men to keep up the defence of the Nurses' Home. As fierce fighting continued throughout the evening, Éamonn shot an RIC man who was attempting to force an entry through the front door.[86]

Eventually, the British commanders got word that the precious convoy of ammunition and its escort had managed to gallop across Rialto Bridge and into the safety of the Royal

Hospital Kilmainham, while the Volunteers had been distracted defending their own positions. Lieutenant Monk Gibbon, filthy and deaf from the fighting, later wondered whether it had ever been necessary to halt the convoy. For a second time that week, the British troops were ordered to withdraw from the South Dublin Union and by 10.15pm were billeted for the night in the Royal Hospital's Great Hall.[87]

When the attack eased off, the Volunteers ventured cautiously down the stairs and into a yard. Some of the men wanted to evacuate the Union, but just then, Éamonn came along. Volunteer Michael Lynch recalled that 'I never saw him looking in better spirits, though worn out and tired. He said: "They will never get in. We have them licked."' [88] Throughout the night, the Volunteers did their best to give first aid to Brugha, who was suffering massive blood loss and becoming delirious.[89]

While Éamonn and Cathal Brugha were in the middle of the fighting in the South Dublin Union, their wives waited out the week together, not knowing the fate of their husbands. Brugha's wife, Caitlín, didn't learn of her husband's injuries until the following evening when her brother, Fr Kingston, called to see her. Áine Ceannt recalled that, 'He tried to make light of the injuries and Mrs Brugha, though anxious, was reassured.' Caitlín was expecting a baby at the time and had a bad fright one day when, out for a walk with her sister and a friend, they were challenged to halt up the road from the house. They took to their heels and ran, practically falling in the front door when Áine opened it to their frantic ringing. Throughout the week the anxious women could hear the noise of fighting in the city and could see fires burning in the distance. The flames that Áine and Caitlín saw probably came from Sackville Street, where many of the buildings were on fire following incendiary and artillery fire from the *Helga*.[90]

Friday, 28 April

In the pre-dawn of Friday morning, the new British Commander-in-Chief, General Sir John Maxwell, arrived in Dublin. Although operational responsibility for the suppression of the Rising remained with General Lowe, the Government had appointed Maxwell as Military Governor with sweeping powers under martial law. He immediately confirmed that he would not be satisfied with anything short of unconditional surrender and would 'not hesitate to destroy all buildings within any area occupied by the rebels'.[91]

Isolated under continuous sniper fire from the Royal Hospital Kilmainham, the Volunteer garrison in the South Dublin Union knew nothing of the plans of the new British Military Governor nor of the fate of their fellow Volunteers. They could hear only the sound of gunfire and see 'the gleam of many fires in the city'.[92] All they knew was that the British had, for the second time, withdrawn from the buildings immediately surrounding the beleaguered Nurses' Home, which were left abandoned to their traumatised former occupants.

With careful nursing from his comrades, Brugha had, miraculously, survived the night. On Friday morning, Éamonn arranged for a procession led by Fr Gerhart, wearing his priest's stole and carrying a Red Cross flag for protection, to take the delirious Brugha to one of the Union hospitals. He was later brought under British guard to Dublin Castle's hospital from where, some months later, he was released. His wounds mended slowly and, although he never recovered the full use of his injured leg, against all the odds he survived.[93]

The witness statements by members of the 4th Battalion, although written many years later when the heroism of the martyred leaders of the Rising had been established in the public mind, unanimously testify to the esteem in which their men held both Éamonn and Cathal Brugha. John Styles referred to Éamonn as 'the most unselfish man I ever met … He never thought of himself, gave everything he possessed to his men and the cause he had so much at heart.' Of Brugha he said: 'He was a very determined man who did not know what fear was.'[94] Another said of Éamonn that 'during the whole week he was an example of cool daring and seemed to bear a charmed life. Nothing daunted him.'[95]

Recent assessment by academic historians of Éamonn and Cathal Brugha's leadership skills during the intense fighting in the South Dublin Union has also been positive. Brian Barton, in his authoritative account of the courts martial that followed the Rising, referred to Éamonn and Cathal Brugha's 'heroic and inspirational leadership'. Of Éamonn, he said that, 'during the Rising he revealed the necessary qualities of energy, resourcefulness, resilience and physical courage to inspire confidence and win the admiration of his unit'. He pointed out that, 'unlike other Military Council members, such as Pearse and MacDonagh, he was by instinct a soldier, a man of action'.[96] Charles Townshend commented: 'The comparatively small garrison of the Union was energised by the leadership style of Ceannt and his Vice-Commandant, Cathal Brugha.'[97]

With Brugha dispatched to comparative safety, Éamonn found himself increasingly isolated as leader of the small garrison. Although quite different in personality, he and Brugha had been friends and comrades for many years. Without him, Éamonn carried the lonely burden of motivating his men through days of anxious waiting under constant sniper fire. He was expecting another serious assault at any minute. He set his men to digging trenches behind the Nurses' Home to provide an escape route to comparative safety if, as he clearly expected, the 'big guns are used against us'.

In front of his men, Éamonn was determined to continue to be the self-possessed leader – coolly planning, controlling and responding in the face of overwhelming odds. He was, however, only human and found himself coping with a reality that was beyond his inexperienced imagination. That Friday afternoon, Volunteer Joseph Doolan found Éamonn alone 'in a small room by himself, his rosary beads in his hands and the tears rolling down his cheeks and face'. Doolan retired without disturbing him. [98]

It did not help that Éamonn was still isolated from his other senior officers, Captains Seamus Murphy and Con Colbert, by then together in Marrowbone Lane. Their own efforts to contact Éamonn in the South Dublin Union had failed repeatedly. Unknown to Éamonn, the two men had become so frustrated by their enforced waiting game that they planned to leave the distillery on Sunday and fight their way to join Éamonn and the rest of the battalion in the South Dublin Union.

In the Union itself, that Friday evening, no further assault had materialised and Éamonn gathered his men for their usual evening prayers. After they had recited the Rosary, he talked to them about the events of the previous day. He told them that he had heard word across the wall from James's Street that in spite of the fires in the centre of the city, the Volunteers were holding their own.

Éamonn's words to his men were motivational, but quite wrong. A number of garrisons found themselves in a similar position to Éamonn's – cut off from their own outposts, under sustained sniper fire but little or no artillery bombardment, and confident that they could continue to hold their positions. Like Éamonn, however, none of them realised that General Lowe had identified the GPO and the Four Courts as the greatest strategic threats and was concentrating his resources on them.

Saturday, 29 April

With the British action focused on the city centre, the South Dublin Union was quiet on Saturday. The garrison remained on alert and, under Éamonn's direction, did their best to repair their defences and armaments in the expectation of another assault.

The staff of the Union had by and large been confined to their quarters during the fighting, except for forays out to care for their charges.[99] On Saturday, the rumour went around among them that 'the place would be blown up by heavy gunfire from the British at the Old Men's Home, Kilmainham [British military headquarters] if the Volunteers did not surrender by 3pm'. The ward master Patrick Smyth later recalled that the staff all went to Confession, 'to prepare for whatever was to happen'.[100]

The Volunteers had also heard the rumours but believed there would be advance notice of an attack in order to allow the residents of the Union to be evacuated. There was some talk, in which Éamonn was not involved, of making a break for it themselves and fighting their way out to the country.

As the day went on, however, nothing materialised and only the constant sniper fire broke the uneasy peace. The waiting game continued. After evening prayers that night, Éamonn told them that a big attack could come at any moment and 'when the attack came every man was to keep cool and hold on to his post no matter what the odds. We [are] winning.' [101]

It was not only the Volunteers whose nerves were stretched to breaking point that Saturday. In the Robert Street Malt Store, part of Guinness's brewery near Marrowbone Lane, two long-standing brewery employees with no connections to the insurgents – William Rice and CE Dockery – together with two soldiers – Lieutenant A Lucas and Lieutenant Worswick of the 2nd King Edward's Horse – were shot and killed by Quartermaster Sergeant Robert Flood of the Royal Dublin Fusiliers. Sergeant Flood was later court martialled on a charge of murder. His defence, which was not unreasonable given the events of the week, was that he thought the men were Sinn Féiners who were going to let the rebels into the brewery. He was acquitted. [102]

In the Volunteer outpost in Marrowbone Lane all was quiet except that 'a few stray soldiers came within rifle range and got hit'. [103] Rose McNamara, one of the Cumann na mBan volunteers, recalled that the only thing captured on Saturday was a load of cabbage! Fears that a potential spy in the form of a 'masculine looking woman', seen along by the canal, were checked out but proved groundless.[104]

In the city, Pearse and Connolly were increasingly concerned at the number of innocent civilians who had already been killed and wounded, and with the fate of the men who had put their trust in them as leaders. The members of the Provisional Government who were present – Éamonn and Thomas MacDonagh being absent at their posts – held a 'council of war' in No.16 Moore Street, where they had established their headquarters after fleeing the burning GPO.[105] Surrender was abhorrent to them all, particularly Tom Clarke, but in the end they decided by a majority to seek surrender terms from the British. Pearse signed the formal surrender document before being driven to the British military headquarters to sign a further surrender document in front of General Maxwell.[106] Volunteer Quartermaster Michael Staines, together with Diarmuid Lynch and a team of stretcher-bearers, took Connolly to the hospital in Dublin Castle.[107] It was there that Connolly endorsed the surrender document, but only for the men under his command.[108]

Sunday, 30 April

It was mid-afternoon of the following day, Sunday, before the garrison in the South Dublin Union heard news of the surrender. The men in the boardroom were keeping watch over James's Street when they saw Commandant Thomas MacDonagh, from the Jacob's factory garrison, and Fr Aloysius, a

Capuchin priest, walking down the street with a white flag.

Fr Aloysius and his fellow priest Fr Augustine were based in Church Street, not far from Moore Street, but had not heard news of the surrender until early on Sunday morning. They were convinced that the Volunteers in Church Street would not accept the surrender unless they saw a copy signed by Pearse. They walked to Dublin Castle where General Lowe, seeing an opportunity to use their good offices to deliver the surrender order to commandants Éamonn Ceannt and Thomas MacDonagh, placed his car at their disposal. To allay their concerns regarding the authenticity of the surrender, Lowe arranged for them to see James Connolly before driving on to see Pearse at Arbour Hill Detention Barracks. Pearse explained the decision of the Provisional Government:

> In order to prevent the further slaughter of Dublin Citizens and in the hope of saving the lives of our followers now surrounded and hopelessly outnumbered, the members of the Provisional Government present at Headquarters have agreed to an unconditional surrender and Commandants of the various districts in the City and Country will order their Commands to lay down arms.[109]

The members of the Provisional Government and signatories of the Proclamation clearly expected that their own lives would be forfeit, but hoped that those of the rank and file would be spared.

The two priests took the surrender notice back to Church Street, then on to Jacob's factory. There, General Lowe met with Commandant Thomas MacDonagh at noon. In the face of MacDonagh's disbelief and dismay, they adjourned to Lowe's car and an armistice was negotiated until 3pm to enable MacDonagh to contact Éamonn, in the South Dublin Union, and the outpost in Marrowbone Lane. Before leaving, MacDonagh told his devastated men, many of whom wanted to fight on, that they had 'fought a good fight, held out for one glorious week, and achieved what they [had] meant to accomplish'.[110]

When the car got close to the South Dublin Union, a barricade blocked their way and the two priests, accompanied by MacDonagh, General Lowe and two other British officers, went the rest of the way on foot.[111] Fr Aloysius waved his white flag in front of the building and MacDonagh kicked and knocked at the gate. Initially there was no response, but when they tried again at an entrance further along the road, the door was opened.[112]

When MacDonagh and Éamonn had greeted each other, MacDonagh broke the news of the surrender. Éamonn read Pearse's message with dismay but quickly pulled himself together. Determined to choreograph a defiant and dignified military bearing for his battalion's last appearance on the streets of Dublin, he told the British officers that if he did surrender, it would only be on certain conditions.

He insisted that the British troops be withdrawn from the streets, and that he be allowed to march the South Dublin Union garrison to collect their colleagues at Marrowbone Lane distillery before making their way, as a single body, to their ultimate destination.

The British were uneasy. They didn't know where the distillery was and were afraid that they might be fired upon. Éamonn insisted that he would continue fighting if he was not granted these concessions. Eventually it was agreed that one of the British officers would remain with Éamonn in the SDU while the rest of the party – MacDonagh, the two priests and the other two British officers – would go on to alert the Marrowbone Lane garrison of the surrender.[113]

Éamonn collected his men in one of the dormitories on the ground floor. He read out Pearse's surrender on behalf of the Provisional Government, by which, as a member, he was bound. Volunteer James Coughlan later recalled that Éamonn told them, however, that he, himself, 'would not *order* them to surrender', and that 'any man wishing to make his getaway could do so – but that, having behaved like soldiers from the beginning, he would like [them] to behave like soldiers to the end. "As for us", he said, referring to the signatories of the proclamation, "we know what will happen to us", and then referring to the Volunteers, he said that he expected "our friends in America" would look after our dependants.'[114] Joseph Doolan recalled Éamonn telling them that 'you men will get a double journey but we, the leaders, will get a single journey'.[115] Most of the men agreed to surrender. Volunteer Peadar Doyle rationalised that they 'had stood together all through the fight and ought to stand together to the end'.[116]

Not everyone agreed, particularly since there was no military presence to enforce the surrender.[117] William T Cosgrave recalled that Éamonn himself was not favourable to the surrender and found support among some of the other Volunteers.[118] Lieutenant Sean McGlynn was 'entirely against it' – he believed that the 'known leaders would have to forfeit their lives', and he favoured getting away or fighting it out. Éamonn realised that McGlynn's real concern was for his wife and family. 'There and then,' recalled McGlynn, 'he gave me two gold sovereigns to send home to my wife.'[119]

Éamonn was not the only one concerned with the fate of the men. Lieutenant Cosgrave, a councillor in Dublin Corporation, later referred to Volunteer Michael Lynch, a Corporation clerk who had been in the boardroom during the week, as 'a proper fool' for not trying to get away into his aunt's quarters. His aunt was a ward mistress employed in the Union and had given Lynch 'a feed' late on the Thursday night.[120] Lynch chose reluctantly to surrender, and Cosgrave noted that 'eventually there was a general acquiescence to surrender'.[121]

Éamonn told the men to collect their guns and belongings and to line up in front of the Nurses' Home within half an hour. He counted them off. There were forty-two men present out of the original strength of between fifty and sixty. One of the British officers, Major Rotherham, who accepted the surrender, remarked, 'I see you are getting your men together.' Éamonn calmly replied that they were all present. Rotherham was astounded by the tiny band that had held off two major assaults by the British Army.[122]

Leaving by the front gate of the Union, the garrison formed disciplined 'fours' and, carrying their rifles, marched towards Marrowbone Lane. Volunteer Ignatius Callender, who had been delivering dispatches around the city, was passing St James's Chapel when he 'saw Éamonn Ceannt and his gallant little band marching towards the city (possibly for Dublin Castle). They looked a bit haggard – but proud as they followed their gallant leader, who was marching side by side with a British Officer.'[123]

Fr Augustine and the British officers had notified those in Marrowbone Lane of the order to surrender. It came as a surprise to the garrison, which, Volunteer Robert Holland recalled, 'was still in great spirits, eating cakes that the girls had baked, and getting ready for a *céilidhe*'. He recalled that after the senior officers had received the news, Colbert told him, 'Bobby, I do not know what to say or think but, if what I think comes true, our cause is postponed to a future generation.'[124]

Annie O'Brien, who was a member of Cumann na mBan, remembered that 'the news was received very badly and there was great disappointment'. She was looking out the window when Éamonn and his men arrived at the distillery. She thought that Éamonn 'was like a wild man, his tunic was open, his hair was standing on end and he looked awful. He hated the task of asking the garrison to surrender.'[125]

When Lily O'Brennan, who had also been there all week, ran up to Éamonn, he told her to go home and to take a message to Áine. But Lily was caught up in the excitement and insisted that 'having come out with the men we were determined to surrender with them and take the consequences'. She fell in with the other Cumann na mBan women who were marching out behind the Volunteers.[126]

There were about 145 men and women in the distillery, so the battalion that Éamonn led had more than trebled in size. The wounded, including Captain Douglas ffrench Mullen, were transported to hospital and the battalion moved off towards Bride Street near St Patrick's Cathedral. Volunteer Peadar Doyle remembered that 'all along the route to St Patrick's Place we were greeted with great jubilation, particularly in the poorer areas'.[127]

As they reached Bride Street, Volunteer Thomas Doyle recalled, 'Éamonn Ceannt and General Lowe marched at the head of the men. Éamonn looked great; he had his shirt thrown open; his tunic thrown open and was swinging along at the head of his men. He looked a real soldier.'[128]

Fr Augustine recalled:

> The whole column marched splendidly with guns slung from their left shoulders and their hands swinging freely at their sides. They wore no look of defeat but rather that of victory. It seemed as if they had come out to celebrate a triumph and were marching to receive a decoration. Ceannt was in the centre of the front with two others at his side. But my eyes were riveted on him so tall was his form, so noble his bearing and so manly his stride. He was indeed the worthy Captain of a brave band who had fought a clean fight for Ireland.'[129]

The British military were lined up along the street, with bayonets fixed. As Éamonn's column made its way to St Patrick's Park beside St Patrick's Cathedral, the British fell in behind them, cutting off any possibility of retreat. Éamonn ordered the battalion to lay down their arms and equipment. Lieutenant Henry Murray recalled that many were humiliated but discipline was maintained.[130] The Volunteers were disarmed and their names and addresses were taken. Éamonn gave up his gun and then his belt to a British officer who also tried to divest him of his Volunteer uniform.[131]

In St Patrick's Park, the 4th Battalion formed up behind Commandant Thomas MacDonagh's 2nd Battalion, who were already in place. The two battalions were marched away together. The legal historian Seán Enright has pointed out that 'this precise sequence of events led army officers to lose track of who had surrendered from which garrison and this would have consequences for the trials which followed'.[132]

The journey from St Patrick's Park to Richmond Barracks was 'not so free and easy as the journey from the Union'. They were under very heavy guard, which served as much to protect them from the onlookers' hostility as to police them. Volunteer Robert Holland recalled that they 'were subjected to very ugly remarks and cat-calls from the poorer classes'. [133] Lieutenant William Wylie was one of the commissioned officers in charge.[134] The Volunteers were marched up to High Street, back down James's Street and out through Inchicore, to Richmond Barracks. Many of the men in F Company were from Inchicore and they heard their names called out by bystanders, including old schoolmates – some of the remarks to Volunteers Robert Holland and Peadar Doyle were very rude, and Holland recalled that only the British troops saved them from being manhandled.[135]

Richmond Barracks in Inchicore was a British Army barracks that had the capacity to house up to 1,600 soldiers.[136] During the week after the Easter Rising it became a transit point for some three thousand men who had either been involved in the fighting or had found themselves caught up in the subsequent arrests. It also became the venue for the field courts martial of the leaders of the Rising. The British

Army were completely unprepared to deal with the situation, and while some Volunteers bitterly criticised the conditions in which they were kept, others acknowledged that they were treated as well as could be expected under the circumstances.[137]

When Éamonn and the 4th Battalion arrived at Richmond Barracks, they were housed in large dormitories. Buckets were provided as latrines and Volunteer James Coughlan recalled that:

> For rations we were given British emergency rations, biscuits and canned beef. There were no facilities to even wash our hands and we were kept herded in the same room all day that we slept in at night. Soon the atmosphere became anything but pleasant. Occasionally E. Ceannt would get us to open up all the windows and lead us in such simple physical exercises as we had room to perform.[138]

The men had no idea what to expect and Robert Holland recalled that 'some of them thought they might be shipped to France since they were trained [as soldiers] – or to the colonies'.[139]

Chapter Nine

• • • • • •

May 1916

Trial and Retribution

Monday, 1 May 1916

O n the morning of Monday, 1 May, the citizens of Dublin awoke to a bright spring day and a new reality. The bombardment of the previous week had given way to an eerie silence broken only by occasional sniper fire. The centre of their capital city lay in smoking ruins. Bodies lay buried in rubble. Shocked families mourned loved ones who had been killed or maimed. Across the political and civil divide, some 450 had been killed and 2,600 wounded in Dublin as a result of the Rising.[1]

Some, like Nurse Margaret Keogh and the three inmates of the South Dublin Union,[2] two passers-by in St James's Street and the Guinness employees in the Robert Street Malt Store, were innocent bystanders caught in the conflict.

Most innocent of all were the forty children killed in the city, mostly by gunfire. One little boy, John Foster, was only two years and ten months old when he was shot by a Lancer while sitting in his pram in Church Street.[3]

The rebels who had catapulted into action just one week earlier had surrendered unconditionally. They had received a mixed reception from Dubliners as they were marched into detention. In some of the poorer areas the wives and families of enlisted soldiers, the 'separation women', were particularly vicious in their hostility.[4] In the well-off areas, the hostility was deep but expressed behind closed doors and lace curtains. In lower-middle-class areas and even in some poorer areas, the reaction was muted and even quietly supportive. It was clear that many of those marching under military escort, though dirty and dishevelled, were clerks and tradesmen, civil servants and apprentices – husbands and fathers, sons and daughters of respectable families. As the writer James Stephens had noticed earlier in the week, attitudes of Dubliners towards them were slowly changing from disapproval and astonishment at their actions to grudging respect for their achievements.

Chief Secretary Augustine Birrell submitted his resignation on Monday morning. When Under-Secretary Matthew Nathan's resignation followed quickly, the final abdication of civil authority was complete. The Military Governor, General Maxwell, was firmly in command. The entire country was under martial law.

Maxwell was determined to crush rebellious sentiment.

Arrests were soon widespread. Although the number of Volunteers who had mobilised outside the capital city during Easter week was limited, with the exceptions of Galway, north Dublin, Meath and Wexford, within weeks 3,500 people had been arrested throughout the country for complicity in the Rising. The vast majority, particularly outside Dublin, had nothing to do with it. Even in Dublin many innocent men were caught up in the indiscriminate sweep of arrests. On Tuesday afternoon, Fr Augustine was hearing confessions in Richmond Barracks when one detainee, an Irish-speaking customs official, told him that he had been brought there by the military because copies of *An Barr Buadh* and other Irish papers had been found in his lodgings.[5]

Out in Dartry, Áine and Caitlín Brugha were frantic for news of their husbands. On Sunday, Áine had learned for the first time that Éamonn's name had been signed to the Proclamation. On Monday she heard from some priests in Rathgar that 'the men would be tried and the leaders were to be tried by field general court-martial'.[6]

Over in Drumcondra, Éamonn's brother Michael's anxiety about his brother was compounded by the shortage of food, heat and light. The gas had been turned off and coal was in short supply. He was cut off from news and unable to pass the military cordon to get to his work in City Hall. In the absence of accurate news, wild rumours flourished. Michael had no idea whether the fighting would reignite to engulf them or whether their family, the family of one of the rebel leaders, would be caught up in reprisals. He captured this anxiety graphically in his diary:

> Fearing that there would be a battle all around us, we carried out a rapid mobilisation on our own account. I got all our spare Bank Notes and some gold, and my Life Insurance Policies and Post Office Saving Bank book, together in my coat: Mother [his wife Julia] stuffed 2 pillow cases with flour, bread, sugar, tinned food etc. and we made ready for a hasty flight if necessary.

In spite of his initial scepticism about the Rising, when Michael heard about the Volunteers' unconditional surrender he

> couldn't credit they'd surrender after their brave stand all the week. At the same time, I was convinced that one more week would see us all near starvation and that that would finish it. As it was, only for the looting in the city, the poor would have been in a terrible way.[7]

In Richmond Barracks, Éamonn and the other detainees were woken that Monday morning to a breakfast of hard tack and tea – in a bucket. For their noontime dinner, the same fare was supplemented by bully beef in a small tin. The beef was shared between two men and the tin used afterwards as a makeshift cup.

Later in the day, the men were escorted into the barracks gymnasium. Volunteer Lieutenant Henry Murray remembered that while they waited to see what would happen:

> The main body of the prisoners were despondent but the leaders, notably Éamonn Ceannt, Major MacBride and Con Colbert were resigned and cheerful, their invariable answer to the natural questioning of the men as to their fate being that 'they will probably shoot us and let you fellows off with a few months in jail or internment for the duration of the war'. Éamonn Ceannt in particular urged the men in my presence to look to the future and not to regard the Rising as the end but rather as the commencement of a fresh and better effort; at the same time he expressed his personal view that the surrender had been a mistake and that he would have preferred to continue the fight. This attitude of Éamonn Ceannt and the gallant and cheerful bearing of Con Colbert impressed the men and an air of quiet determination rapidly succeeded the previous general despondency.[8]

Around midday, the men were seated in rows when a group of British officers and plainclothes detectives from the Dublin Metropolitan Police, known as 'G men', picked out those they believed to be leaders or known agitators. This was a critical precursor for General Maxwell's plan to bring the ringleaders to trial as early as possible. Although none of the leaders had tried to conceal their rank – Éamonn, in uniform, had openly marched at the head of the 4th Battalion alongside General Lowe – there were now hundreds of men all jumbled together in serried rows. Most were scruffy, unshaven and difficult to identify. Some wore uniforms, while others were in their everyday clothes. Most were unwilling to help their captors. Éamonn had told his men that each of them was to make the best defence possible. They took him at his word.[9]

Volunteer James Coughlan remembered that, even while Éamonn was being selected for trial, he was determined to look after the welfare of 'the humblest of those who had served him':

> When E Ceannt was picked out, he called the attention of the senior officer present to one of our garrison, a volunteer named Fogarty, who had become mentally deranged [following the shooting of Frank Burke].[10]

Eventually, after the selection process was finished, some two hundred Volunteers, including Éamonn and the other leaders, had been segregated out. They were escorted to an office, where they were left standing under guard from 6pm to 9pm. They had had nothing to eat since noon. The men were then called into another office one by one and informed of the prosecution case against them. Éamonn asked whether it was a court and whether he was bound to answer. Being told 'no' in each case, he said that he would reserve his defence.[11]

Over the next few days, the remaining detainees were marched in groups to the North Wall and dispatched by ship to prisons throughout England, Scotland and Wales.[12]

In the meantime, General Maxwell was making hasty arrangements for the field courts martial. Although he had planned to start the first court martial on Monday, he faced legal difficulties and a shortage of qualified and experienced officers. With no support available from England, he had to rely on Brigadier General Charles Blackader and Brigadier Ernest Maconchy to chair the two courts martial. Although both men had experience in courts martial, neither had any legal training. The historian Brian Barton has also noted that, although the rules for conducting courts martial state that 'members of a court … must not be personally interested in any manner in the case to be tried by them', both men had been in command of troops brought over from England to suppress the Rising.[13] Maxwell's two prosecuting counsel were William Wylie and Ernest Longsworth. Both men were commissioned officers of the Officer Training Corps at Trinity College Dublin and both were members of the Irish Bar, specialising in civil law. Neither man had any experience of court-martial work.[14]

The legal problem facing Maxwell stemmed from the fact that courts martial under the auspices of the Defence of the

Realm Act could only impose a death penalty where there was evidence that the relevant actions were carried out 'with the intention of assisting the enemy: Germany'.[15] Although there was much to suggest German involvement, there was little actual proof.

Until, that is, Maxwell got his hands on a letter written by Patrick Pearse to his mother from Richmond Barracks. The postscript to the letter said that the German expedition, on which Pearse had relied, 'actually set sail but was defeated by the British fleet'.[16] Although General Maxwell withheld the letter from Mrs Pearse, a typed transcript was included in the evidence against Pearse at his court martial.[17]

Tuesday, 2 May 1916

On Tuesday morning at about 9am, Éamonn, William Cosgrave, Phil Cosgrave, Peadar Doyle and others were escorted to another room in the barracks where three officers were seated behind a table with the fourth, Lieutenant William Wylie, to one side. The officer in the centre told them that they were about to be tried by field court martial, and that they had the right to object, not to the process but to any individual as a member of the court. Éamonn and his colleagues had no objections but asked whether they were entitled to legal representation. The court seemed unclear on this point.[18]

They were later escorted to join the other detainees on

a green space in the middle of Richmond Barracks. Some time later, Volunteer Gerald Doyle joined them. He had been brought under armed escort from Kilmainham Jail, where he had been detained since being taken prisoner at the Rialto gate of the South Dublin Union early the previous week. Éamonn, who until then had no way of knowing the fate of the men he had left to guard the gate on Easter Monday, asked Doyle how he came to be brought to Richmond Barracks in handcuffs. Doyle relayed the story of their futile attempt to defend the gate, followed by their arrest and detention. Doyle particularly wanted to assure Éamonn that, although their captors had questioned Doyle and his comrades closely, determined to find out who had been in command in the South Dublin Union, they learned nothing, since the men had agreed in advance that they would give nothing away.[19]

The courts martial began on the afternoon of Tuesday, 2 May. By the time they were finished, 186 men and one woman, Countess Constance Markievicz, had been tried and fifteen men, including Éamonn Ceannt, had been executed. The first of the leaders to be tried were Patrick Pearse, Tom Clarke and Thomas MacDonagh. The charge against each was that he 'did an Act to wit, did take part in an armed rebellion and in the waging of war against His Majesty the King such act as to be calculated to be prejudicial to the Defence of the Realm and being done with the intention and for the purpose of assisting the enemy'.

Wednesday, 3 May 1916

In the pre-dawn hours of Wednesday, 3 May, Patrick Pearse, Tom Clarke and Thomas MacDonagh were executed by firing squad.

Volunteer Gerald Doyle and his comrades, who had spent the night in Kilmainham Jail, met Éamonn later in Richmond Barracks and told him of the executions. Éamonn mourned his friends, but when they told him of Clarke's parting words – 'This is not the end of our fight for Irish freedom, only the beginning' – Éamonn 'gave a great smile'.[20]

All day Wednesday, Éamonn and his comrades waited as, in turn, they were marched into their trials and marched away again afterwards. Although prepared for the worst and now aware that three of his closest friends and collaborators had already been executed, Éamonn had always been determined to 'make a fight for his life'.

In spite of the dire circumstances in which he found himself, he set about defending himself in his usual calm, methodical way. He knew the charges against him. He also knew by then, following a conversation between the equally methodical William T Cosgrave and the prosecuting officer, Lieutenant Wylie, that they were to be tried by field general court martial. According to Cosgrave's account of the meeting, 'no person was allowed to appear and speak on behalf of a prisoner, but each prisoner would be permitted to bring a friend with him, whom he could consult and who would be free to advise the prisoner but not to address the court'. [21]

Although denied legal representation at the court martial itself, Éamonn and Cosgrave were each determined to base their defence on the best legal advice they could acquire. They were also prepared to use the good offices of their contacts in Dublin Corporation. Éamonn, of course, was a long-standing Corporation employee and Cosgrave a long-standing Sinn Féin Councillor. Major John MacBride, who was also an employee of Dublin Corporation and anxious not to lose his job if he received a prison sentence, joined them in this. Cosgrave recalled that MacBride did not appear to be as keenly interested as the other men, both of whom were acutely aware that their lives, rather than their careers, were at stake.

Cosgrave sent messages to 'a solicitor, a Barrister, Mr J Ronayne BL, and Dr L Sherlock who was at that time the most influential member of Dublin Corporation'. The solicitor never turned up, but Alderman Lorcan Sherlock and barrister John Ronayne came within the hour. So did the Lord Mayor of Dublin, Sir James Gallagher, who, like Sherlock, was prepared to speak on Cosgrave's behalf. Cosgrave asked Ronayne, 'who was most anxious to be helpful', to advise the three men on their defence. There is no record of Éamonn's discussion with Ronayne, but much can be inferred from the methodical and carefully worded defence at his court martial.

Éamonn's trial started on Wednesday, 3 May 1916. Brigadier General CG Blackader (President), Lieutenant Colonel G German, and Lieutenant Colonel WJ Kent presided. The charge was the same as for the other leaders. Éamonn pleaded, 'Not guilty.'

The prosecution relied on the deposition of Major JA Armstrong, Inniskilling Fusiliers, who had been present at the surrender of both the 2nd and 4th Battalions in St Patrick's Park. The evidence Armstrong produced in the case of Thomas MacDonagh, his second in command, Major MacBride and Éamonn, was similar in each case. It was both circumstantial and, in Éamonn's case at least, totally inaccurate.[22] He testified that:

> The British troops were fired on, the fire came from the neighbourhood of Jacob's Factory. Several casualties occurred. I was under fire. I was present about 5 p.m. when the party from Jacob's Factory surrendered.
>
> I directed an officer to make a list of the unarmed men. The accused [Éamonn] surrendered as one of the party and was at the head of it, his name was not on the unarmed list. There was an armed list made and his name appears at the head and from information he is described as commandant. I asked him to give orders and he did so, they were obeyed.

Under cross-examination from Éamonn, Major Armstrong admitted that he had 'arrived at a list of armed men by a process of elimination only, and a recollection of men seen with arms, the accused was one of them'. He said that Éamonn did not have a rifle but that he took either a revolver or an automatic pistol from his pocket and laid it on the ground.

In his defence, Éamonn called on Major John MacBride who testified that he knew Éamonn intimately and was in no doubt as to his identity. He said that he, MacBride, was in Jacob's factory and left the premises between 4pm and 5pm on Sunday afternoon: 'The accused was not in my company before I left. It was impossible for the accused to be in Jacob's factory without my knowledge, he had no connection with the party that occupied Jacob's factory.' Under cross-examination, MacBride said: 'I have not the slightest knowledge that he is Commandant of the 4th Battalion. I saw him in uniform at the time the surrender took place.'

At this point, the court record, presumably in some discomfiture, noted that:

> The Prisoner [Éamonn] calls on Thomas MacDonagh who was not available as he was shot this morning. The Court adjourns this case for further evidence.[23]

While Éamonn's fate was postponed until the following day, William Cosgrave's court martial continued. Cosgrave 'made no admissions' and stated that the charge against him of assisting the enemy was baseless, unsustained and utterly unfounded. The Lord Mayor and Alderman Sherlock testified to his good character. The court sentenced him to death with a recommendation for mercy. Twenty-two men were tried that day. The field courts martial imposed the death sentence on twenty of them.

Éamonn spent Wednesday night in Richmond Barracks with MacBride, the two Cosgrave brothers (William and Phil) and three others in a room at the top of the barracks' stairway. Éamonn and William Cosgrave discussed Éamonn's court martial. Éamonn correctly believed that some of the charges against him were 'faulty, inadmissible or unsubstantiated'. Cosgrave advised him that he should have objected and that he would have expected the court to disallow at least two of the charges. Éamonn knew that Cosgrave was much better versed on legal matters than he was and asked him to stand as his 'soldier's friend' at the court martial when it resumed the following day. Cosgrave was willing, but it was not to be.[24]

Thursday, 4 May 1916

The following morning, the news filtered through that Joseph Plunkett, Edward Daly, Michael O'Hanrahan and Willie Pearse had been executed at day break.[25]

Until his court martial reconvened, Éamonn remained with the other prisoners who were awaiting trial. He scribbled a quick note in the hope that it would find its way to Áine:

> Trial about to be resumed at 10 this [Thursday] 4 May. I am cheerful and happy and hope Áine and Rónán also are so. Whatever befalls I shall try to accept my fate like a man and commend you and Rónán to the sympathy of our relatives and friends. *Slán leat.* Do not fret, Éamonn[26]

Éamonn's court martial resumed at 12.45pm. Although William Cosgrave had been willing to stand, the court rejected Éamonn's request for a 'soldier's friend' on the technical ground that he should have made the request the previous day. Éamonn called two further witnesses, both of whom confirmed that he had not been present in Jacob's factory.

Once the testimony had been given, Éamonn summarised the case in his defence. He stated that he had produced three witnesses who swore that he had not been in, nor had he surrendered from, Jacob's factory. He could not, therefore, have had anything to do with the firing from that building that resulted in casualties to British troops. He pointedly noted that he could have produced a fourth witness, the by now executed Thomas MacDonagh, in corroboration, but that he was 'not available'. Éamonn did not accuse Major Armstrong of lying, but of being deceived in his thinking. He said that the evidence against him was inconclusive, that there was at least reasonable doubt, and that he should be given the benefit of the doubt. He admitted to surrendering to the military authorities but denied acting in order to assist the enemy. He noted, again pointedly, that the Crown had not even tendered any evidence in that regard. He said that he had given away his pistol and that 'the Volunteer uniform more often than not does not indicate the rank of the wearer'. He admitted that 'I came at the head of two bodies of men but was only connected with one body.'[27]

The legal historian Seán Enright has summed up Éamonn's closing address as 'remarkable in its clarity'.[28] In a paper on the legality, or otherwise, of the Easter 1916 court martial proceedings, Supreme Court Justice Adrian Hardiman described Éamonn's efforts to defend himself as 'very clever', particularly in respect of his cross-examination of Major Armstrong. Hardiman also noted that 'the military and legal authorities did not believe that some of the verdicts could withstand legal scrutiny'.[29] Although Maxwell had initially promised to make the court records publicly available, the British government was advised, in 1917, that it should not release the proceedings of Éamonn's court martial into the public domain. Their advice rested, in particular, on the haste with which Thomas MacDonagh had been executed, thus making it impossible for Éamonn to fully defend his case.[30]

Ultimately, Éamonn's defence, like those of his co-conspirators, could only ever have been a technical one.

The military authorities were understandably confused, and in spite of their attempts to interrogate Volunteers such as Gerald Doyle, they had not been able to establish exactly who had been in charge of the garrison in the South Dublin Union.

Yet Éamonn had never attempted to hide his membership of the Irish Volunteers (or any other nationalist organisation with which he was associated, with the important exception of the IRB and its Military Council). He had marched at the head of his battalion through the streets of Dublin on many occasions. His name, albeit in printed rather than handwritten form, was clearly on the Proclamation. It declared him to be a member of the Provisional Government – if asked, he would not have denied it. In notes on the back of his court martial charge sheet Éamonn had jotted: 'shall not deny anything proven or admit what is not proven'.[31] Éamonn had also, according to the subsequent recollections of his own men, fatally wounded a member of the RIC during the attack on the Nurses' Home, though he was not charged with this.

Ironically, in the context of the prosecution's evidence, some of the ambiguity caused by Major Armstrong's testimony could easily have been clarified. The prosecuting counsel at Éamonn's court martial, Lieutenant William Wylie, was the responsible officer who had actually written down Armstrong's disputed notes during the surrender in St

Patrick's Park. He might have clarified the confusion as to where and with whom Éamonn had been fighting during the previous week, but as the legal historian Seán Enright has pointed out:

> It was a long-standing rule of common law that a lawyer might appear as an advocate or as a witness but could never be both. Wylie was the one officer who might positively prove the case against Ceannt but could say nothing.[32]

Throughout the courts martial before which he appeared, William Wylie made sincere efforts to assist, or at a minimum, be fair to, the accused. He was impressed by Éamonn's demeanour, which he considered to be the most dignified of the accused. Wylie later wrote in his memoirs that Éamonn showed no sign whatever of nervousness or faltering in front of the court.[33] Ultimately, the court, which was beginning to suspect that Éamonn was playing for time, found him guilty as charged. He was sentenced to death by being shot.

While Éamonn was pleading his case, the constant stream of men into, and back from, their own courts martial continued. John MacBride's earlier nonchalance during his meeting with the barrister John Ronayne proved misplaced. The precise circumstances of MacBride's involvement in the Rising are unclear.[34] His own testimony suggests that he had little part in planning the Rising and only happened upon Thomas MacDonagh en route to Jacob's factory on Easter

Monday and believed it his duty to join in. Ultimately he himself believed that his pro-Boer stance against the British in the South African war was the final straw that led to the confirmation of his sentence by General Sir John Maxwell, a veteran of that war. He was probably correct.

Most of the men who had been sentenced to death that day were taken to Kilmainham Jail, arriving around 8pm. Because of the fact that his trial had run on, Éamonn may have remained in Richmond Barracks or alternatively been transferred to Kilmainham overnight and returned to Richmond Barracks in the morning.[35] Later that night, alone among them, MacBride was told that his sentence had been confirmed. William Cosgrave was in the cell beside Mac-Bride and, when, at daybreak on Friday morning, he heard him being taken out for execution, Cosgrave would have fully expected that it would be his turn next. But that afternoon he heard that his own sentence had been commuted to penal servitude for life.[36]

Friday, 5 May 1916

General Maxwell had confirmed MacBride's sentence in haste. He had been called to Westminster to attend a Cabinet meeting the following day. The politicians in Westminster were growing uneasy at the speed and secrecy with which the executions of the first seven leaders had been carried out. With more, including Éamonn, sentenced to death on

Friday, and boatloads of men being shipped over to prisons in England, Scotland and Wales, General Maxwell received a telegraph from Downing Street warning him to avoid 'anything which might give rise to a charge of hasty procedure or want of due care and deliberation in confirming sentences'. Prime Minister Asquith also warned, presciently, that 'anything like a large number of executions would excite a swift revulsion of feeling', and 'sow the seeds of lasting trouble in Ireland'. The Cabinet ultimately gave Maxwell discretion to continue, subject to the death sentence being inflicted only on 'ringleaders and proven murderers'.[37]

Éamonn, Con Colbert and Sean Heuston, together with Michael Mallin, whose court martial took place on Friday, had to wait anxiously until Maxwell returned to learn whether he would confirm their sentence, or whether they had any hope of it being commuted to a lengthy prison term. The decision of the Cabinet made it almost impossible that Éamonn's sentence, at least, would be commuted. He himself was under no illusions, although he tried to allay Áine's fears. Some time that Friday afternoon, he scribbled a note to her:

> Writing in English to say I am well but expecting the worst – which may be the best. Everyone amazingly cheerful and resigned to their several fates. Can see there is a 'reign of terror' outside. Everyone seems to be here in Richmond Barracks. Lily probably in Kilmainham. I saw her. Not much comfort here, but I sleep well and we get

ample rations. Make Mrs B's [Áine's mother] mind easy. I'm sure she's worrying. Tell Rónán to be a good boy and remember Easter 1916 forever. I'm in excellent form. I'm sure all relatives etc. will be looked after later on. Don't expect you'll see no. 2 [Dolphin Terrace] as you left it. Probably looted by this. *Adieu* or *au revoir* – I don't know which. Mr M A Corrigan, Solicitor, 3 St Andrews Street (undertakers also) might get you or Richard to see me. Éamonn Ceannt

Later, at 4pm, he wrote again:

Trial closed. I expect the death sentence, which better men have already suffered. My only regret is that I have now no longer an opportunity of showing how I think of you now that the chance of seeing you again is so remote. I shall die like a man for Ireland's sake. Éamonn Ceannt.[38]

Saturday, 6 May 1916

Éamonn spent the weekend in Kilmainham Jail, awaiting confirmation of his fate. The exact day and time of his transfer from Richmond Barracks to Kilmainham is difficult to establish. One report puts it late on Friday evening.[39] Gerald Doyle, however, recalled seeing Éamonn in Richmond Barracks on Saturday, 6 May, both before and after Doyle's own court martial.

Even at this late stage, there continued to be some doubt in the official mind as to Éamonn's whereabouts and rank during Easter week. Gerald Doyle's court martial took place on Saturday morning and he later maintained that the authorities were still trying to 'fix Willie Cosgrave as the Officer in Charge of the South Dublin Union'.[40] This is not surprising since Cosgrave was with Éamonn at the surrender to General Lowe and, as a well-known Sinn Féin Councillor on Dublin Corporation, he had a higher public profile than Éamonn, a clerk in the same organisation. Cosgrave's Sinn Féin affiliation would also have counted against him – the Rising was now mistakenly fixed in the public mind as a 'Sinn Féin rebellion'.

On Saturday evening, Éamonn at last had a visit from his beloved wife, Áine. She had been waiting anxiously for news of Éamonn all week. With the city still in chaos, it was impossible to separate fact from rumour. The military were everywhere and police cordons were erected across the main thoroughfares. It was difficult to get around or through the city. She spent most of the week on the south side with Caitlín Brugha in Dartry, while the rest of the Kent family were clustered on the north side around Drumcondra.

The family's worst fears seemed to be realised when they read of the executions of Pearse, MacDonagh and Plunkett. However, Wednesday's paper reported that Prime Minister Asquith, in the House of Commons, had said that Éamonn was sentenced to three years' penal servitude. Michael Kent wrote in his diary: 'For the time being our hearts bounded with joy.'[41] When Áine read the newspaper reports, she was delighted and relieved but, charitably, 'thought it very hard that Thomas MacDonagh, who to my mind had not been so deeply involved until the last moment, should have suffered execution'.[42]

On Thursday, the day on which Éamonn's trial started, they got their first real news when the Lord Mayor, Sir James Gallagher, told Michael Kent that he had seen Éamonn during his visit to Richmond Barracks and that he had been brought in for trial.[43]

On Friday, Áine, who was still harbouring the hope that her own husband was en route to prison rather than a death sentence, 'piloted Mrs Brugha to the Union to see her husband'. On her way back to the Brugha home in Dartry, she called into her own home in Dolphin Terrace. Éamonn's fears, that it would no longer be as Áine had left it on Easter Monday morning, were realised. She found the little house:

> … a wreck, having been raided by the military. Our food had been spilt, that is to say tea and sugar were inches deep on the floor, our tinned foods had been taken out and evidently a bayonet run through each of them, and doors and windows were smashed, but these had been boarded up by neighbours. The brass buttons, which I had removed from

Éamonn's uniform, to replace them by green, had been taken from the place I had left them.

Áine's neighbours told her that a young woman who lived next door had been so frightened by the raid that she'd 'had a seizure and died immediately'.[44]

Even if the object of the raid had been to collect evidence of Éamonn's role in the Rising, as the appropriation of his uniform buttons suggests, the wanton destruction was evidence of the deep-seated anger felt by the British military towards the leaders of the Rising – a venture they saw as treasonable. The Ceannt house was not the only one to be ransacked.

Áine set out early on Friday morning to cross the city to Éamonn's sister Nell's home in Drumcondra. That evening they went together to the Capuchin priests in Church Street who had been ministering to the men in Richmond Barracks and Kilmainham Jail. Word had gone out around Dublin that the Capuchins were acting as go-betweens for the prisoners and their families. There they met Fr Albert. He warned them not to believe what they read in the newspapers and to be careful with what they themselves said. Unable to get back across the city to Dartry, Áine spent the night in Drumcondra with Nell. Early on Saturday morning, not wishing to outstay her welcome with Caitlín Brugha, she gathered up her mother, her son, Rónán, and their belongings and went to join Éamonn's family in Drumcondra. Áine's sister

Lily, who had been with the garrison in Marrowbone Lane, was still detained in Kilmainham Jail with the other Cumann na mBan prisoners.

In Drumcondra, Áine stayed with Nell and her husband, Jack Casey. Éamonn's just-widowed brother, retired RIC Constable JP, was also staying in the house. The other Kent brothers, Michael and Dick, lived with their families nearby.

Later that day, Áine met with John Ronayne, the barrister who had advised Éamonn. He told her that Éamonn's trial was over and that 'he had to take his hat off to Éamonn for being so cool'.[45] Áine and Dick took a taxi to Richmond Barracks where – following an introduction from an old friend, Johnny Foley, who had been Secretary to the Lord Mayor – the Provost Marshal, Lord Powerscourt, greeted them with civility. He didn't know the result of Éamonn's court martial, but sent Áine to Kilmainham Jail with a note to the Governor asking that they be given permission to visit Éamonn.[46]

On Saturday night, Áine saw Éamonn for about twenty-five minutes in his cell in Kilmainham. The cell was upstairs in the prison, probably No. 88.[47] There was no seating in the cell, no bedding, not even a bed of straw. Éamonn's Sam Browne belt was gone and his uniform was torn. A soldier stood at the door all through the visit and they had no privacy. When Áine asked Éamonn whether the Rising had 'been an awful fiasco', he insisted, 'No, it was the biggest thing since '98.'

Although Éamonn certainly expected that General Maxwell would confirm his death sentence as soon as he returned from London, he didn't want to take all hope away from Áine. In an attempt to establish the truth about the newspaper report of his prison sentence, he told her to contact Sir Charles Cameron, the former Corporation Chief Medical Officer. Áine was still haunted by the knowledge that Muriel MacDonagh had been unable to visit her husband, Thomas, on the night before his execution and before she left him, she made Éamonn promise that, whatever happened, he would send for her.[48]

Sunday, 7 May

On Sunday, while Éamonn and his fellow prisoners were attending Mass in the chapel in Kilmainham Jail, Áine made her forlorn way back across the city to Sir Charles Cameron's home in Ballsbridge. He could throw no light on Wednesday's newspaper report but promised to find out what he could. That afternoon, Áine was sitting in Nell's back room when a soldier from the Royal Dublin Fusiliers arrived at the door. Her worst fears were allayed when he turned out to be on a mission from Éamonn's brother Bill. Based with his regiment of the Royal Dublin Fusiliers in Cork, Bill was out of touch with events in Dublin and was anxious for news of his brother. Áine passed on what news she could and the man promised to relay it back.[49] Áine's relief was short-lived.

Prime Minister Asquith was right in expecting that the executions would revolt Irish public opinion and 'sow the seeds of lasting trouble in Ireland'. During Sunday afternoon, Fr Aloysius sent a message to John Dillon, the IPP MP. Dillon fundamentally disagreed with the methods used during the Rising but admired the courage and conviction of the leaders. He promised to do anything he could to prevent further executions. Dillon telegraphed to John Redmond in London but, for Éamonn, Colbert, Heuston and Mallin, it was already too late.[50]

As soon as General Maxwell returned from London, he confirmed their death sentences. Their executions were scheduled for daybreak the following day. During the latter part of Sunday, following the procedure laid down for the executions, the four men were moved to new cells, closer to the execution yard. Éamonn was in cell no. 20. A note that he wrote to Áine in that cell at 4pm suggests that Éamonn knew Maxwell's verdict at that stage.

Éamonn was meticulous to the last about setting his affairs in order. He told Áine to tell their son, Rónán, that his father was dying for Ireland and that he would understand when he 'gets sense and wisdom'. He told Rónán to take care of his mother. He wrote his final will, leaving all he possessed to his wife. He advised Áine to cash in his two insurance policies, to see if there was any help available from his old colleagues in the Dublin Municipal Officers' Association, and to get his brother Dick to help her to access financial assistance from any Dependants' Fund that might be organised. He left his watch chain to Rónán and asked Áine to give Mick (Michael), Richard (Dick), Nell, Lily, Mrs Brennan, John P (JP) and Bill 'some small token of me with my blessing'.[51]

At approximately 10pm that Sunday night, the summons that Áine had been dreading all week arrived. An army officer knocked at the door of Nell's house, this time with news for Áine that her husband wanted to see herself and Nell. Dick was waiting for them in the car. They went on to collect Michael.

Michael Kent's diary provides a graphic account of that terrible night. He had been sitting at home with his boots off when:

> A knock came to the front door and an official envelope was handed into me. 'On His Majesty's Service.' Inside a few lines from the Governor of Kilmainham Jail to say my brother, Éamonn, wished to see me. I never in my whole life experienced my heart sinking right down into my boots 'till that night. I knew 'twas all up with poor Ned [Éamonn]. Quickly I got ready, and, with a few comforting words from Mammy [his wife, Julia], I went out into the wild wet night and was shown into the waiting motor car by a policeman, the driver being a soldier. Inside were poor Éamonn's wife, Fanny [Áine], also Nell and Dick. We were all as dumb as dogs. The car was stopped every quarter of a mile or so by

sentries in the middle of the road, their rifles pointing and bayonet fixed. 'Halt! Who comes there?' Then the grinding noise as the motor pulled up, the policeman's answer (as he stuck his head out sideways under the flap): 'King's Messenger! King's Messenger!' The half audible answer of the sentry as he stepped out of the way: the grinding noise again, and then away into the darkness, only to repeat the same process again and again and again. The last two days and nights, and today, it has rained without ceasing. Arrived at the Jail we stumbled across closhes [sic] of water, were challenged through the grill gate, admitted, and handed up our letters, names registered, lanterns procured, and then down the dark corridors into the bowels of this hellish abode, 'till recently, of criminals, across a wide hall, wary of the raised gratings in the floor and up to the iron grill and door of one of the endless cells. Great God! To think poor Ned is locked and barred in that silent tomb. The keys rattle, doors open, and we enter to find poor Éamonn after rising from a little table, lit by one candle, where his correspondence is arrayed, several envelopes addressed in his fine clear style, with – apparently – letters enclosed, and one large sheet partly written on. He received us and shook hands quite calmly and, after a word or two, put his arm around Áine, bent down with a sweet smile and kissed her lovingly. They were lovers again – he wanted those few minutes – and seeing them wrapped in one another, we turned away and conversed near the two sentries at the door (who stayed all the time) while Éamonn and Áine sat on the edge of the low plank bed in the corner, and had their last quarter of an hour on earth together. We were allowed 20 minutes. A few minutes before time was up Ned called us over and we knelt around him for our last chat. He said Father McCarthy, who was with him, hinted there was hope of a reprieve, and the soldiers made such remarks as 'It's a long way to Tipperary'. Eamonn spoke in a quiet matter-of-fact-I'm-merely-telling-you-what-I've-heard sort of a way; there was something strained in his manner and, it was evident from his letter afterwards, he had absolutely no hope but wanted to keep up poor Fanny's heart, and ours too, fearing a scene. I never saw him look so well, he was wearing the grand green uniform of the Irish Volunteers, his moustache was trimmed and his face looked tanned and healthy. His was the grand, noble face: nothing in his life to be ashamed of: his gentle kindly eyes looked out calmly on God's world, fearing none save God. When the sentry said kindly that time was up, we stood up and had a few words more: Éamonn said he asked for Father Augustine and he hadn't come. When this was told to the sentry by Dick he offered to take him to the Commandant to see about it and this appeared to please Éamonn. Then we shook Éamonn heartily by the hand: Dick saying when Éamonn mentioned Fanny that he would look after her: after he kissed Áine, we passed out of the cell but I waited to tell him the news of a great fund of a Million dollars opened in America and finally I said, 'We'll go home and pray for you till 4 o'clock in the morning.' To this he answered, gratefully, 'Aye do.' After we left the cell, and before the sentry shut the door, I looked back at poor Ned and that picture I shall bear with me to the end. He stood sideways, right side towards me, the candles showing him up clearly from the exterior darkness, looking down at the little table where he had been writing, wrapped in thought, silent, a pucker at the base of the fore-head, just at the nose. My heart welled up with infinite pity for the poor, poor lad that I brought to school, but, control-ling myself, I said out loudly, almost fiercely, '*Beannacht Dé leat*' [God's blessings on you] and back he answered at once in his old calm, quiet way, as if he were saying Good-Night, '*Go soirbhidh Dia duit*' [May God favour you]. Dick saw the Commandant and learned that Fr Augustine had been sent for and would be with Éamonn at one o'clock, and went back and told this to poor Ned, so that he saw him last of us all. The same dumb, weary drive home – twice as long as the car broke down and we had to wait for another at Conyngham Road.[52]

During their private conversation, Éamonn told Áine that all the talk of a reprieve, and the fact that only one execution had taken place on Friday, was disturbing him. He told her,

'I was quite prepared to walk out of this at a quarter to four in the morning but all this talk has upset me.' Áine found out the following day that, when Dick Kent spoke to the Commandant about Fr Augustine, he was told to tell his brother that 'there is no reprieve'. It was up to Dick then to confirm the news that his brother had all along expected.[53]

When his family left, Éamonn spent some time with Fr Augustine before the stalwart priest went to comfort the other condemned men. Éamonn returned to the half-written sheet of paper that Michael had seen in his cell. It was a letter in which he addressed the people of Ireland. Uniquely among the leaders of the Rising, he expressed his deep regret at being ordered to surrender. To the Irish people he wrote:

Kilmainham Jail, 7 May 1916

I leave for the guidance of other Irish revolutionaries who may tread the path which I have trod this advice, never to treat with the enemy, never to surrender at his mercy but to fight to a finish. I see nothing gained but grave disaster caused by the surrender which has marked the end of the Irish Insurrection of 1916 – so far at least as Dublin is concerned. The enemy has not cherished one generous thought for those who, with little hope, with poor equipment, and weak in numbers, withstood his forces for one glorious week. Ireland has shown she is a Nation. This generation can claim to have raised sons as brave as any that went before. And in the years to come, Ireland will honour those who risked all for her honour at Easter in 1916. I bear no ill will against those whom I have fought. I have found the common soldiers and the higher officers human and companionable, even the English who were actually in the fight against us. Thank God soldiering for Ireland has opened my heart and made me see poor humanity where I expected to see only scorn and reproach. I have met the man who escaped from me by a ruse under the Red Cross. But I do not regret having withheld my fire. He gave me cakes!!

I wish to record the magnificent gallantry and fearless, calm determination of the men who fought with me. All, all, were simply splendid. Even I knew no fear, nor panic, nor shrank from no risk [sic], even as I shrink not now from the death which faces me at daybreak. I hope to see God's face even for a moment in the morning. His will be done.

All here are very kind. My poor wife saw me yesterday and bore up – so my warder told me, even after she left my presence. Poor Áine, poor Rónán. God is their only shield now that I am removed and God is a better shield than I. I have just seen Áine, Nell, Richard and Mick and bade them a conditional good-bye. Even now they have hope!

Éamonn Ceannt[54]

His last letter was to Áine, the wife and love who had supported him unquestioningly from their earliest days together. It was written at 2.30am:

My dearest wife Áine

Not wife but widow before these lines reach you. I am here without hope of this world and without fear, calmly awaiting the end. I have had Holy Communion and Fr Augustine has been with me and will be back again. Dearest 'silly little Fanny'. My poor little sweetheart of – how many – years ago. Ever my comforter, God comfort you now. What can I say? I die a noble death, for Ireland's freedom. Men and women will vie with one another to shake your dear hand. Be proud of me as I am and ever was of you. My cold exterior was but a mask. It has served me in these last days. You have a duty to me and to Rónán, that is to live. My dying wishes are that you shall remember your state of health, work only as much as may be necessary and freely accept the little attentions which in due time will be showered upon you. You will be – you are, the wife of one of the leaders of the Revolution. Sweeter still, you are my little child, my dearest pet, my sweetheart of the hawthorn hedges and Summer's eves. I remember all and I banish all that I may be strong and die bravely. I have one hour to live, then God's judgement and, through his infinite mercy, a place near your poor Granny and my mother and father and Jem and all the fine old Irish Catholics who went through the scourge of similar misfortune from this Vale of Tears into the Promised Land. *Bíodh misneach agat a stoirín mo Chroidhe. Tóig do cheann agus bíodh foighde agat go bhfeicfimíd a chéile arís i bhFlaithis Dé tusa, mise agus Rónán beag beag bocht. Adieu,* Éamonn[55]

When Fr Augustine returned from supporting the other condemned men and witnessing their executions, Éamonn gave him the letters to deliver to Áine. Fr Augustine walked with Éamonn down the corridor to the jail yard. Éamonn's hands were then tied behind his back and a cloth around his eyes. A small square of white paper was pinned to his coat to act as a target. The firing party officer and the firing party of twelve men stood at a distance of ten paces.[56] Éamonn held Fr Augustine's crucifix in his hands and was seated on a soapbox in front of the firing squad.

Éamonn Ceannt was executed between 3.45am and 4.05am on Monday, 8 May 1916.[57] His last words were 'My Jesus Mercy'.[58]

Although no longer able to be with him, Éamonn's wife and family kept vigil throughout the night. When Michael got home it was almost midnight. He said the rosary with his wife and her family. After his wife Julia had gone to bed, Michael prayed on.

I prayed on as I had never prayed before … I said five rosaries, as many or more litanies, and numerous other prayers … Sometimes kneeling, occasionally sitting and, every hour or so, going into the parlour to look out between the laths of the venetian blind at the coming dawn for Éamonn's last earthly dawn. Coming on to 4 o'clock, I redoubled my prayers and made special appeals to the great object of my particular devotion, the Sacred Heart of Jesus. When 3.45 passed I said to myself, 'Well, I suppose it's all over now, and I won't know a thing about it – no matter – I'll pray on until 4 o'clock and then I'll go to bed.' So I started off once more when, in the perfect stillness of the morning, soon afterwards, I heard clearly the faint click of a rifle: 'twas faint, but in that solemn stillness, perfectly distinct. Instantly my whole nerves seemed to contract up into my heart and I pulled out my watch – seven minutes to four. I put out the lights and, as I went upstairs and into bed I cried bitterly from the depths of my heart. But God's will be done.[59]

Over in Nell's house, Áine too was praying through the night. At 6am, as the curfew was lifted, she and Nell made their way to Church Street. The rain had stopped and it was a glorious summer morning. Fr Augustine, exhausted from his traumatic night, had said Mass and gone to bed. Áine told them not to disturb him, but said that she only wanted to know the truth about her husband. She was told, 'He is gone to Heaven.'[60]

Chapter Ten

· · · · · ·

Aftermath

After the final executions on 12 May, General Maxwell ordered that the bodies of Éamonn and his fellow rebels should not be released to their families. He feared that the graves would be turned into martyrs' shrines to which annual processions would be made. He ordered that the executed men be buried in a mass grave in Arbour Hill Prison, in quicklime and without coffins.[1]

On the face of it, Maxwell seemed to have had little to fear in terms of a public reaction. The Unionist newspapers were scathing in their denunciation of the rebellion and its leaders, and even the nationalist papers initially came out in support of the executions. Appearances could be deceiving, however. Maxwell, who had been chosen to suppress the rebellious sentiment in the aftermath of the Rising precisely because he had no 'history' in Ireland, had little understanding of how quickly and fundamentally the national mood could change. He soon became aware that the politicians were getting nervous about events in Dublin. Immediately after the first executions, John Redmond of the IPP, a man who had unequivocally condemned the rebels, warned that the executions would destroy all hope of constitutional politics.

Prime Minister Herbert Asquith was so concerned at the potential public outcry that he initially postponed the executions of MacDiarmada and Connolly before finally agreeing that they should go ahead.[2] After the two were executed at daybreak on 12 May, he travelled to Dublin to review the situation for himself.

The process of transforming Irish public opinion in favour of the rebels gathered impetus when thousands of other men and a small number of women, most of whom had done little other than support the principle of independence for Ireland, were arrested. Maxwell was fearful that the bush fire of the Rising would reignite, and he had instituted a countrywide sweep of 'all dangerous Sinn Féiners … [including] those who have taken an active part in the movement although not in the present rebellion'.[3] Some 3,430 men and 79 women were arrested, among them Arthur Griffith, the Sinn Féin party leader, who had played no part in the Rising. John Dillon, Deputy Leader of the IPP, warned Maxwell that such indiscriminate actions would 'madden the Irish people … [and] if Ireland were governed by men out of Bedlam, you could not pursue a more insane policy'.

The truth of Dillon's assertion fully dawned on the Prime Minister when, shortly after his arrival in Ireland, he realised that most of the remaining prisoners were young country lads who should never have been arrested in the first place. There were no further executions and 1,424 of the 3,430 men arrested were released almost immediately.

However, there were still two thousand Irishmen and a handful of women in prisons in England, Scotland and Wales. Better than any other training college, their experience there would, in time, equip them to pick up the baton of the men of 1916.[4]

Before long, public opinion began to change. This was brought about by the cumulative effect of the executions and internments, together with the restrictions of martial law, and the murder, while he was trying to stop the looting, of the pacifist and women's rights advocate Francis Sheehy-Skeffington by a British officer.

On Sunday, 18 June, Áine and other family members attended a Requiem Mass for Éamonn at Church Street. Fr Albert and Fr Aloysius told the congregation about the piety and bravery of Éamonn and the other men whom they had accompanied to their deaths. Requiem Masses were held around the city for all of the executed men and provided a focus for the growing sympathy for the rebels. They would also prove to be an inspiration for many of those who later followed in their path. The Roman Catholic hierarchy had initially condemned the Rising but, influenced by the executions and arrests, some of the bishops were changing their stance. Although there remained a deep-seated unease with

the use of physical force, gradually physical force republicanism became fused in the minds of many people with 'the
more populist faith and fatherland tradition.'[5]

Supporters of constitutional politics among the nationalist community began to wonder whether they had been
misguided and whether people like Éamonn might have
been right: that only the threat of violence – from the Ulster
Unionists – or the very *act* of violence by the Irish Volunteers, could bring about Home Rule. As the historian Ronan
Fanning has argued, 'It was a time when violence and the
threat of violence trumped democratic politics.'[6]

It was not long before all sides of the nationalist community
began to come together to support the dependants of the men
who had taken part in the Rising. Áine Ceannt and the other
widows, mothers, sisters and children of the executed men – as
well as the wives and dependants of the men still in prison –
had, in most cases, been left virtually penniless. In Áine's case,
her home had also been ransacked and she was living with her
in-laws. On the day after Éamonn's execution Michael Kent
accompanied Áine and Rónán to the office of the City Treasurer to collect a cheque for £4 14s., which brought Éamonn's
pay up to the day of his death.[7] But when she tried to cash in
Éamonn's insurance policy, the Scottish Amicable Life Assurance Society advised her that 'in view of the circumstances of
the death of the assured' they were under no liability in respect
of the life insurance policy taken out by her husband.[8]

The DMOA, the professional body in which Éamonn had been hugely involved, recorded a vote of sympathy 'with Mrs Kent on the death of Mr E Kent and with Mrs MacBride on the death of Mr J MacBride' but declined to establish a general fund for the relief of dependants in distress after the rebellion. It was only at the annual general meeting the next December, and following protests from one of the officials, who was also a member of the IRB, that the Association approved some financial assistance for Éamonn's widow and child.[9]

The various groups that emerged to help those left destitute eventually merged to form the Irish National Aid and Volunteer Dependants' Fund (INAVDF). It was this fund that ultimately provided Áine and Rónán, as well as the other dependants, with a measure of financial security. Áine received support from various sources that provided her with an annual income of approximately £60–£75. This was more than many widows got at the time, but compares poorly with Éamonn's income from the Corporation at the time of his death of £220 per annum.[10]

Her own work on the committee of the INAVDF introduced Áine, who had previously lived a relatively private, domestic life, to a nationwide organisation that was charged with dispersing significant amounts of money sent from all four corners of the globe. It was under the patronage of the Roman Catholic Church, and its committee included public figures and professional men. For Áine Ceannt, this was the first step towards a new public role that she could never have anticipated in the early days of her marriage to Éamonn.

On his return from prison in England, Michael Collins was appointed to the post of paid Secretary to the INAVDF.[11] As well as being an extremely efficient administrator – Áine called him 'an untiring worker' – Collins and others were soon using the fund, and its contacts with the returned internees, to revitalise the struggle for an independent Ireland which Éamonn and his colleagues had started. While Áine sat on the committee, her sister Lily worked with the fund as Secretary to the Distribution Committee and helped with the task of finding jobs for the internees after their release. Both women remained closely involved with Cumann na mBan. The following year, 1917, Áine was elected Honorary Treasurer and later Vice-President, a post that she held until 1925. Lily was a member of the Executive Committee and in 1918 became the first paid Secretary of the organisation.[12] In October 1917, at the first Árd Fheis of the Sinn Féin Party after the Rising, Áine and three other members of Cumann na mBan were co-opted onto the party's Standing or Executive Committee. In 1918 Áine successfully contested an election for the Rathmines Urban District Council on behalf of Sinn Féin, and, in 1920, was elected its Vice-Chairman.

During the War of Independence Áine acted as an arbitrator for Dáil Éireann's Labour Department in wage disputes between employers and employees.[13] While much of this work took place in Dublin, it also took Áine to various parts of the country. On one occasion she visited Castleconnell, near Limerick, to arbitrate in a dispute between the owner of a fishery and his workers. While there she broke her ankle. During the long journey back to Dublin, the car in which they were travelling was stopped and searched several times by the military. The confidential files escaped detection because they were being used as a 'cushion' for Áine's broken ankle.[14]

Áine's ankle came in useful again shortly afterwards when her house was raided by the Black and Tans during a search for Michael Collins. While they were looking in the wrong place for Collins, they might have found some incriminating papers that Lily had brought home about her work of finding employment for former members of the RIC who had been involved in a mutiny in Listowel. Áine, with her broken ankle propped up in front of her, sat on the papers, which remained safe during the search of the house.[15]

Lily was working at the time in the Department of Labour under the auspices of Countess Markievicz as Minister for Labour. Countess Markievicz had decided to set up an employment bureau for the men of the IRA and the women of Cumann na mBan. Lily, who had previously been occupied through the INAVDF in helping the former internees find new employment opportunities, was put in charge of the bureau. She established a dressmaking workroom in the premises of the Irish Women Workers' Union, which was

soon a hive of activity. One of Lily's more unusual assign-
ments was on behalf of Michael Collins who needed to find
a reliable parlourmaid for Mr Alfred Cope in Dublin Castle.[16]
Cope was a senior member of the Dublin Castle administration and it was a considerable advantage for Collins to have
his own spy in Cope's household. During the War of Independence, Lily, like other members of Cumann na mBan,
also acted as a courier and helped to move wounded men
who were on the run from houses and hospitals that were no
longer considered to be 'safe'.[17]

The sisters still lived together, having moved from Dolphin's Barn to Oakley Road in Ranelagh. Their home,
which was frequently raided, provided a refuge for men
and women on the run prior to and during the War of
Independence.

In 1921 Áine was appointed to the post of Acting Secretary (the Secretary having been arrested) to the General
Council of County Councils.[18] She also acted as a district
judge, initially for the South City area, and then for Rathmines and Rathgar, in the courts established by the Dáil
(the Provisional Government set up after the 1918 general
election). The Dáil Courts were established in August 1919;
the judges were appointed by the Dáil and were paid for
their services. They were required to swear allegiance to
the Republic.

When the War of Independence ended on 11 July 1921,

peace negotiations between Dáil Éireann and the government at Westminster eventually led to the negotiation of a Treaty in December 1921. Lily acted as a secretarial assistant to the delegation while they were in London.

Like many of the widows and relatives of the 1916 leaders, Áine believed that the Treaty had achieved too limited a degree of independence and was a betrayal of all that for which Éamonn had died. Áine was a regular participant in executive committee meetings of Sinn Féin after the signing of the Anglo-Irish Treaty and worked diligently with those Republicans opposed to the Treaty. She chaired the Cumann na mBan meeting at which it was discussed and overwhelmingly rejected. She and Lily took the Republican side in the Civil War that followed (June 1922 to May 1923). Lily worked with the Republican publicity staff and was arrested in the offices of Sinn Féin in November 1922. She was held prisoner in Kilmainham Jail, Mountjoy Jail and the North Dublin Union.[19]

Lily remained in jail until October 1923, during which time Áine's house was frequently raided. Writing to Lily in March 1923, Áine told her that 'all the books were scattered down the stairs'. Áine got the house back in order only to be raided again 'by troops in mufti. They did not remain long as there is nothing now to raid except the debris collected in the hall.' Windows were smashed and Áine's mother was 'perished, sitting in the kitchen with no window'. Many of Éamonn's papers were destroyed and Áine mourned the loss of the little gold brooch that Éamonn had brought her from Paris.[20]

Just as the Easter Rising of 1916 had left many distressed widows and dependants, so too had the War of Independence and the subsequent Civil War. When the Civil War came to an end, both Áine and Lily gradually withdrew from republican politics. Áine devoted the remainder of her public life to working with the Irish White Cross for the relief of children who had lost their fathers and breadwinners during the violence of the revolutionary decade. She published an account of the work of that organisation, *The Story of the Irish White Cross, 1920–1947*, in 1948.[21] Áine died in February 1954. She was in poor health and heartbroken by the deaths of her two sisters, Lily and Kathleen, both of whom died in the same month, May 1948.

Áine's son, Rónán, obeyed his father's last wish and remained with his mother throughout her life, initially in Oakley Road, Ranelagh, and later in Churchtown. He attended Trinity College and qualified as a solicitor in 1935. He never married and died childless in 1974.

The difficulty of being the son of a hero was touchingly portrayed by Rónán in a letter written to a friend of his parents, Máire nic Shiúbhlaigh, that was recently published in the *Irish Examiner*:

From time to time, for years past, I have wondered if mamy [sic] was, in a way, not disappointed in me for not having shown myself as fine a man as my father was … It might have seemed to her that my lack of forcefulness etc., as compared with my father's courage was a bit of a 'let-down'.[22]

Even in later life, a slight tinge of bureaucratic unease hovered over Áine and Rónán as the widow and son of a 'rebel'. During the Second World War, Ireland remained neutral but tensions were high and the government was on the alert for any signs of German spies. Áine and Rónán were living in their home, Inis Ealga, in Churchtown, when, in June 1940, the Garda Siochána received reports that:

Suspicion has been aroused regarding visitors at unusual hours at 'Inis Ealga', the residence of Éamonn [this should read *Rónán* but appears to be a Freudian slip on the part of the Gardaí], Solicitor, Law Department of Dublin Corporation and his widowed mother.

The Gardaí were concerned that an amateur wireless enthusiast had picked up messages in morse code from 'somewhere in the Dundrum area'. The Garda report stated that several sources had suggested that:

Mr Ceannt is very interested in Pro-Nazi ideas and he may be used by foreign sources for their own purposes. Subject is the son of one of the 1916 leaders who was executed by the British and is stated to be a staunch supporter of the elected Government and the policy of neutrality but information suggests otherwise. There is no suspicion of IRA connection on the part of Mr Ceannt.

The military made certain technical tests in the area and in June the Ceannt house was searched by military intelligence. Rónán received them politely. He had been listening peacefully to a musical broadcast – the gramophone was equipped to receive radio programmes from abroad but not to transmit. Rónán assured the search party that he was not at all interested in pro-Nazi ideas and that he would be 'the first to notify the Gardaí of anything he might learn regarding invasion'![23]

Conclusion

Éamonn Ceannt's participation in the Easter Rising of 1916 has been somewhat a mystery; he has only appeared sporadically in many of the works about the revolutionary period with the honourable exception of William Henry's biography, *Supreme Sacrifice: The Story of Éamonn Ceannt 1881– 1916*.[24] Where his role has been documented, the focus has been on what he did rather than why he did it. He has been described as 'a more shadowy figure than the other leaders',[25] 'more naturally a physical force man than any of the other leaders',[26] and 'a frustrated young Dublin clerk … [who] was almost fanatically devoted to the cause'.[27]

Unlike some of his colleagues, there is no evidence that Éamonn had any interest in making a 'blood sacrifice'. He was no romantic intellectual, nor was he a teacher, a committed socialist or a despotic revolutionary. A committed cultural nationalist, Éamonn was a highly intelligent, capable, meticulous bureaucrat turned soldier, with a strong sense of duty and of right and wrong. Although not a committed socialist, he was a 'staunch believer in the need for organisation in defence of one's rights'.[28]

The establishment of the Irish Volunteers in November 1913 meant that Éamonn at last had an 'Irish army' that he could join with a clear conscience. Even then Éamonn publicly communicated his hope that the Volunteers would not have to fight.[29] It was the outbreak of the war in Europe – and the immense propaganda campaign that resulted in thousands of Irish men joining the British Army – that led Éamonn to believe in the inevitability of armed conflict between the Irish Volunteers and the British Army. Once the war had started, and he was appointed to the Military Council of the IRB, he was irrevocably committed to a policy of physical force.

It was in his combined roles as Commandant of the 4th Battalion of the Irish Volunteers and member of the IRB Military Council that Éamonn found his true destiny. He reached maturity during a time and place where militarism was glorified and where a man was expected to do his duty by defending his country – if necessary by fighting and dying in that cause. He genuinely believed that he was part of a conventional Irish army engaged in a legitimate form of warfare.[30]

And he was good at it. The men who served under him recognised him as an excellent leader. Once the Rising took place he remained 'cool and cheerful' under pressure.[31] Apart from his leadership strengths, however, Éamonn's military strategy, like that of the other rebel leaders, cannot go unchallenged. The historian Fearghal McGarry has pointed out that the Military Council's decision to stage the Rising in densely populated parts of Dublin's inner city conflicted with their perception of themselves as a conventional military force fighting by conventional means. He questioned, in particular, the morality underlying the choice of the South Dublin Union – a small 'town' with 3,000 inhabitants, many of whom were mentally and physically vulnerable.[32]

In the case of the South Dublin Union, the evidence suggests that, although the speed with which the attack took place made it impossible to evacuate inmates, genuine attempts were made to protect them from the worst of the fighting. In spite of the ferocity of the two main engagements and the ongoing sniper activity throughout the week, the toll of dead and injured was considerably less than might have been expected. The Minutes of the Board of Guardians of the South Dublin Union recorded, on 17 May 1916:

> That as a result of the late disturbances there were killed, or
> died of their wounds, two British Officers, three soldiers, one

RIC man, six Irish Volunteers or Sinn Féiners, and Nurse
Keogh. Nine wounded soldiers and five Sinn Féiners were
treated in [the] hospitals. All have now been removed save
one (a Sinn Féiner). Three male inmates were also killed.[33]

Militarily, the Union provided a strategically located and
highly defensible site and the tactics adopted by Éamonn,
together with his Vice-Commandant, Cathal Brugha, and the
other senior officers, and the genuine bravery they showed
in their implementation, enabled them to hold out against
vastly superior forces on two separate occasions. The fact
remains, however, that on both these occasions the British
military failed to press home their advantage. On the Tuesday
of Easter week and later on the Thursday, the British forces
were withdrawn by their superiors rather than overcome by
the Irish Volunteers.

In the end, Éamonn was not an experienced military tac-
tician, nor was he an intellectual, nor a sophisticated political
analyst. He was a committed activist and a propagandist who
believed that an Ireland governed by a parliament elected
by the people of Ireland on behalf of the people of Ireland
would provide economic and social independence of action
that no Westminster government would ever permit.

He obeyed the order of his peers on the Provisional Government to surrender, albeit reluctantly, but claimed and
won the right to march his garrison to the point of surrender as a disciplined force of soldiers. In so doing he maxim-

ised the propaganda value of his final act as a commandant in an Irish army.

In his final letter he expressed the hope that 'in the years to come, Ireland will honour those who risked all for her honour at Easter in 1916.' In the century since his execution, the memory of the men and women who fought and died during Easter Week 1916 has waxed and waned. Their actions and their legacy have been celebrated and repudiated in turn. This book has sought to assess the actions and the motivations of one man, Éamonn Ceannt, in the context of his time and place. It is based on the evidence of his diaries, letters, articles and speeches and on the memories of those who knew him.[34]

Be skilled in the art of war so that there may be no war. Live plainly so that you may be strong and hardy. Be not given to vain boasting. Do not tarry long in taverns, nor take counsel with those who would wish you ill. Keep your own counsel. Be simple, be efficient, be noble, and the world of Ireland is yours …

Éamonn Ceannt, *The Irish Volunteer* inaugural edition, 7 February 1914

Appendix

*'Let those who come after see to it that
his name not be forgotten'*

On 24 April 1917, exactly a year to the day after the Easter Rising
in Dublin, Éamonn's brother, Bill, was killed in action on the Western Front during the Battle of Arras. News of his death reached his
family on 8 May, the anniversary of Éamonn's execution.[1]

Bill, a professional soldier, had spent the war with the 3rd
Reserve Battalion of the Royal Dublin Fusiliers, most of it in
County Cork. The battalion was a training unit for troops before
they were posted to the front. Bill would have seen thousands of
young men going out to war, many of whom, if they came back at
all, returned maimed in mind and body.

Although his family bitterly believed that Bill's final posting was
'because he was poor Éamonn's brother and had sent food into
one of the Sinn Féin prisoners in the barracks at the time of the
Rising', the timing of his posting and the evidence of Bill's own
letters from the front suggest another interpretation.[2]

On 11 September 1916 Bill was posted to France, where he
was attached to the 1st Battalion. The Allied forces, including the
Royal Dublin Fusiliers, had suffered massive losses since the start
of the Battle of the Somme in July 1916 and were drawing heavily on their reserve troops. Although Bill was in his mid-forties,
he had nearly twenty years of experience to contribute and he
was quickly promoted to Acting Company Sergeant Major. In
November, having been seriously wounded during the Battle of

the Somme, he was promoted in the field. A few weeks before he was wounded he wrote to his brother Michael: 'My regiment is just after coming from the Somme for a rest . . . Well, the conditions are fearful . . . Up to your knees in mud and water, practically no cover now on account of the quick advances . . . It has been teeming rain for weeks back and the ever constant thunder of all kinds of shells . . . Dante's Inferno could only be in the halfpenny place.'

In spite of the horrors he was enduring, he told Michael: 'Well, I had to come out, I couldn't see my way to stick it out at home.'[3]

William was lucky to survive his first few months in France. During the Battle of the Somme (1 July to 24 November) the Allies had suffered 400,000 casualties, captured 120 square miles of land, and advanced six miles – forty men killed or wounded for every yard advanced.[4]

When the Allies engaged in a new offensive – the Battle of Arras – in early 1917, Bill's luck finally ran out. On 24 April he was 'struck down in an advance on the enemy lines in France by machine-gun bullets, the latter striking him just at the bottom of the chest ... After dark a "few of the lads" went out and buried him.'[5]

His name was recorded on the Arras Memorial, where the Commonwealth War Graves Commission 'remembers him in perpetuity'. His family received a scroll numbering him among those who answered the call of King and Country. It admonished 'Let those who come after see to it that his name not be forgotten.'[6]

Ironically, the legacy of Easter 1916 in Dublin – his brother Éamonn's 'war' – meant that, except to his family, Bill's name and the names of many thousands of Irish men who were killed and maimed in World War 1 were the names that would, for too many decades, be forgotten.

Notes

CHAPTER ONE

1 Elizabeth Malcolm, *The Irish Policeman* (Dublin, 2006), p129.

2 National Library of Ireland (hereinafter NLI), Papers of Éamonn and Áine Ceannt, and of Kathleen and Lily O'Brennan (hereinafter Ceannt Papers), MS 41,479/8, Transcript of Shorthand Notes taken down by Michael Kent.

3 National Archives of Ireland (hereinafter NAI), RIC General Register of Service, James Kent, Number 27,415.

4 NLI Ceannt Papers MS 41,479/8, Transcript of Shorthand Notes taken down by Michael Kent; NLI Ceannt Papers MS 41,479/8, *Irish Press*, May 1932, Letter from James G Skinner, Clonmel, Co Tipperary; NAI Census of Ireland 1901 and 1911.

5 James Kent was fortunate to be part of the first generation of Irish children to benefit from the establishment of the national school system in 1831, see John Coolahan, *Irish Education: Its History and Structure* (Dublin, 2005), p58.

6 Thomas Fennell, *The Royal Irish Constabulary* ed. Rosemary Fennell (Dublin, 2003), p9.

7 Marriage Certificate of James Kent and Johanna Gallway.

8 Fennell, *The Royal Irish Constabulary* p9. For purposes of comparison, had James remained a farm labourer, he would have earned between 9s to 12s per week (c. £26 per annum), H D Gribbon, *Economic and Social History, 1850-1921* in W E Vaughan Ed. *A New History of Ireland VI, Ireland under the Union 1870-1921*, (Oxford, 2012), p319.

9 Fennell, *The Royal Irish Constabulary*, p40. This ban was lifted following the 1882 Report of the Committee of Inquiry into the Royal Irish Constabulary (1883) – see Elizabeth Malcolm, *The Irish Policeman,* (Dublin, 2006), p135.

10 Fennell, *The Royal Irish Constabulary,* pp8, 14 and 15.

11 Petty Sessions Order Books CSPS 1/4988, 24 October 1872 and CSPS 1/2325, 22 September 1877, www.findmypast.ie accessed 15 October 2012.

12 As above.

13 As above.

14 Malcolm, *The Irish Policeman,* p95.

15 Fennell, *The Royal Irish Constabulary*, p89.

16 Malcolm, *The Irish Policeman,* p94.

17 F S L Lyons, *Ireland since the Famine* (Glasgow, 1973), p165.

18 Fennell, *The Royal Irish Constabulary*, p98.

19 NLI Ceannt Papers MS 41,479/8, What I remember about Éamonn by Michael Kent.

20 Áine Ceannt, BMH WS 264.

21 Kent-Gallagher Family Papers, Draft Article by Lily O'Brennan – possibly the basis for an article in the *Limerick Leader*, Saturday 14 July 1934.

22 Elizabeth Malcolm, *The Irish Policeman,* p170.

23 NAI RIC General Register of Service, James Kent, Number 27,415.

24 Elizabeth Malcolm, *The Irish Policeman,* p212.

25 Kent-Sheehy Family Papers, Kent Family, Short Biographical Details by Rónán Ceannt, 25 January 1973. This family tree, compiled by Rónán, is known to be inaccurate in some respects so cannot be entirely relied upon. It is the only surviving record, however, of Bill Kent's life before he joined the Royal Dublin Fusiliers.

26 NAI RIC General Register of Service, John Patrick Kent, Number 54068.

27 Mary Daly, *Dublin: The Deposed Capital, A Social and Economic History 1860–1914* (Cork, 1984), p1.

28 Daly, *Dublin: The Deposed Capital,* p16.

29 *An Encounter,* in James Joyce, *Dubliners,* Wordsworth Editions Ltd, 1993, London, p10.

30 NLI Ceannt Papers MS 41,479/8, Transcript of Shorthand Notes taken down by Michael Kent.

31 Thom's Directory of Ireland, 1895–1914; Death Certificate of Johanna Kent, 16 February 1895.

32 *Araby*, in James Joyce, *Dubliners*, Wordsworth Editions Ltd (London, 1993), p18.

33 Sean Ó Ceallaigh, BMH WS 1765.

34 Coolahan, *Irish Education*, p61. These prizes were initially intended only for boys but were, following pressure from a delegation led by Belfast womens' rights campaigner Isabella Tod, extended to include girls.

35 NLI Ceannt Papers MS 13,069/44.

36 UCC Multitext project in Irish History, http://multitext.ucc.ie, accessed 24 July 2014.

37 NLI Ceannt Papers MS 13,069/44–45.

38 Death Certificate of Johanna Kent, 16 February 1895.

39 NLI Ceannt Papers MS 41,479/8, What I remember about Éamonn by Michael Kent.

40 NLI Ceannt Papers MS 13,069/44 – this appears to come from notes for an essay or a debate on the merits of education.

41 NLI Ceannt Papers MS 13,069/44, draft letter to a friend.

42 NLI Ceannt Papers MS 13,069/44.

43 Allen Library, Ceannt Collection. E Ceannt Handwritten School Diary.

44 Barry M. Coldrey, *Faith and Fatherland; The Christian Brothers and the Development of Irish Nationalism, 1838–1921* (Dublin, 1988), p113.

45 Allen Library, Ceannt Collection. E Ceannt Handwritten School Diary.

46 *Chums* was a British boys' weekly newspaper that had gained in popularity after serialising Treasure Island by Robert Louis Stevenson in 1894.

47 NLI Ceannt Papers MS 13,069/44–45.

CHAPTER TWO

1 NLI Ceannt Papers MS 41,479/8, Draft article by Lily O'Brennan.

2 Kent-Sheehy Family Papers, Kent Family – Short Biographical Details by Rónán Ceannt, 25 January 1973.

3 NAI 1901 Census of Ireland.

4   Áine Ceannt, BMH WS 264.

5   NLI Ceannt Papers MS 41,479/8, Draft article by Lily O'Brennan.

6   Áine Ceannt, BMH WS 264.

7   Local Government (Ireland) Act, 1898.

8   Daly, *Dublin: The Deposed Capital,* p207.

9   The United Irish League was a nationalist political party. It was originally founded by William O'Brien and, by the early part of the twentieth century had outgrown its agrarian roots to become the main support organisation behind the Irish Parliamentary Party.

10 Dublin City Library and Archive, Dublin Corporation Reports 1900, Vol. 3, p759–762.

11 Dublin City Library and Archive, Reports and Printed Documents of the Corporation of Dublin, 1910, Vol 2, p82 and p216.

12 NLI Ceannt Papers MS 13,069/43, Memorandum and Articles of Association of the Dublin Municipal Officers' Association.

13 Áine Ceannt, BMH WS 264.

14 NLI Ceannt Papers MS 41,489/8, Éamonn Ceannt – An Impression by J Monks, a Corporation Colleague.

15 Áine Ceannt, BMH WS 264.

16 F S L Lyons, *Culture and Anarchy in Ireland, 1890–1939* (Oxford, 1979), pp44–45.

17 Ruth Dudley Edwards, *Patrick Pearse: The Triumph of Failure* (Dublin, 1990), p26.

18 NLI Ceannt Papers MS 41,479/8, Recollections of A Gaelic Leaguer.

19 As above. The fact that contemporaries remembered Éamonn's adoption of the Connaught dialect reflects the underlying fractures within the League that would later lead to fundamental disagreements. The Munster speakers, centered around the Keating Branch, became 'a kind of élite within an élite and disparaged the speakers of other dialects, especially those of Connaught Irish.' See The Gaelic League in Dublin 1913: Twenty Years A-Growing?, talk given by Séamas Ó Maitiú in Dublin City Hall on 9 April 2013.

20 *An Claidheamh Soluis*,Vol, III, No. 2, 23 March 1901, p25.

21 *An Claidheamh Soluis,* Vol. II, no. 33, 27 October 1900, p521.

22 NLI Ceannt Papers MS 41,479/8.

23 As above.

24 NLI Ceannt Papers MS 41,479/8.

25 *An Claidheamh Soluis*,Vol. II, No. 38, 1 December 1900, p603.

26 *An Claidheamh Soluis*,Vol.V, No. 14, 14 June 1903.

27 *An Claidheamh Soluis*,Vol. II, No. 43, 5 January 1901, p684.

28 *An Claidheamh Soluis*,Vol.V, No. 4, 4 April 1903, and Vol.VI, No. 21, 30 July 1904, p5. The Executive Council was composed of 30 members, 15 Resident and 15 (increased to 30 in 1905) Non Resident.

29 NLI Ceannt Papers MS 41,479/8, What I remember about Éamonn by Michael Kent.

30 As above.

31 As above.

32 Áine Ceannt, BMH WS 264.

33 Kent-Gallagher Family Papers, Cumann na bPíobairí Pamphlet signed by Edward T. Kent, Hon. Secretary.

34 Áine Ceannt, BMH WS 264.

35 Kent-Gallagher Family Papers, Cumann na bPíobairí Pamphlet signed by Edward T. Kent, Hon. Secretary.

36 NLI Ceannt Papers MS 13,069/33, List of Lantern Slides for Bagpipe Lecture.

37 NLI Ceannt Papers MS 13,069/33, Notes for a set of articles on Union or War pipes (undated).

38 NLI Ceannt Papers MS 13,069/27.

39 Kent-Gallagher Family Papers, Cumann na bPíobairí Pamphlet signed by Edward T. Kent, Hon. Secretary.

40 NLI Ceannt Papers MS 13,069/32.

41 Irish Theatre Institute – Playography Ireland, www.irishplayography.com/play accessed on 26th March 2013.

42 The Oireachtas was a festival of competitions in Irish music, dance, poetry and prose which was held annually by the Gaelic League from 1897.

43 *An Claidheamh Soluis*, Vol. V, No. 11, 28 May 1903.

44 NLI Ceannt Papers MS 41, 479/8.

45 NLI Ceannt Papers MS 13,069/49, 'The first night I arrived in Galway as a Gaelic Leaguer by Éamonn Ceannt', annotated on verso of final page 'read by Éamonn before Clontarf Branch about 11–12 years ago, Richard Kent 3/6/1916'.

46 Áine Ceannt, BMH WS 264.

47 NLI Ceannt Papers MS 41,478/1.

48 NLI Ceannt Papers MS 13,069/2, Letter from Éamonn Ceannt to Frances O'Brennan on 15 May 1904.

49 NLI Ceannt Papers MS 13,069/5, Envelope addressed by Éamonn Ceannt to Frances O'Brennan.

50 NLI Ceannt Papers MS 13,069/3, Letter from Éamonn Ceannt to Frances O'Brennan on 10 December 1903.

51 NLI Ceannt Papers MS 13,069/3, Letter from Éamonn Ceannt to Frances O'Brennan on 12 December 1903. The novel Knocknagow by Charles Kickham, published in 1879, had been given to Éamonn by his sister. Its attack on the landlord system and accurate portrayal of rural life in Ireland made it very popular in Irish homes.

52 NLI Ceannt Papers MS 13,069/3, Letter from Éamonn Ceannt to Frances O'Brennan on 24 December 1903.

53 NLI Ceannt Papers MS 13,069/3, Letter from Éamonn Ceannt to Frances O'Brennan on 31 March 1904.

54 NLI Ceannt Papers MS 13,069/5, Letters from Éamonn Ceannt to Frances O'Brennan on 2 May and 11 May 1904. Reckitt's Blue Bag which 'laundered white's whiter', was a common feature of households throughout the British Isles until the 1970s. The idea of making a relatively simple product

in Ireland rather than importing the British product was a driving force for Éamonn. In a postcard to Áine he included a design which described it as 'Made in Ireland by Irish Labour.'

55 NLI Ceannt Papers MS 13,069/53, Diary 1905 belonging to Éamonn Ceannt.

56 As above.

57 As above.

58 NLI Ceannt Papers MS 13,069/27.

59 NLI Ceannt Papers MS 13,069/53, Diary 1905 belonging to Éamonn Ceannt.

60 NLI Ceannt Papers MS 13,069/27, Letters from M O Duibhginn to Éamonn Ceannt on 8 and 20 April 1905.

61 NLI Ceannt Papers MS 13,069/32, Cumann na bPíobairí Annual Report 1905–1906.

62 NLI Ceannt Papers MS 13,069/53, Diary 1905 belonging to Éamonn Ceannt.

63 NLI Ceannt Papers MS 13,069/60.

64 Dublin City Library & Archive, Reports and printed documents of the Corporation of Dublin, Vol. II 1910, Dublin, 1911.

65 NLI Ceannt Papers MS 13,069/52.

66 NLI Ceannt Papers MS 41,479/8.

67 NLI Ceannt Papers MS 13,069/10.

68 As above.

69 *An Claidheamh Soluis*, Vol. VII, No. 32, 21 October 1905, p7.

70 *An Claidheamh Soluis*, Vol. VII, No. 34, 4 November 1905, p9.

71 NLI Ceannt Papers MS 41,479/8.

72 Áine Ceannt, BMH WS 264.

CHAPTER THREE

1 NLI Ceannt Papers MS 13,069/10, Letter to Éamonn Ceannt from Peter Murray on 18 November 1906.

2 *An Claidheamh Soluis*, 9 September 1905, p8.

3 *An Claidheamh Soluis*, 1 September 1906, p7.

4 NLI Ceannt Papers MS 13,069/12.

5 *An Claidheamh Soluis,* 6 October 1906, p9.

6 *The Freeman's Journal*, October 1906

7 *An Claidheamh Soluis*, 20 October 1906, p7.

8 *The Freeman's Journal*, 11 August 1906, p17.

9 *An Claidheamh Soluis*, 10 November 1906, p10.

10 NLI Ceannt Papers MS 13,069/37.

11 NLI Ceannt Papers MS 13,069/50.

12 Lyons, *Culture and Anarchy*, p64.

13 Lyons, *Ireland since the Famine*, p242.

14 At an earlier stage in his career Pearse himself had launched what his biographer, Ruth Dudley Edwards, would call, 'an ill informed adolescent attack' on Yeats for plays, poetry and theatre that Pearse regarded as un-Irish. Edwards noted that Pearse would come to regret this when he came to know Yeats later in their respective careers. See Ruth Dudley Edwards, *Patrick Pearse: The Triumph of Failure* (Dublin, 2006), p30.

15 *An Claidheamh Soluis*, 13 April 1907, p9.

16 NLI MS 13,069/12.

17 UCD Archives, P13/71, Papers of Lily O'Brennan.

18 *An Claidheamh Soluis*, 27 April 1907, p7–8.

19 Michael Laffan, *The Resurrection of Ireland, The Sinn Féin Party 1916–1923* (Cambridge, 2005), p25.

20 As above, p23–26.

21 NLI MS 41,479/6.

22 Martin Maguire, *Servants to the Public: A History of the Local Government and Public Services Union 1909–1990* (Dublin, 1998), p27.

23 *An Claidheamh Soluis*, 6 June, 1908, p14.

24 Timothy McMahon, *Grand Opportunity – The Gaelic Revival and Irish Society 1893–1910* (Syracuse, 2008), p87 and p89, ebook edition.

25 *An Claidheamh Soluis,* 8 August 1908, p9.

26 *An Claidheamh Soluis,* 22 February, 1908, p12.

27 NLI Ceannt Papers MS 41,479/8 Éamonn Ceannt's visit to Rome by P J Daniels.

28 Áine Ceannt, BMH WS 264. The costume and a set of Éamonn's bagpipes are in the National Museum of Ireland, Collins Barracks.

29 Pope Pius X was known for his conservative views. In April 1907, his papal decree *Ne Temere,* which restricted mixed marriages, raised concerns among Irish Protestants about the dangers of Rome Rule in the context of Home Rule.

30 Sean T Kelly, BMH WS 1765. Sean T O'Kelly joined the IRB in 1901 and in 1905 he was a founder member of Sinn Féin. He became a Sinn Féin member of Dublin Corporation in 1906 and joint secretary in 1908.

31 Áine Ceannt, BMH WS 264.

32 NLI Ceannt Papers MS 13,069/46, A trip to Rome (Turas go dtí an Róimh).

33 NLI Ceannt Papers MS 41,479/8, Éamonn Ceannt's Visit to Rome by P. J Daniels.

34 NLI Ceannt Papers MS 13,069/46, A trip to Rome.

35 *Irish Independent,* 2 September 1908.

36 NLI Ceannt Papers MS 41,479/8, Éamonn Ceannt's Visit to Rome by P. J Daniels.

37 NLI Ceannt Papers MS 13,069/10, Various Letters.

38 *Sinn Fein,* No. 136, 12 December 1908, p2.

CHAPTER FOUR

1 *An Claidheamh Soluis,* Vol X, 6 February 1909, p9.

2 *Irish Independent,* 19 March 1909, p5.

3 Timothy McMahon, *Grand Opportunity – The Gaelic Revival and Irish Society 1893–1910* (Syracuse, 2008), p76, ebook edition.

4 Joost Augusteijn, *Patrick Pearse: The Making of a Revolutionary* (London, 2010), p120.

5   *An Claidheamh Soluis,* Vol. XI, No. 29, 25 September 1909, p12.

6   Joost Augusteijn, *Patrick Pearse: The Making of a Revolutionary* (London, 2010), pp140–143.

7   *An Claidheamh Soluis,* 19 June–2 October 1909.

8   Áine Ceannt, BMH WS 264.

9   Sean Ó Ceallaigh, BMH WS 1765.

10 Sinn Féin's policy of abstention from the Westminster Parliament did not extend to local government within Ireland. The party saw an opportunity in county councils of gaining much needed practical knowledge of government. In January 1906 the Party won four seats on Dublin Corporation which, together with five former Nationalist (IPP) candidates who allied themselves with Sinn Féin, made it the second largest party behind the Nationalists United Irish Party (UIP) in the Corporation. Their criticism of UIP slum landlords and patronage won them more allies from the small group of Labour members. See Joseph V O'Brien, *Dear Dirty Dublin: A city in distress 1899–1916*(Berkeley and Los Angeles, London, 1982), p90.

11 NLI Ceannt Papers MS 13,069/43.

12 *Sinn Féin,* No. 140, 9 January, 1909, p1.

13 *Sinn Féin,* No. 140, 9 January 1909, p1.

14 Dublin City Library and Archives, Minutes of the Municipal Council, 15 March 1909.

15 National Archives of Ireland, DMOA executive committee minutes, 16 October 1908, 10 February 1909 and 3 March 1909, cited in Martin Maguire, *Servants to the Public: A History of the Local Government and Public Services Union 1901–1990* (Dublin, 1998), p18.

16 Dublin City Library and Archives, Reports and Printed Documents of the Corporation of Dublin, Vol. II, 1910. Éamonn and Michael both had been 'classified' i.e. had been approved for a higher scale of increment based on satisfactory performance. City Treasurer Eyre was one of a small number of higher officials whose salaries ranged from £750–£2,000 per annum, see O'Brien, *Dear Dirty Dublin,* op. cit.

17 Kent-Gallagher Family Papers, Letter from Dublin City Treasurer to Edmund Kent (Éamonn Ceannt) dated 29th November 1909.

18 *Irish Independent,* 4 March, 1910.

19 *Irish Independent,* 2 April, 1910.

20 *Irish Independent,* 4 April, 1910.

21 *Irish Independent,* 26 April, 1910.

22 NLI Ceannt Papers MS 41,479/8.

23 Maguire, *Servants to the Public,* p18.

24 NLI Ceannt Papers MS 13069/49. Éamonn described intensive cultivation as 'producing two or three crops of lettuce or other marketable vegetable where in the ordinary course of nature only one would have appeared. This is not done by conjuring tricks or by the aid of the black art. The result is achieved by hurrying up poor mother earth and making her bustle with the times instead of allowing her the leisure she enjoyed in primitive ages.'

25 Kent-Gallagher Family Papers, Diary of Michael Kent.

26 To fully understand the fragility of the IPP's hold over the Liberal Government during this period, see Ronan Fanning, *Fatal Path: British Government and Irish Revolution 1910–1922* (London, 2013), Chapter Two.

27 Southern Protestants, who were predominantly Unionist, numbered c.250,000, Ref. *Census of Ireland*, 1911, quoted in J. J. Lee, *Ireland 1912–1985: Politics and Society* (Cambridge, 1989).

28 Ulster Protestants, predominantly Unionist, numbered c. 891,000, Ref. *Census of Ireland*, 1911, quoted in J. J. Lee, *Ireland 1912–1985: Politics and Society* (Cambridge, 1989).

29 Fanning, *Fatal Path*, p50.

30 Áine Ceannt, BMH WS 264.

31 Laffan, *The Resurrection of Ireland*, p31.

32 Lyons, *Ireland since the Famine*, p136.

33 Lyons, *Ireland since the Famine*, p315.

34 Marnie Hay, *Bulmer Hobson and the Nationalist Movement in Twentieth Century*

Ireland (Manchester, 2009), Chapter Three.

35 Helen Litton, *16 Lives: Thomas Clarke* (Dublin, 2014), p100.

36 Hay, *Bulmer Hobson*, pp96–97.

37 *Kildare Observer,* 24 June 1911.

38 *Sinn Féin,* 29 June 1911, quoted in Gerard MacAtasney, *Seán MacDiarmada: The Mind of the Revolution* (Manorhamilton, Co. Leitrim), p53.

39 Áine Ceannt, BMH WS 264.

40 MacAtasney, *Seán MacDiarmada*, p53.

41 Áine Ceannt, BMH WS 264. There is no mention of this in Ruth Dudley Edwards' biography and Augusteijn suggests that Pearse did not play an active part in the Committee, Augusteijn, p234

42 *Irish Freedom,* June, 1911.

43 *Sunday Independent,* 18 June 1911.

44 The permission of the Paving Committee of Dublin Corporation was required to dig up the road to erect the poles.

45 Áine Ceannt, BMH WS 264.

46 *Sinn Féin,* 1 July 1911.

47 *Sinn Féin,* 15 July 1911.

48 *Irish Freedom,* July, 1911. The matter was explained more objectively in *The Freeman's Journal,* 6 July 1911 when the matter came to court. The gentleman in question, Mr Seamus O'Duffy of Reuben Avenue, was the Hon Secretary of the National Council of Sinn Féin, and the charge was that he didn't have the necessary license to sell postcards. He was released with a caution.

49 Dublin City Library and Archives, Reports of Dublin Corporation, III of 1911, Report of the Estates and Finance Committee.

50 Kent-Gallagher Family Papers, Diary of Michael Kent.

51 Hay, *Bulmer Hobson*, pp100–101.

52 *An Claidheamh Soluis,* 29 July 1911.

53 *An Claidheamh Soluis,* 16 September 1911.

54 *An Claidheamh Soluis,* 14 October 1911.

55 For the background to the role of the National Board in Irish education, see Lyons, *Ireland since the Famine,* Chapter 3 (iii). The National Board was appointed by the Lord Lieutenant and, as Lyons pointed out, had made significant contributions to the cause of education for Irish children since the early part of the 19th Century. In so doing, however, it managed to lock horns with the Catholic Church, which was determined to retain control of the education of Catholic children, and of nationalist Ireland, which accused it of doing nothing to differentiate the education of Irish children from those of English children. The latter was true to a significant extent as Irish history, music and poetry did not figure in the curriculum of the National Schools (unlike to independent Christian Brothers' schools) although, under pressure from the Gaelic League, from 1904 on the Board decided to allow 'the teaching in Irish speaking and bilingual districts of both Irish and English to all classes, and the teaching of other subjects trough the medium of either language'.

56 *Irish Independent,* 7 September 1911.

57 *Freeman's Journal,* 13 December 1911.

58 Dudley Edwards, *Patrick Pearse,* p. 182.

59 *Irish Independent,* 2 October 1911.

60 *Sinn Féin,* 9 September, 1911.

61 *Sinn Féin,* 23 September, 1911.

62 *Sinn Féin,* 30 September 1911.

63 *Sinn Féin,* 7 October 1911.

64 *Sinn Féin,* 7 October 1911.

65 *Sinn Féin,* 11 November 1911.

66 Áine Ceannt BMH WS 264. In her statement many years later to the Bureau of Military History, Áine Ceannt said that, 'on 12/12/12 there appears an entry in Éamonn Ceannt's diary – "is iongantach an lá é seo, is iogantach an lá dom-sa freisin é". My [Áine's] reading of this entry is that on that date Éamonn Ceannt joined the IRB.' The year recalled by Áine

(1912) appears to be incorrect. MacDiarmada's biographer, Brian Feeney (*16 Lives: Seán MacDiarmada* (Dublin 2014), dates MacDiarmada's illness – he was stricken by polio – to August 1911 and says that he was released from hospital in December 1911 – which would accord with the date of the Aonach. Another interpretation of this important date has been provided by Bulmer Hobson's biographer, Marnie Hay (op. cit). Hay also questioned the accuracy of Aine's statement. She pointed out that, in later accounts of the affiliation of members of the Provisional Committee of the Irish Volunteers, Hobson sometimes lists Éamonn as an IRB member and sometimes as unaffiliated. She attributed this to Hobson's uncertainty as to whether Éamonn was sworn into the IRB before or after the establishment of the Irish Volunteers in November 1913. She suggests that the year listed in Áine's Witness Statement may reflect a typographical error or a lapse of memory. Hobson, a former Sinn Féiner, was a longstanding and influential member of the IRB. While it may seem surprising that Hobson was unaware of the date of Éamonn's affiliation, it is worth remembering that the IRB was a secretive body composed of cells whose membership was not know to each other. There were c. 750 members based in Dublin (Hay p.102) and it is possible that, although in the tiny world of advanced nationalism, Hobson would have certainly known Éamonn, he would not necessarily have been aware that he had been sworn into the Brotherhood. In addition, as Hay points out (Hay, p.108) relations between Hobson and MacDiarmada had begun to deteriorate during 1912 and Hobson may well not have been aware of all of MacDiarmada's recruiting activities. Other than the question of the year, the account of the meeting with Seán MacDiarmada as described by Áine has a ring of truth.

67 Kent-Gallagher Family Papers, Diary of Michael Kent.

CHAPTER FIVE

1 Roy Jenkins, *Churchill* (London, 2002), p235.

2 Fanning, *Fatal Path*, p63.

3 *Freeman's Journal,* 1 April 1911.

4 For a detailed explanation of the tactics of the British Government during this period see Fanning, *Fatal Path*.

5 *Irish Independent,* 15 April 1912.

6 NLI Ceannt Papers MS 13,069/47.

7 Death Certificate of James Kent.

8 *Freeman's Journal,* 21 March 1912.

9 Kent-Gallagher Family Papers, Diary of Michael Kent.

10 *Irish Independent, 19 March 1912.*

11 Dudley Edwards, *Patrick Pearse,* p164.

12 *An Barr Buadh,* 16 March 1912.

13 *An Barr Buadh,* 12 April 1912.

14 *An Barr Buadh,* 19 April 1912.

15 *An Barr Buadh,* 18 May 1912.

16 Letter from Greg Murphy quoted in Augusteijn, *Patrick Pearse,* p235 and Dudley Edwards, p158.

17 Although Éamonn was clearly one of those whose access to education had benefitted from aspects of the system of secondary (Intermediate) Education that resulted from the Intermediate Education (Ireland) Act, 1878, the system was far from perfect. The limitations of the system led to the establishment of a Commission on Intermediate Education in 1898, which identified, inter alia, the focus on cramming and rote learning and led to certain changes in the system. The subsequent legislation and regulations failed to get to the root of the problem. Among Irish-Irelanders the Intermediate system was seen as training Irish boys for service to the Empire or the British and Irish Civil Service. See Coolahan, *Irish Education: Its History and Structure* (Dublin, 1981). Pearse, based on his research into alternative education systems, trenchantly criticised the Intermediate system in his essay *The Murder Machine* (1916).

18 *Irish Independent,* 11 June 1912.

19 Fanning, *Fatal Path,* p74.

20 *Sinn Féin,* 12 October 1912.

21 *Sinn Féin, 7 December 1912.*

22 *Sinn Féin,* 27 January 1912.

23 *Freemen's Journal,* 19 December 1912.

24 Fanning, *Fatal Path,* p79–80.

25 Timothy Bowman, *The Ulster Volunteers 1913–1914: Force or Farce?* in History Ireland, Issue 1, 2002.

26 Charles Townshend, *Easter 1916: The Irish Rebellion* (London, 2006), p36.

27 BMH WS 0004, Diarmuid Lynch.

28 Townshend, *Easter 1916,* p37.

29 UCD Archives P163/1, Sinn Féin Minutes, Quarterly meeting of the National Council, 20 January 1913.

30 Áine Ceannt, BMH WS 264.

31 UCD Archives P163/1, Sinn Féin Minutes, meeting of the National Council, 23 January 1913.

32 BMH WS 0263 Thomas Slater.

33 NLI Ceannt Papers MS 13,069/51, Returned cheques.

34 Thomas Slater, BMH WS 0263.

35 UCD Archives P163/1, Sinn Féin Minutes – Special Congress re the Political Situation, 22 March 1913.

36 UCD Archives P163/1, Sinn Féin Minutes – meeting of the National Council, 3 April 1913.

37 UCD Archives P163/1, Sinn Féin Minutes – meeting of the National Council, 15 May 1913.

38 UCD Archives P163/1, Sinn Féin Minutes – meeting of the National Council, 13 February 1913

39 UCD Archives P163/1, Sinn Féin Minutes – meeting of the National Council, 27 February 1913.

40 Séamus Ó Maitiú, 'A spent force? *An Claidheamh Soluis and the Gaelic League in Dublin 1893–1913'* in *1913 A Capital in Conflict: Dublin City and the 1913 Lockout,* ed. Francis Devine (Dublin 2013).

41 *Sinn Féin*, 15 February 1913.

42 *An Claidheamh Soluis,* 12 July 1913.

43 *An Claidheamh Soluis,* 12 July 1913.

44 *Sinn Féin,* 12 July 1913.

45 *Freeman's Journal,* 31 July 1913.

46 *Irish Independent,* 1 August 1913.

47 *Sinn Féin,* 19 July 1913.

48 Quoted in Dudley Edwards, p231.

49 *An Claidheamh Soluis,* 8 November 1913.

50 For a more in-depth understanding of the response of nationalism to the radicalisation of the working class see Adrian Grant, *Irish Republican Socialism 1909–36* (Dublin, 2012), pp51–58.

51 *Irish Freedom,* October 1913.

52 Brian Feeney, *Seán MacDiarmada* (Dublin, 2014).

53 Hay, *Bulmer Hobson*, p105.

54 Áine Ceannt, BMH WS 264.

55 Hay, *Bulmer Hobson*, p110.

56 *An Claidheamh Soluis,* 1 November 1913.

57 Piarais Beaslai, The Founding of the Irish Volunteers, *Irish Independent,* 5 January, 1953.

58 Sean Fitzgibbon, BMH WS0130.

59 NLI Ceannt Papers MS13,069/42.

60 The O'Rahilly, 'The Secret History of the Irish Volunteers (Dublin 1915)' cited in F X Martin, *The Irish Volunteers 1913–1915* (Dublin, 1963).

61 *The Irish Volunteer,* 20 June 1914.

62 The O'Rahilly, 'The Secret History of the Irish Volunteers', op. cit.

63 Áine Ceannt, BMH WS 264.

64 *The Irish Volunteer,* 20 June 1914.

65 Áine Ceannt, BMH WS 264.

66 NLI Ceannt Papers MS 13,069/44.

67 Allen Library.

68 Gerry Golden, BMH WS 0521.

69 For an overview of the steps taken by the IRB to influence the Irish Volunteers throughout Ireland see Fearghal McGarry, *The Rising: Ireland: Easter
1916* (Oxford 2010), pp45–47.

70 Liam Tannam, BMH WS 0242.

71 Kent-Gallagher Family Papers, Diary of Michael Kent.

CHAPTER SIX

1 For an understanding of the political developments in Europe at this period
leading to outbreak of war, see William Mulligan, *The Origins of the First
World War: New Approaches to European History* (Cambridge, 2010).

2 The honourable exceptions were the women workers in Jacob's Biscuit
Factory who held out until the following March and even then were
subjected to humiliating re-entry requirements – see Conor Mulvagh, 'We
must look beyond 1913 and learn the lessons from the Lockout', The Jour-
nal.ie, 6 April 2014.

3 For a detailed understanding of the political background from the perspec-
tive of Westminster see Fanning, *Fatal Path*.

4 Fanning, *Fatal Path*, p112.

5 *The Irish Volunteer,* 20 June 1914.

6 *The Irish Volunteer,* 7 February 1914.

7 Dudley Edwards, *Patrick Pearse,* p209.

8 *The Irish Volunteer,* 17 February 1914.

9 *The Irish Volunteer,* 24 February 1914.

10 Fanning, *Fatal Path*, p123.

11 As above, p118.

12 The AOH was a secretive Catholic nationalist organisation, which had its
roots in Ulster in the 19th century where it positioned itself up in opposition

to the Orange Order. It was closely associated with Joseph Devlin and the Irish Parliamentary Party (IPP) and was strongly opposed to the secular Irish Republican Brotherhood (IRB).

13 Colonel Maurice Moore, ex Connaught Rangers and Gaelic Leaguer, was the senior military man on the Provisional Committee of the Irish Volunteers.

14 Bulmer Hobson, BMH WS 0050.

15 *Irish Independent,* 9 June 1914.

16 *Freeman's Journal,* 10 June, 1914.

17 Bulmer Hobson, BMH WS 0050.

18 For a more detailed account of these discussions see Hay, *Bulmer Hobson,* pp129–131 and Townshend, *Easter 1916,* pp52–53.

19 Michael Judge was a member of the Ancient Order of Hibernians (AOH).

20 Honor O Brolchain, *16 Lives: Joseph Plunkett* (Dublin, 2012).

21 Bulmer Hobson, BMH WS 0050.

22 Letter from Pearse to McGarrity quoted in Dudley Edwards, *Patrick Pearse,* p211.

23 Bulmer Hobson, BMH WS 0050.

24 *The Irish Volunteer,* 11 July 1914.

25 Donal O'Hannigan, BMH WS 0161.

26 Henry S Murray, BMH WS 0300.

27 Letter from Pearse to McGarrity, 17 July, 1914 quoted in Dudley Edwards, *Patrick Pearse,* p215.

28 For a detailed account of the adventure see Lyons, *Ireland Since the Famine*, pp325–328.

29 Áine Ceannt, BMH WS 264.

30 Donal O'Hannigan, BMH WS 0161.

31 As above.

32 Seamus Kenny, BMH WS0158.

33 Joseph O'Connor, BMH WS0157.

34 Joseph Doolan, BMH WS 0199. There is some uncertainty whether it was the RIC or the Coastguard that fired off the rockets. Another Volunteer (Thomas McCarthy, BMH WS 0307) recalls that it was the Coastguard.

35 Joseph O'Connor, BMH WS 0157.

36 Seamus Kavanagh, BMH WS 0208.

37 Thomas McCathy, BMH WS0307.

38 *The Irish Volunteer,* 1 August 1914.

39 Henry S Murray, BMH WS0300.

40 Áine Ceannt, BMH WS 264.

41 Seamus Daly, BMH WS0360.

42 Sean Prendergast, BMH WS0755.

43 Patrick Egan, BMH WS 0327

44 *The Irish Volunteer,* 1 August 1914.

45 Hay, *Bulmer Hobson,* p162.

46 James J Burke, BMH WS 1758.

47 *Irish Independent,* 29 August 1914.

48 Sean Fitzgibbon, BMH WS 0130.

49 Thomas McCarthy, BMH WS 0307.

50 Townshend, *Easter 1916,* p61.

51 Sean T O'Kelly, BMH WS 1765.

52 Fanning, *Fatal Path,* p133–135.

53 *Irish Independent* 24 September 1914.

54 *Irish Independent* 18 September 1914.

55 Dudley Edwards, *Patrick Pearse,* pp219–220.

56 *Irish Independent,* 26 September 1914.

57 Dudley Edwards, *Patrick Pearse,* p200.

58 Townshend, *Easter 1916,* pp64–65.

59 Garry Holohan, BMH WS 0328.

60 *Irish Independent,* 24 September, 1914.

61 The other signatories were The O'Rahilly, Thomas MacDonagh, Joseph Plunkett, Piaras Beaslai, M J Judge, Peter Paul Macken, Sean Fitzgibbon, P H Pearse, Padraic O'Riain, Bulmer Hobson, Éamonn Martin, Con Colbert, Seán MacDiarmada, Seamus O'Conchubhair, Liam Mellows, Colm O'Loghlainn, Liam Ua Grogan and Peter White.

62 Joost Augusteijn, *Patrick Pearse,* p260 (ebook edition).

63 *Irish Independent,* 29 September, 1914.

64 George Irvine, BMH WS 0265.

65 Helen Litton (ed.), *Kathleen Clarke, Revolutionary Woman* (Dublin, 2008).

66 Henry S Murray, BMH WS 0300.

67 Sean T O'Kelly, BMH WS1765.

68 Desmond Ryan (ed.), *Labour and Easter Week, A selection from the writings of James Connolly, with an introduction by William O'Brien* (Dublin, 1949). There is some uncertainty as to who organised the meeting on 9 September. Sean T O'Kelly believed it was Seán MacDiarmada while William O'Brien believed it to have been Éamonn. The likelihood is that the overall initiative came from Clarke and MacDiarmada and Éamonn, who was 'well acquainted' with William O'Brien, organised his participation together with that of James Connolly. James Connolly had been living in Belfast but had arrived in Dublin during August. He spoke to William O'Brien 'about acting with all those who would favour organising for an insurrection'. O'Brien told him he would should only talk to those with influence and mentioned Clarke and MacDiarmada. He offered to put him in contract with them through Éamonn Ceannt, 'who was a member of the Executive of the Irish Volunteers as well as a leading member of the IRB'.

69 Dudley Edwards, *Patrick Pearse,* p208 and p213. Sean O'Casey, in particular displayed animosity towards the Volunteers. After his resignation as Secretary of the ICA on 24 July 1914, Dudley Edwards says that 'the greatest bar to co-operation disappeared'.

70 Sean T O'Kelly, BMH WS 1765.

71 Desmond Ryan, op. cit.

72 Pádraig Yeates, *A City in Wartime: Dublin 1914–1918* (Dublin, 2012). Yeates noted that 'among corporation employees who did not have to worry about job security or what their employer thought, only 169 had joined the forces by 1916'.

73 Sean T O'Kelly, BMH WS 1765.

74 *The Irish Volunteer,* 10 October, 1914.

75 Kevin O'Sheil, BMH WS 1770.

76 In the battle of Omdurman (Soudan) 1898, Kitchener lost 47 men killed and 382 wounded. The opposing force of Mahdists/Dervishes (religious nationalists) lost 10,000 killed, 13,000 wounded and 5,000 taken prisoner. Churchill was among those who criticised the brutal treatment of the wounded by Kitchener's forces after the battle. (Roy Jenkins, *Churchill* (London, 2002), p41). As a boy, Éamonn had won a pocket-money prize from *Chums* magazine entitled Fame and Glory in the Soudan War. He had clearly not forgotten it.

77 *The Irish Volunteer,* 17 October, 1914.

78 Marnie Hay, *Bulmer Hobson,* p164.

79 *Irish Volunteer,* 31 October 1914.

80 *The Irish Volunteer,* 14 November 1914. The other appointments were: General Secretary, Bulmer Hobson (IRB); Press Secretary, Patrick Pearse (IRB); Publication Secretary, Pádraig Ó Riain (IRB); Affiliation Secretary, Sean Fitzgibbon; Musketry Training, Seamus O'Connor (IRB); Organisation: Michael J Judge; Purchase of Arms, Eoin MacNeill and The O'Rahilly; Joseph Plunkett, by now a member of the IRB, was later appointed to the Executive Committee as Co-Treasurer with The O'Rahilly.

81 NLI Ceannt Papers MS 13,069/40.

82 Yeates, *A City in Wartime,* p50.

83 *The Irish Volunteer,* 14 November 1914.

84 NLI Ceannt Papers MS 13,069/58.

85 Dudley Edwards, *Patrick Pearse,* p228.

86 Charles Townshend, *Easter 1916,* p93.

87 F.X. Martin (ed.), *Eoin MacNeill on the 1916 Rising,* HIS, xii (1961), cited in Hay, *Bulmer Hobson,* p173.

88 NLI Ceannt Papers, MS 13,069/42.

89 *The Irish Volunteer,* 19 December 1914.

90 Michael T Foy and Brian Barton, *The Easter Rising* (Stroud, 2011), p21. Townshend, *Easter 1916,* notes that in his biography of Tom Clarke, Le Roux called this group a committee of the Volunteers rather than the IRB.

91 Letter from Pearse to McGarrity, 19th October 1914, quoted in Dudley Edwards, *Patrick Pearse,* p. 224. Dudley Edwards comments that, in so doing, Pearse was apparently unaware that Hobson had fallen from favour with the activists within the IRB.

92 Tom Burke, *The 2nd Battalion Royal Dublin Fusiliers and the Tragedy of Mouse-trap Farm, April and May 1915* (Dublin, 2005). One of those who died at Mousetrap Farm was Sgt. William Malone, from Dublin. His brother, Michael was in the Irish Volunteers and died almost exactly a year later in 1916 during the fighting on Northumberland Road against the Sherwood Foresters.

93 Yeates, *A City in Wartime*, p54.

94 Burke, *The 2nd Battalion Royal Dublin Fusiliers.*

95 Fanning, *Fatal Path*, p137.

96 Yeates, *A City in Wartime*, p50–51.

97 Joe Lee, *Ireland 1912–1985, Politics and Society* (Cambridge 1990), p23.

98 *The Irish Volunteer,* 16 January 1915.

99 *The Irish Volunteer,* 6 February 1915.

100 *The Irish Volunteer,* 16 February 1915.

101 *The Irish Volunteer, Supplement,* 20 February 1915.

102 *The Irish Volunteer,* 20 February 1915.

103 NLI Ceannt Papers MS 13,069/38.

104 Hay, *Bulmer Hobson,* p168.

105 NLI Ceannt Papers MS 13,069/59.

106 *The Irish Volunteer,* 20 March 1915.

107 Longford, Éamonn de Valera, quoted in Dudley Edwards, *Patrick Pearse,* p229.

108 Helen Litton, *Edward Daly* (Dublin, 2013), p67.

109 NLI Ceannt Papers MS 13,069/38.

110 *The Irish Volunteer,* 3 April 1915.

111 NLI Ceannt Papers MS 13,069/42, Photostat Orders from Pearse to Commandant, 4th Battalion, Re: Easter Manoeuvres 1915.

112 Memoirs of Séan T O'Kelly, *The Irish Press,* 11 July 1961, quoted in Gerard MacAtasney, *Seán MacDiarmada,* p90.

113 *An Claidheamh Soluis,* 7 August, 1915. MacDiarmada had been in prison since the previous May, charged under the Defense of the Realm Act (DORA) with making a seditious speech discouraging recruitment to the British Army.

114 BMH CD 316/2 – Booklet, Souvenir Publication.

115 Le Roux, *Tom Clarke,* quoted in Dudley Edwards, *Patrick Pearse,* p234.

116 Micheál Ó Droighneáin, BMH WS 374.

117 *Irish Independent,* 5 July 1915.

118 Laurence Nugent, BMH WS 0907.

119 *The Irish Volunteer,* 21 August 1915.

120 Sean T O'Kelly, BMH WS 1765.

121 *The Irish Volunteer,* 21 August 1915.

122 NLI Ceannt Papers MS 13,069/36, Circular letter from Éamonn Ceannt, 10 November 1915.

123 NLI Ceannt Papers MS 13,069/36.

124 Micheál Ó Droighneáin, BMH WS 374.

125 J J O'Connell, MS of 'History of the Irish Volunteers', (NLI, BH, MS

13,169), quoted in Marnie Hay, *Bulmer Hobson,* p171.

126 Mortimer O'Connell, BMH WS 0804.

127 Townshend, *Easter 1916*, pp95–111. Based on the fairly sketchy evidence that survives, Townshend has compiled the most comprehensive analysis to date of the plan and its objectives, assumptions, choices and chances of success. No copy of the plan survives however and Townshend concludes that, although it is possible to speculate on the basis on which the planners reached their decisions e.g. the central role of Dublin and the decision on which structures to occupy within Dublin, no reliable evidence of such assessments survives.

128 O Brolchain, *16 Lives: Joseph Plunkett*, p310.

129 O Brolchain, *16 Lives: Joseph Plunkett*, p320.

130 Sean T O'Kelly, BMH WS 1765.

131 Diarmuid Lynch, BMH WS 0004.

132 Dr Patrick McCartan returned to Dublin in 1905 from the US, where he had been a member of Clan na Gael. He joined the IRB and became editor of *Irish Freedom* and a member of the Supreme Council from late 1914.

133 Dudley Edwards, *Patrick Pearse*, p242.

134 Townshend, *Easter* 1916, p116.

135 Diarmuid Lynch, BMH WS 0004.

136 O Brolchain, *16 Lives: Joseph Plunkett*, p324.

137 Micheal O'Droighneain, BMH WS 374. O'Droighneain's statement is corroborated by that of the courier sent with the letter, Mrs Martin Conlan, BMH WS 419.

138 Joseph Doolan, BMH WS 0199.

139 *The Irish Volunteer,* 6 November 1915.

140 As above.

CHAPTER SEVEN

1 BMH WS 1765, Sean T O'Kelly.

2 Foy and Barton, *The Easter Rising,* p33.

3 Townshend, *Easter 1916,* p108.

4 Collins, *16 Lives: James Connolly,* p255.

5 Lyons, *Ireland Since the Famine,* p46.

6 Diarmuid Lynch, BMH WS 00004.

7 Áine Ceannt, BMH WS 0264.

8 William O'Brien, BMH WS 1766.

9 Plunkett Dillon, *All in the Blood,* p198.

10 Áine Ceannt, BMH WS 0264.

11 Frank Robbins, BMH WS 0585.

12 Brian Hughes, *16 Lives: Michael Mallin* (Dublin, 2012), pp109–110.

13 Plunkett Dillon, *All in the Blood,* p198.

14 Áine Ceannt, BMH WS 264. In a letter to the editor of the *RTE Guide* dated 24 April 1967 (Kent-Gallagher Family Papers), Áine's son, Rónán, suggested an alternative scenario for Connolly's departure. He recalled that Constance Markievicz, while staying in the Ceannt family home during the Civil War, had recounted meeting Connolly on the Sunday morning in the Coghlan house, looking dirty and disheveled. He said to her 'Con, I've been in Hell, in Hell'. Markievicz believed that Connolly's absence had been voluntary. That he 'had been anxiously been awaiting news that the Citizen Army had carried out his long standing instructions to go out and capture Dublin Castle in the event of his absence for three days or more, and that he had been gravely disappointed when the Citizen Army had held their hands'.

15 George Irvine, BMH WS 0265.

16 Áine Ceannt, BMH WS 264.

17 NLI Ceannt Papers MS 13,069/39.

18 Gerald (Gary) Byrne, BMH WS 014.

19 Donal O'Hannigan, BMH WS 0161.

20 Michael Staines, BMH WS 0284. Since the 'Headquarter's Staff' of the Irish Volunteers were not aware of the plans for the Rising, this may be an exam-

ple of the confusion in the minds of IRB members as to whose orders they were following. It may on the other hand reflect the fact that Staines' recollections at the time (July 1949) of his Statement to the Bureau of Military History were not entirely clear.

21 Áine Ceannt, BMH WS 264.

22 Henry S Murray, BMH WS 0300.

23 Michael Lynch, BMH WS 0511.

24 Henry S Murray, BMH WS 0300. In his Witness Statement Murray provided a clear description of the organisation of the Battalion and the names and responsibilities of the senior officers. He notes that E Company, under the Captainship of Patrick Pearse was in actuality a Headquarters' company and attached to the 4th Battalion in name only. The company formed part of the GPO Garrison during Easter Week.

25 As above.

26 Laurence O'Brien, BMH WS 0252.

27 Áine Ceannt, BMH WS 264.

28 Sean Cody, BMH WS 1035.

29 Áine Ceannt, BMH WS 264.

30 Harry Nicholls, BMH WS 0296.

31 Annie Mannion, Matron SDU, BMH WS 0297.

32 William T Cosgrave, BMH WS 0268.

33 Thomas Doyle, BMH WS 0186.

34 Paul O'Brien, *Uncommon Valour, 1916 and the Battle for the South Dublin Union* (Dublin, 2010).

35 John J Styles, BMH WS 0175.

36 Michael Staines, BMH WS 0284.

37 Hay, *Bulmer Hobson*, p185.

38 Foy and Barton, *The Easter Rising*, p45.

39 Lyons, *Ireland Since the Famine*, p350.

40 Christopher Byrne, BMH WS 0167.

41 Edward O'Neill, BMH WS 0203.

42 John J Styles, BMH WS 0175.

43 Áine Ceannt, BMH WS 264.

44 Donal O'Hannigan, BMH WS 0161.

45 Brigid Martin, BMH WS 0398.

46 Bulmer Hobson, BMH WS 0081.

47 Hay, *Bulmer Hobson,* p187.

48 Áine Ceannt, BMH WS 264.

49 There remains some doubt as to the exact date on which this meeting took place and whether, as seems doubtful, any actual signatures were appended to an original document – see John O'Connor, *The 1916 Proclamation* (Dublin, 1999). Michael Molloy (BMH WS 0716), one of the compositors who printed the proclamation recalled that the signatures were on a separate piece of paper that he later destroyed, see also Brian Barton, *The Secret Court Martial Records of the Easter Rising.* Éamonn's colleague, William T Cosgrave (BMH WS 0268), claimed that he had spoken to Éamonn during the course of Éamonn's trial and that Éamonn said that he had not signed the Proclamation. Cosgrave recalled that he said that 'He subscribed to his name being put to it. He had been unable to attend at the time the signatures were being put to the Proclamation; but the naked fact is that he wrote his name to the Proclamation.' It should be noted that this conversation took place within the context of a possible charge being considered at Éamonn's trial.

50 Hay, *Bulmer Hobson,* p187.

51 Áine Ceannt, BMH WS 264.

52 Patrick Egan, BMH WS 0327.

53 Foy and Barton, *The Easter Rising,* p51.

54 Áine Ceannt, BMH WS 264.

55 Monsignor Patrick Browne, BMH WS 0729.

56 Fearghal McGarry, *The Rising: Ireland, Easter 1916* (Oxford 2010), p117.

57 Hay, *Bulmer Hobson,* p188.

58 Áine Ceannt, BMH WS 264.

59 Townshend, *Easter 1916*, p132.

60 Foy and Barton, *The Easter Rising*, p48.

61 Mrs Frank Fahy, BMH WS 0202.

62 Patrick Egan, BMH WS 0327.

63 Áine Ceannt, BMH WS 264.

64 Hay, *Bulmer Hobson*, p191.

65 Townshend, *Easter 1916*, p134.

66 Áine Ceannt, BMH WS 264.

67 As above.

68 UCDA, EMacN, LAI/G/117, Seamus O'Connor , BMH WS, 14 June 1948, quoted in Hay, *Bulmer Hobson*, p194.

69 Mrs Bulmer Hobson (Clare Gregan), BMH WS 0685, quoted in Foy and Barton, *The Easter Rising*, p55.

70 Áine Ceannt, BMH WS 264.

71 Diarmuid Lynch, BMH WS 0004.

72 Sean McGarry, BMH WS 0368.

73 Augusteijn, *Patrick Pearse,* p307 (ebook edition).

74 John J Styles, BMH WS 0175.

75 Seamus Kenny, BMH WS 0158.

76 Patrick O'Daly, BMH WS 0220.

77 Áine Ceannt, BMH WS 264.

78 Foy and Barton, *The Easter Rising*, p58.

79 Townshend, *Easter* 1916, p136.

80 Colm O'Lochlainn, BMH WS 0751.

81 Áine Ceannt, BMH WS 264.

82 Kent-Gallagher Family Papers, Diary of Michael Kent.

83 Sean T O'Kelly, BMH WS 1765.

84 Liam O'Briain, BMH WS 0007.

85 Foy and Barton, *The Easter Rising*, p62.

86 The precise sequence of events that night remains unclear. This account is based on a collation of witness statements written by a number of the participants many years later. Kathleen Clarke later recalled that she had turned up at the meeting with a message for her husband Tom. She recalled (Kathleen Clarke, *Revolutionary Woman*, ed., Helen Litton) that Pearse, Plunkett, Diarmuid Lynch and others were also present in the flash lit room. She said they told her they hadn't wanted to wake her husband Tom since he badly needed his sleep.

87 BMH, Recording of Áine Ceannt.

88 Áine Ceannt, BMH WS 264.

89 Nora Connolly, BMH WS 0268.

90 Sean McGarry, BMH WS 0368.

91 Foy and Barton, *The Easter Rising*, p65.

92 BMH WS 0167 Christopher Byrne.

93 Kent-Gallagher Family Papers, Diary of Michael Kent.

94 Peadar S Doyle, BMH WS 0155.

95 Áine Ceannt, BMH WS 264.

96 Kent-Gallagher Family Papers, Diary of Michael Kent.

CHAPTER EIGHT

1 Liam O'Flaherty, BMH WS 0248.

2 NLI MS 41,479/7 Transcript of a radio broadcast by Lily O'Brennan.

3 Áine Ceannt, BMH WS 264.

4 Peadar Doyle, BMH WS 0155.

5 William T Cosgrave, BMH WS 0268.

6 Henry S Murray, BMH WS 0300.

7 The Rialto section of the Grand Canal Main Line was closed in 1974 and now forms part of the route of the Red Line Luas tramway.

8   Seamus Murphy, BMH WS 1756.

9   NAI BG/Bg 79* Box 22, Minutes of the Board of Guardians of the South Dublin Union, 5 January–28 June 1916, Book no. 39.

10 The Capuchin Annual 1966.

11 George Irvine, BMH WS 0265.

12 Michael Lynch, BMH WS 0511.

13 NLI Ceannt Papers MS 41,479.

14 Peadar S Doyle, BMH WS 0155.

15 As above.

16 NLI Ceannt Paper s MS 41,479.

17 William T Cosgrave, BMH WS 0268.

18 For an overview of the action during Easter week at the other Rising sites see Foy and Barton, *The Easter Rising* and Townshend, *Easter 1916,* as well as Paul O'Brien, *Uncommon Valour, Shootout: The Battle For St. Stephen's Green, 1916, Field of Fire: The Battle of Ashbourne, 1916, Crossfire: The Battle for the Four Courts, 1916* and *Blood on the Streets: 1916 and the Battle for Mount Street Bridge.* William Henry, *Supreme Sacrifice, The story of Éamonn Ceannt,* includes an account of the Rising in Galway.

19 The Capuchin Annual 1966.

20 The Capuchin Annual 1966.

21 Thomas Doyle, BMH WS 0186. The reference to the Pope's Blessing relates to a visit that Papal Count George Noble Plunkett, Joseph Plunkett's father, had paid to Rome shortly before the Rising – see Townshend, *Easter 1916*, p123.

22 William Murphy, BMH WS 0352.

23 Peadar S Doyle, BMH WS 0155.

24 James Coughlan. BMH WS 0304. Volunteer Michael Lynch (BMH WS 0511) recalled that the doctor was covered by a gun held by Volunteer James Foran.

25 O'Brien, *Uncommon Valour,* p26.

26 Paul O'Brien, *Uncommon Valour,* p30. The mistaken view that Sinn Féin, a political party with no connection with the Irish Volunteers or the IRB, was

responsible for the Rising, quickly became the accepted narrative and would have important implications for the party in the elections in 1918.

27 As above.

28 James Coughlan, BMH WS 0304.

29 NLI Ceannt Papers MS 41,479/8, Sean McGlynn to Ed Keegan.

30 BMH WS 0265 George Irvine.

31 As above.

32 James J Burke, BMH WS 1758.

33 The Capuchin Annual 1966.

34 Dan McCarthy, BMH WS 0722.

35 James Coughlan, BMH WS 0304.

36 William T Cosgrave, BMH WS 0268.

37 Fanning, *Fatal Path,* pp139–140.

38 Áine Ceannt, BMH WS 264.

39 Kent-Gallagher Family Papers, Diary of Michael Kent.

40 William T Cosgrave, BMH WS 0268.

41 James Coughlan, BMH WS 0304.

42 Paul O'Brien, *Uncommon Valour,* p58.

43 James Foran, BMH WS 0243.

44 Michael Staines, BMH WS 0284.

45 NLI Ceannt Papers, MS 41,479/8; Michael Lynch, BMH WS 0511.

46 Peadar Doyle, BMH WS 0155.

47 BMH WS 0297 Annie Mannion.

48 As above.

49 S Geoghan, *The Campaigns and History of the Royal Irish Regiment, Vol. II* (London, 1927) quoted in Paul O'Brien, *Uncommon Valour,* p62.

50 Townshend, *Easter* 1916, p190.

51 Anne Maddock O'Reilly, *St James's Gate, 1914–1918: Guinness Brewery during the Great War,* unpublished MA dissertation, UCD School of History and

Archives, 20010–11. Before the Rising, Éamonn had rejected the Guinness Brewery as a strategic outpost for want of adequate supplies. His concern may have been justified since it is unlikely that the Brewery Manager would have been as hospitable to the Volunteers as he was to the British Army.

52 Townshend, *Easter 1916*, p186–189.

53 Liam O'Flaherty, BMH WS 0248.

54 Laurence O'Brien, BMH WS 0252.

55 William T Cosgrave, BMH WS 0268.

56 Charles J O'Grady, BMH WS 0282.

57 Kent-Gallagher Family Papers, Diary of Michael Kent.

58 Christopher Byrne, BMH WS 0167.

59 NLI Ceannt Papers MS 41,479/7.

60 Henry S Murray, BMH WS 0300.

61 Christopher Byrne, BMH WS 0167.

62 NLI Ceannt Papers MS 41,479/7.

63 Robert Holland, BMH WS 0280.

64 William Cosgrave, BMH WS 0268.

65 NLI Ceannt Papers MS 41,479/1.

66 Seán Enright, *Easter Rising 1916, The Trials* (Sallins, 2014), p11.

67 McGarry *The Rising,* pp167–168.

68 James Stephens, *The Insurrection in Dublin* (Dublin 1916) quoted in Townshend, *Easter 1916*, p267.

69 Townshend, *Easter* 1916, p196.

70 As above, p192.

71 McGarry, *The Rising,* p168.

72 Michael Lynch, BMH WS 0511.

73 James Foran, BMH WS 0243.

74 NLI Ceannt Papers MS 41,479/8.

75 William T Cosgrave, BMH WS 0268.

76 Peadar S Doyle, BMH WS 0155.

77 Oates, W.C., *The 2/8th Battalion,* The Sherwood Foresters in the Great War series (London, 1929), quoted in Paul O'Brien, *Uncommon Valour*, p74.

78 Davis Coakley, 'A Question of Integrity: Sir Francis Fletcher Vane and the 1916 Rebellion' in *Borderlands: Essays on Literature and Medicine in Honour of J.B. Lyon*, ed. Davis Coakley and Mary O'Doherty (Dublin, 2002), p96.

79 Vane, Sir F., Letters to his Wife, April and May 1916 (Carlisle), quoted in Coakley, 'A Question of Integrity', p96–97.

80 As above.

81 William T Cosgrave, BMH WS 0268. The evidence as to who gave the order to retreat is confusing. James Coughlan agreed with Cosgrave that it came from Brugha.

82 James Coughlan, BMH WS 0304.

83 William T Cosgrave, BMH WS 0268.

84 James Coughlan, BMH WS 0304.

85 Joseph Doolan, BMH WS 0199.

86 James Coughlan, BMH WS 0304. A small number of RIC men, who had been doing a course in Portobello Barracks, were pressed into service with the Munster Fusiliers to help and had taken part in the assault on the Nurses' Home. The man was wearing RIC trousers and a khaki tunic – a combination that Coughlan noted would become well known as Black and Tan in the coming years.

87 Gibbon, M., *Inglorious Soldier. An Autobiography,* (London, 1968), cited in Paul O'Brien, *Uncommon Valour*, p82.

88 Michael Lynch, BMH WS 0511.

89 William T Cosgrave, BMH WS 0268.

90 Áine Ceannt, BMH WS 264.

91 Townshend, *Easter 1916*, p208.

92 William T Cosgrave, BMH WS 0268.

93 Joseph Doolan, BMH WS 0199.

94 John J Styles, BMH WS 0175.

95 NLI Ceannt Papers MS 41,479/8. Sean McGlynn to Ed Keegan (1936, May 24).

96 Brian Barton, *The Secret Court Martial Records of the Easter Rising* (Gloucestershire, 2010), p229.

97 Townshend, *Easter 1916*, p203.

98 Joseph Doolan, BMH WS 0199.

99 Annie Mannion, BMH WS 0297.

100 Patrick Smyth, BMH WS 0305.

101 NLI Ceannt Papers MS 41,479/1.

102 Maddock O'Reilly, *St James's Gate, 1914–1918*.

103 Robert Holland, BMH WS 0280.

104 Rose McNamara, BMH WS 0482.

105 Honor O Brolchain, *16 Lives: Joseph Plunkett* (Dublin, 2012).

106 Foy and Barton, *The Easter Rising*, p206.

107 Michael Staines, BMH WS 0284.

108 Fr Augustine, BMH WS 0920.

109 As above.

110 As above.

111 Fr. Aloysius, BMH WS 0200.

112 NLI Ceannt MS 41,479/8. Letter to Rónán Ceannt from Michael J Kelly.

113 NLI Ceannt Papers MS 41,479/8.

114 James Coughlan, BMH WS 0304.

115 Joseph Doolan, BMH WS 0199.

116 Peadar S Doyle, BMH WS 0155.

117 As above.

118 William T Cosgrave, BMH WS 0268.

119 NLI Ceannt Papers MS 41,479/8.

120 Michael Lynch, BMH WS 0511.

121 William T Cosgrave, BMH WS 0268.

122 Joseph Doolan, BMH WS 0199. This account is borne out by a number of the volunteers present including Michael Lynch (BMH WS 0511) and James Coughlan (BMH WS 0304), as well as the SDU Wardmaster, Patrick Smyth (BMH WS 0305).

123 Ignatius Callender, BMH WS 0923.

124 Robert Holland, BMH WS 0280.

125 Annie O'Brien, BMH WS 0805.

126 NLI Ceannt Papers MS 41,479/7.

127 Peadar S Doyle, BMH WS 0155.

128 Thomas Doyle, BMH WS 0186.

129 Fr Augustine, BMH WS 0920.

130 Henry S Murray, BMH WS 0300.

131 Fr Augustine, BMH WS 0920.

132 Seán Enright, *Easter Rising 1916*, p24.

133 Robert Holland, BMH WS 0280.

134 William Cosgrave, BMH WS 0268.

135 Robert Holland, BMH WS 0280; Peadar S Doyle BMH WS 0155.

136 Richmond Barracks, which would have looked very similar to today's National Museum at Collins' Barracks, was taken over by the army of the Irish Free State in 1922 and renamed Keogh Barracks. It was later acquired by Dublin Corporation for public housing and became known as Keogh Square. Keogh Square was demolished in 1969 and replaced by St Michael's Estate. At that time three of the buildings that had formed the barracks were acquired by the Christian Brothers and became a school for boys. The school has since closed. St Michael's Estate was partially redeveloped under a Public Private Development plan.

137 Henry S Murray, BMH WS 0300.

138 James Coughlan, BMH WS 0304.

139 Robert Holland, BMH WS 0280.

CHAPTER NINE

1 *Statistical Tables for the Dublin Metropolitan Police for the Year 1916,* Cmd. 30, 1919, quoted in Seán Enright, *Easter Rising 1916.*

2 NAI, BG/Bg 79★, Box 22, Minutes of the meeting of the Board of Guardians of the SDU on 17 May 1916.

3 *Irish Times,* 22 March 2014.

4 Separation women were in receipt of separation allowances while their husbands were in the British Army. Without these allowances they and their children would have been in danger of starvation.

5 Fr Augustine, BMH WS 0920.

6 Áine Ceannt, BMH WS 264.

7 Kent-Gallagher Family Papers, Diary of Michael Kent.

8 Henry S Murray, BMH WS 0300.

9 Peadar S Doyle, BMH WS 0155.

10 James Coughlan, BMH WS 0304.

11 William T Cosgrave, BMH WS 0268, Appendix A.

12 Thomas Doyle, BMH WS 0186.

13 Barton, *The Secret Court Martial Records,* p41.

14 Seán Enright, *Easter Rising 1916,* pp28–29.

15 As above.

16 As above, p30.

17 Barton, *The Secret Court Martial Records,* p121.

18 William T Cosgrave, BMH WS 0268, Appendix A.

19 Gerald Doyle, BMH WS 1511.

20 As above.

21 William T Cosgrave, BMH WS 0268.

22 Barton, *The Secret Court Martial Records,* p121.

23 PRO WO71/348 Trial of E. Ceannt (E Kent), Prisoner Number Thirty-two

24 William T Cosgrave, BMH WS 0268.

25 Gerald Doyle, BMH WS 1511.

26 NLI Ceannt Papers MS 13,069/8

27 PRO WO71/348 Trial of E. Ceannt (E Kent), Prisoner Number Thirty-two

28 Seán Enright, *Easter Rising 1916,* p166.

29 Adrian Hardiman, '"Shot in Cold Blood": Military Law and Irish Perceptions in the Suppression of the 1916 Rebellion' in *1916 The Long Revolution,* ed. Gabriel Doherty and Dermot Keogh (Cork, 2007).

30 Barton, *The Secret Court Martial Records*, p234.

31 Piaras F MacLochlainn, *Last Words – Letters and Statements of the Leaders Executed after the Rising at Easter 1916 (*Dublin, 1990), p134.

32 Seán Enright, *Easter Rising 1916,* p164.

33 León Ó Broin, *W. E. Wylie and the Irish Revolution 1916–1921* (Dublin, 1989) p24–25. Wylie's experience with the Kent brothers led him to conclude that 'Ireland was a funny country'. Éamonn's brother, Dick, became Wylie's registrar in the Land Commission court many years later. When Wylie was appointed Judge of the Land Commission in 1920, he promoted Dick to the head of the records branch. Wylie served with Áine Ceannt on the organising committee of the Irish Red Cross Society. He judged her to be a 'fine businesswoman… she showed not sign of bitterness and they both got along famously.' Brian Barton has pointed out that Wylie's memoirs were published in 1939 when his memory was 'increasingly erratic and defective, so should not be taken as entirely accurate.

34 Brian Barton, *The Secret Court Martial Records*, p212.

35 Gerald Doyle, BMH WS 1511, says that about 25 prisoners, including himself and Éamonn, 'were *brought* to Richmond Barracks' on the morning of 5 May which may suggest that they had spent the night in Kilmainham and were returned to Richmond Barracks for court martial.

36 William T Cosgrave, BMH WS 0268.

37 Townshend, *Easter 1916*, p280.

38 NLI Ceannt Papers MS 13,069/8.

39 Brian Barton, *The Secret Court Martial Records*, p235.

40 Gerald Doyle, BMH WS 1511.

41 Kent-Gallagher Family Papers, Diary of Michael Kent.

42 Áine Ceannt, BMH WS 264.

43 Kent-Gallagher Family Papers, Diary of Michael Kent.

44 Áine Ceannt, BMH WS 264.

45 Kent-Gallagher Family Papers, Diary of Michael Kent.

46 Áine Ceannt, BMH WS 264.

47 UCD Archives p13/29, Extract from a letter from Lily O'Brennan to her mother and sister, Áine (Fanny).

48 Áine Ceannt, BMH WS 264.

49 As above. Unable to do anything for Éamonn, Bill seems to have done what he could for their namesake, Thomas Kent. Kent was from Castlelyons, near Fermoy, in Co Cork. He and his brothers, David, William and Richard were enthusiastic Irish Volunteers. Following the Rising in Cork they had returned home but found the house surrounded by soldiers who were rounding up anyone connected with the nationalist cause. A gun battle ensued, during which R.I.C. Head Constable W.C. Rowe was shot dead. Thomas and William Kent were arrested; David was wounded; and Richard was mortally wounded trying to escape. Tried by courts martial in Cork, William was acquitted, but Thomas was sentenced to death. Thomas Kent was executed in Cork on Tuesday 9 May 1916. Although there is no reference to it in his Army records, Áine recalled later that Bill Kent was disciplined on the charge of stealing food from the regimental canteen to give to Thomas Kent while he was in custody. Bill insisted that he had bought the food with his own funds but the charge stood.

50 Fr. Aloysius, BMH WS 0200.

51 Piaras F MacLochlainn, *Last Words*, p138.

52 Kent-Gallagher Family Papers, Diary of Michael Kent.

53 Áine Ceannt, BMH WS 264.

54 NLI Ceannt Papers MS 3198.

55 NLI Ceannt Papers MS 13,069/9.

56 Based on the procedures adopted by the British military authorities for the execution of those sentenced to death and on the account provided to Lieutenant Robert Barton by Major Heathcote, the officer in charge of the firing parties. See Barton, *The Secret Court Martial Records*, pp70–80.

57 Barton, *The Secret Court Martial Records*, p237.

58 Áine Ceannt, BMH WS 264.

59 Kent-Gallagher Family Papers, Diary of Michael Kent.

60 Áine Ceannt, BMH WS 264.

CHAPTER TEN

1 Barton, *The Secret Court Martial Records*, p81.

2 Barton, *The Secret Court Martial Records*, p90. Barton pointed out that it would have been difficult for Asquith to argue for their exclusions since they were 'ringleaders' and 'deeply implicated in the insurrection'.

3 Townshend, *Easter 1916*, p273.

4 For an understanding of the impact of these internments see William Murphy, *Political Imprisonment and the Irish, 1912–1921* (Oxford, 2014).

5 McGarry, *The Rising,* p281–282.

6 Fanning, *Fatal Path*, p6.

7 Kent-Gallagher Family Papers, Diary of Michael Kent.

8 NLI Ceannt MS 41,480/1.

9 DMOA, executive minutes, 11 May 1916, 2 June 1916 and 2 December 1916, cited in Maguire, *Servants to the Public,* p31–32.

10 Mary Gallagher, 'A very onerous national trust: the Irish National Aid and Volunteer Dependents' Fund, August 1916–July 1919', unpublished MA dissertation, UCD 2011

11 N.L.I. INAVDF Papers MS 23,469, Minutes of the Executive Committee, 13 February 1917.

12 Sinéad McCoole, *No Ordinary Women, Irish Female Activists in the Revolutionary*

Years 1900–1923 (Dublin, 2004), p190.

13 Shortly after the establishment of the first Dáil, Ireland was again plunged into civil unrest when a guerilla war broke out between the Volunteers – now known as the Irish Republican Army (IRA) – and the British forces (Black and Tans). The war lasted until a ceasefire and truce was agreed by both sides on 11 July 1921.

14 Eilis Ui Chonnaill, nee Ryan BMH WS 0568.

15 Áine Ceannt, BMH WS 264.

16 A British civil servant, Cope was Assistant Under-Secretary in Ireland during the Irish War of Independence.

17 Eilis Ui Chonnaill, nee Ryan BMH WS 0568.

18 Áine Ceannt, BMH WS 264.

19 McCoole, *No Ordinary Women,* p190.

20 UCD Archives P13/29, Papers of Lily O'Brennan.

21 Áine Ceannt, *The story of the Irish White Cross, 1920–1947*

22 *Irish Examiner,* 8 May 2013.

23 NAI, 2001/25/243, Department of Justice File S/585/40. Thanks are due to Professor Fanning for this source material.

24 William Henry, *Supreme Sacrifice, the story of Éamonn Ceannt 1881–1916* (Cork, 2005).

25 Lyons, *Ireland Since the Famine*, p341.

26 F O'Donoghue, 'Ceannt, Devoy, O'Rahilly and the Military Plan', in F X Martin (ed.), *Leaders and Men of the Easter Rising,* pp195–6.

27 Dudley Edwards, *Patrick Pearse.*

28 NLI MS 41,489/8, Éamonn Ceannt – An Impression by J Monks a Corporation Colleague.

29 *The Irish Volunteer* inaugural edition, 7 February 1914.

30 McGarry, *The Rising*, p188.

31 James Coughlan, BMH WS 0304.

32 McGarry, *The Rising, p188.*

33 NAI, BG/Bg 79★, Box 22, Minutes of the meeting of the Board of Guardians of the SDU on 17 May 1916.

34 For an assessment of the value of and the pitfalls associated with the use of the witness statements collected by the Bureau of Military History in 1947, see Fearghal McGarry, *Rebels: Voices from the Easter Rising* (Dublin, 2011), pp ix–xxi.

Appendix

1 Kent–Gallagher Family Papers, Diary of Michael Kent.

2 As above.

3 Kent–Gallagher Family Papers, Letter from Bill Kent to Michael Kent, 5 November 1916.

4 Timothy Bowman, 'The Irish at the Somme', *History Ireland* Issue 4 (Winter 1996), accessed at http://www.historyireland.com/20th-century-contemporary-history/the-irish-at-the-somme/ on 20 April 2014.

5 Kent–Gallagher Family Papers, Diary of Michael Kent.

6 Kent–Gallagher family papers.

BIBLIOGRAPHY

Primary Sources

Allen Library

Archives Department, University College Dublin

Bureau of Military History

Dublin City Library and Archive

Kent-Gallagher Family Papers

Kent-Sheehy Family Papers

National Archives of Ireland

National Library of Ireland

Newspapers and Periodicals

An Barr Buadh

An Claidheamh Soluis

Capuchin Annual

Freeman's Journal

Irish Freedom

Irish Independent

Irish Press

Irish Times

Irish Volunteer

Sinn Féin

Thom's Directory

Printed Publications

Augusteijn, Joost, *Patrick Pearse: The Making of a Revolutionary*, London, 2010

Barton, Brian, *Secret Court Martial Records of the Easter Rising,* Gloucestershire, 2002

Burke, Tom, *The 2ⁿᵈ Battalion Royal Dublin Fusiliers and the Tragedy of Mousetrap Farm, April and May 1915,* Dublin, 2005

Ceannt, Áine, *The story of the Irish White Cross*, 1920–1947

Clarke, Kathleen, ed. Helen Litton, *Kathleen Clarke, Revolutionary Woman, Dublin,* 2008

Coldrey, Barry M., *Faith and Fatherland; The Christian Brothers and the Development of Irish Nationalism*, 1838–1921, Dublin, 1988

Collins, Lorcan, *16 Lives: James Connolly,* Dublin, 2012

Fanning, Ronan, *Fatal Path: British Government and Irish Revolution, 1910–1922*, London, 2013

Daly, Mary, *Dublin, The Deposed Capital: A Social and Economic History 1860–1914*, Cork, 1984

Dudley Edwards, Ruth, *Patrick Pearse: The Triumph of Failure*, Dublin, 1990

Enright, Séan, *Easter Rising 1916: The Trials*, Sallins, 2014

Feeney, Brian, *16 Lives: Seán MacDiarmada*, Dublin, 2014

Fennell, Thomas, ed. Rosemary Fennell , *The Royal Irish Constabulary*, Dublin, 2003

Foy, Michael and Barton, Brian, *The Easter Rising*, Gloucestershire, 2011

Gibney, John, *16 Lives: Sean Heuston*, Dublin, 2013

Hay, Marnie, *Bulmer Hobson and the Nationalist Movement in Twentieth Century Ireland*, Manchester, 2009

Henry, William, *Supreme Sacrifice: The Story of Éamonn Ceannt: 1881–1916*, Cork, 2005

Jenkins, Roy, *Churchill*, London, 2002

Laffan, Michael, *The Resurrection of Ireland, The Sinn Féin Party 1916–1923,* Cambridge, 2005

Lee, Joe, *Ireland 1912–1985, Politics and Society*, Cambridge 1990

Litton, Helen, *16 Lives: Edward Daly*, Dublin 2013

Litton, Helen, *16 Lives: Thomas Clarke*, Dublin, 2014

Lyons, F S L, *Culture and Anarchy in Ireland, 1890–1939*, Oxford, 1979

Lyons, F S L, *Ireland Since the Famine*, Glasgow, 1973

McAtasney, Gerard, *Seán MacDiarmada, The mind of the Revolution*, Leitrim, 2004

McAtasney, Gerard, *Tom Clarke, Life, Liberty, Revolution*, Sallins, 2013

MacLochlainn, Piaras, *Last Words: Letters and Statements of the Leaders Executed after the Rising at Easter,* Dublin, 1971

Maguire, Martin, *Servants to the Public: A History of the Local Government and Public Services Union 1909–1990*, Dublin, 1998

Malcolm, Elizabeth, *The Irish Policeman*, Dublin, 2006

Martin, F X. ed., *Leaders and Men of the Easter Rising*, London, 1967

Martin, F X, *The Irish Volunteers 1913–1915: Recollections and Documents,* Dublin, 1963

McCoole, Sinéad, *No Ordinary Women, Irish Female Activists in the Revolutionary Years 1900–1923*, Dublin, 2004

McGarry, Fearghal, *The Rising: Ireland: Easter 1916*, Oxford, 2010

McGarry, Fearghal, *Rebels*, Dublin, 2011

McMahon, Timothy, Grand Opportunity – *The Gaelic Revival and Irish Society 1893–1910*, Syracuse, 2008

O' Brien, Joseph V., '*Dear Dirty Dublin: A city in distress 1899–1916*, London, 1982

O'Brien, Paul, *Uncommon Valour: 1916 and the Battle for the South Dublin Union*, Cork, 2010

O Brolcháin, Honor, *16 Lives: Joseph Plunkett*, Dublin, 2012

Ó Broin, Léon, *W E Wylie and the Irish Revolution 1916–1921*, Dublin, 1989

Plunkett Dillon, Geraldine, ed., Honor O Brolcháin, *All in the Blood,* Dublin, 2006

Townshend, Charles, Easter 1916, *The Irish Rebellion*, London, 2005

Yeates, Pádraig, *A City in Wartime: Dublin 1914–1918*, Dublin, 2012

Yeates, Pádraig, *Lockout: Dublin 1913*, Dublin, 2000

Index